THE SCANDINAVIAN STATES
AND THE LEAGUE OF NATIONS

THE

SCANDINAVIAN STATES

AND THE

LEAGUE OF NATIONS

BY

S. SHEPARD JONES, (D. Phil. (Oxon.))

DIRECTOR, WORLD PEACE FOUNDATION
BOSTON

GREENWOOD PRESS, PUBLISHERS
NEW YORK

TO MY MOTHER

ACKNOWLEDGEMENTS

I AM deeply indebted to many persons and institutions—especially in Denmark, Norway, Sweden and England—for their assistance, of one kind or another, which has made possible this book. To Professor Amry Vandenbosch, who as early as 1930 directed my attention to the rôle of the secondary Powers in the League of Nations, I owe much for his inspiration as teacher, as also to Professor Sir Alfred Zimmern of New College, Oxford, under whose supervision I wrote my doctoral thesis entitled "The Outlook and Activities of the Scandinavian States in the League of Nations," which forms the basis of the present study.

A number of scholars were kind enough to read an earlier draft of the manuscript and to offer helpful suggestion and corrections. For such services I would thank in particular the following: Dr Christian L. Lange of Norway, Secretary-General of the Inter-Parliamentary Union, Dr Ragnvald Moe, Director of the Norwegian Nobel Institute, Dr Edvard Hambro, Director of Chr. Michelsens Institut for Videnskap og Aandsfrihet, Herr Finn T. B. Friis, Member of the Secretariat of the League of Nations, Sir John Fischer Williams and Professor C. A. W. Manning of England, and Dr Axel Serup of Copenhagen.

I regret that it is not possible to mention all those with whom I had useful conversations during my residence in Stockholm, Copenhagen and Oslo in 1934, 1935 and 1936. My thanks are due in this connection especially to His Excellency Dr Peter Munch, Danish Minister of Foreign Affairs, Stortingspresident Carl J. Hambro, Herr Otto Johansson, Head of the League of Nations Section of the Swedish Foreign Office, Dr Georg Cohn of the Danish Foreign Office, Dr Frede Castberg of the Norwegian Foreign Office, Professor Axel Møller of the University of Copenhagen, Herr Paul Mohn, Editor of *Mellanfolkligt Samarbete*, and Herr Herman Stolpe, Editor, both of Stockholm. In addition I would include Professor W. E. Rappard of Geneva and Herr S. Hartz Rasmussen of the League Secretariat, the latter being especially helpful with matters of bibliography.

My greatest debt is to the Rhodes Trustees, who made possible my study at Oxford and (thanks to gloriously long holidays) on the Continent from 1933 to 1936, as well as to the Norwegian Nobel Committee for its generous grant to assist with the publication of this book. To Miss Hanna Astrup Larsen of the American Scandinavian Foundation I am grateful for a final reading of the manuscript. Herr Max Sørensen of the Danish Ministry of Foreign Affairs and Professor William Witherle Lawrence have also kindly read several chapters.

My thanks go to certain staff members of the following libraries who interested themselves in my researches: the Nobel Institute and the University Library in Oslo, the Royal Library and the Rigsdagsbiblioteket in Copenhagen, the Royal Library in Stockholm, Chatham House, the Bodleian, and the Library of the League of Nations in Geneva.

In revising the manuscript for publication I have greatly benefited from the criticisms of my father, Professor W. B. Jones of Georgetown College, Kentucky, and Miss Josephine Brayton, who has prepared the Index.

S. SHEPARD JONES

Kirkland House,
Harvard University,
October 28, 1938

EXPLANATION OF ABBREVIATIONS

A.J.I.L.—*American Journal of International Law.*

A.C.—Records of the Committees of the Assembly.

A.K.—*Andra Kammarens Protokoll* (Journal of the Swedish Lower Chamber).

A.P.—Records of the Plenary Sessions of the Assembly (thus *2A.4C.*, 17 indicates Records of the Fourth Committee of the Second Assembly, page 17).

B.Y.I.L.—*British Year Book of International Law.*

Conf. D.—Records of the Conference for the Reduction and Limitation of Armaments, 1932 *ff.*

Conf. D/C. G.—Records of the General Commission of the Conference for the Reduction and Limitation of Armaments (for other citations beginning *Conf. D.* see official documents of the same conference).

F.K.—*Första Kammarens Protokoll* (Journal of the Swedish Upper Chamber).

Indst S. (Innst. S.) ;Budgett-innst. S.—These are the official Norwegian abbreviations for the Reports of Committees to the Storting.

Kungl. Maj: ts prop.—Royal Swedish proposition.

L. of N. Doc.—League of Nations Document.

L.N.O.J.—*League of Nations Official Journal.*

Sp. A.—Records of the Special Assembly of the League.

St. med.—Abbreviation used in official documents for *Stortings meddelelse*; in this treatise all uses of this abbreviation are reports of the Norwegian Foreign Office concerning the work of the League of Nations.

St. prp.—*Stortingets proposition* (Norwegian Storting's proposition).

Treaty Series—*League of Nations Treaty Series.*

U.N.F. (1920)—Kungl. Utrikesdepartementets blåböcker rörande Nationernes förbund för år 1920. (Swedish Foreign Office Report on the League of Nations.)

PREFACE

AN eminent Danish writer remarked in 1923 that "even in Europe the sympathies and actions of the Scandinavian countries carry little weight and for America they are of almost negligible interest. This is due to the small number of their inhabitants, their geographical remoteness and the differences in their habits of thought."[1] So it must have seemed to many informed persons in and out of Scandinavia.[2] In contrast with Viking prowess, or with the maritime power of Denmark under Frederik II, or with the rescue of Protestantism by the irresistible Gustavus Adolphus,

[1] Georg Brandes, "Scandinavian Sympathies and Destinies." *Foreign Affairs* New York, Vol. I, p. 30 (June 1923). Brandes was referring to Finland and Iceland too. In the present study, Scandinavian States is understood to mean Denmark, Norway and Sweden. Finland can hardly be classified now as a Scandinavian State. Although about 10 per cent of her population speak Swedish, on political grounds Finland has not, at least until quite recently, been included in the Scandinavian bloc. In September 1934, the conference of Northern Ministers included a representative of Finland for the first time. The neutrality policy of Finland, testified to by the Finnish Foreign Minister in the Finnish Parliament in 1934, makes possible a wider collaboration among the Northern countries. See Foreign Minister Sandler's speech at Uppsala on December 14, 1934. *Mellanfolkligt Samarbete*, December 1934, pp. 320-2.

Iceland is not a member of the League of Nations. See *Folkeforbundets Første Tiaar*, p. 89.

[2] The word "Scandinavia" has come to cause irritation in some circles, particularly in Norway. This is due in part to the tendency of the English press to group Denmark, Norway and Sweden together and to lament England's unfavorable balance of trade with "Scandinavia." Norway, however, unlike Sweden and especially Denmark, gives England no cause for complaint on this ground. See the Letter to the Editor of *The Times* (London) from K. T. Knudsen, president of the Norwegian Chamber of Commerce, London, dated April 25, 1932. *The Times*, April 27, 1932.

As Dr. Edwin Björkman wrote in 1914, "literally speaking, there is no Scandinavia as yet. There is a Scandinavian peninsula and a Scandinavian group of nations, but nothing that may be regarded as a political, economical, or even geographical entity. It is convenient, of course, to have a term that can be applied collectively to the three Northern Kingdoms; and to the world at large such a term has more validity than the nations comprised within it seem willing to admit." "Scandinavia and the War," *Oxford Pamphlets, 1914*.

Despite objections, the author has used the word "Scandinavia" in the above sense.

the influence of Scandinavian countries upon Europe during the decades just preceding the World War was unimpressive. The relative decline of physical power had virtually caused their retirement from European politics, for gradually they had come to realize that henceforth in international politics they could be no more than pawns of the great nations. Happy in their relatively detached geographical position, they clung to a policy of isolation and neutrality after the Franco-Prussian War and soon were almost forgotten by the masters of Europe.

The policy of "no entanglements," however, which had been accepted generally in the Northern countries did not—indeed, could not—effect their isolation from the larger field of play, the field of international commerce. Trade remained, even if Power-politics was abandoned. When the War came in 1914, the vastly increased importance of the trade of the Scandinavian neutrals placed their States prominently in public attention. But their special rôle ended with the conclusion of the War, and with it this increased interest in the Northern countries. They now sat as onlookers, excluded, together with the defeated Powers, from the table around which the victors dictated the terms of peace.

The Peace Treaty, however, altered the international position of the Scandinavian States. It brought into being the League of Nations, which, by modifying the old international system, led to a changed relationship between this system and the Scandinavian States. Having remained detached from the political scene in the old dispensation, they came on stage in the new, hoping that their acceptance of rôles would justify itself by the growth of a new spirit of harmony among the principal actors.

The entry of the Scandinavian States into the League of Nations has in some measure renewed their importance in international affairs. But this importance ought not to be exaggerated. For these States have, in a sense, accepted only *limited* membership in the post-War international system, of which the League of Nations is a part. So far as Power-politics operates within this system, the Scandinavian States remain aloof, even when carried on under the auspices of the League of Nations. Events since 1936, which really marks the end of this treatise, tend to bear out this thesis even more clearly.

This study, then, treats of the outlook and activities of three small States in the League of Nations which hold themselves "above the mêlée of European Power-politics."[3] Because these States are divorced from Power-politics, and because their respective foreign policies are subject to a high degree of democratic control, it is already possible to undertake this study. Some materials bearing on their international relations, especially those in the archives of Foreign Offices, are not yet available, but it is unlikely that they contain secrets which, when made known, will seriously affect the conclusions arrived at in this study.

[3] Alfred Zimmern, *The League of Nations and The Rule of Law*, p. 343.

CONTENTS

I. FOUNDATIONS

CHAPTER I

INTRODUCTION: UNITY AND DIVERGENCY IN SCANDINAVIA

THE history of the League of Nations testifies to a considerable agreement among Denmark, Norway and Sweden on important questions discussed at Geneva since 1920. The similarity of outlook of their delegations has been one reason for the grouping of these States into what is called "the Scandinavian bloc." Although this treatise attempts to show the appropriateness of such an expression, it should be noted that the common attitude of the Scandinavian States in the League has not been accompanied by identical policies and activities. "Scandinavian group politics" does not imply a collective responsibility. Delegations are sent to Geneva by the Governments individually and are authorized to speak only for their own Governments. Yet so pronounced is the agreement on fundamental principles that one often hears the expression "Scandinavian representatives" and "Scandinavian proposals," even in the parliaments of the North where the differences between the sister States are more clearly recognized than at Geneva.[1]

By way of introduction to the study of the rôle of the Scandinavian States in the League, let us rapidly survey the development of their mutual relations and the emergence of a common outlook toward international organization.

[1] It is, strictly speaking, incorrect to refer to a "Scandinavian representative," even as regards the representative of one of the Scandinavian States who is normally occupying a seat on the Council of the League of Nations. The expression "Scandinavian representatives" has a correct usage.

On the incorrect use of the expression "Scandinavian proposal," see the Report to the Storting on the Work of the First Assembly published by the Norwegian *Utenriksdepartement*, wherein Dr Mikael H. Lie stated that the proposals of the Danish, Norwegian and Swedish Governments were collectively and erroneously referred to in the debate of the First Committee as "the Scandinavian proposal" or as "the proposal of the three Northern countries" ("de skandinaviske forslag" eller "forslag fra de tre nordiske land"). *St. med.* nr. 9 (1921), p. 11. See also the debate in the Norwegian Storting initiated by M. Johan Castberg, February 1, 1921. *Stortings Forhandlinger* (1921), Vol. 7a, pp. 70-6.

Despite the "community of race and culture" among Scandinavians, despite "their practical community of language, their extensive, although far from total, community of political position, and their steadily increasing community of economic interests," when the War came in 1914, as indeed today, the peoples of the North continued to "think and speak and act as Swedes, Norwegians or Danes, and not primarily as Scandinavians."[2] The reasons lie deep in their history, which from the Union of Kalmar in 1388 to the dissolution of the Union between Norway and Sweden in 1905 may broadly be described as the triumph of separatism over Scandinavianism. Neither Union was such in the higher sense of the word, for in both that equality of position so essential for generating a true spirit of cooperation was lacking. As a result, both Unions fanned the fire of nationalism which brought their destruction. But despite the fratricidal wars from the days when Engelbrekt led the liberty-loving Dalecarlian peasants against the Danes to the era of Napoleon, the seeds of Pan-Scandinavianism were sown by *litterateurs*. Adam Oehlenschläger, for example, in his poetry "nurtured the popular imagination of a common and glorious past" and Grundtvig "with romantic enthusiasm extolled the excellent Nordic spirit."[3]

This movement, which before the middle of the nineteenth century had been kept alive chiefly by intellectuals, gave hopes about 1850 for an advance on the political front. At this time, the question of a military alliance between Denmark and the Union of Norway and Sweden (which had a foreign policy unified in the common King)[4] became "practical politics." The Danes in the period before the Schleswig-Holstein War were hopeful of using Pan-Scandinavianism as a counter to the rising power of their great neighbour to the South, while Sweden, as a result of her policy which effected the "November Treaty" of 1855, coupled with the unexpected peace which Russia made with her enemies at the beginning of 1856, was alarmed by her own position *vis-à-vis* an unfriendly and now un-

[2] Edwin Björkman, "Scandinavia and the War," *Oxford Pamphlets, 1914*, pp. 3, 4.
[3] Alfred Büscher, "Der Skandinavismus. I. Bis zum Ausbruch des deutsch-dänischen Konfliktes 1848," *Nordische Rundschau* (5), January 1929. Reviewed in *Social Science Abstracts*, Vol. I, 7127, by Andreas Elviken, whose words are quoted.
[4] According to the "Riksakt" of August 6, 1815, the Crown in person was vested with the care of foreign affairs of Norway and Sweden. There was one foreign minister for the two countries. See Møller, *International Law*, Vol. I, p. 92.

embarrassed Russia. Accordingly, in the spring of 1857, King Oscar invited his Danish colleague, Frederik VII, to form a Scandinavian alliance which was to include a guarantee of Schleswig; but Frederik rejected the overture on the ground that Holstein had been omitted, and the negotiations failed.[5]

This rebuff to Pan-Scandinavianism was shortly followed by what proved to be its death-blow as a political force aiming at unification. When Denmark was attacked by Prussia and Austria in 1864, the King of Norway and Sweden, restrained by the force of isolationism, was unable to keep his promises of assistance.[6] Thenceforth it was clear that there would be no unification in Scandinavia comparable to that in progress in Germany and Italy. The memory of the bitter disappointment felt by the Danes, moreover, lingered on as a hindrance to closer understanding in the North.[7]

The tide of nationalism was running strong. Vigorously it beat against that remnant of political unity still existing in Scandinavia at the beginning of the twentieth century.[8] The dissatisfaction of Norway with her position of inferiority in respect to the control of foreign affairs led to the dissolution of the Union with Sweden in 1905.[9] Although this separation was to remove a barrier to voluntary cooperation between the sister nations, the immediate effect was to increase bitterness and to introduce divergency of foreign policy. In addition, Swedish opinion grew cool towards Denmark, who had sympathized with the efforts of the Norwegians for independence.[10]

[5] Svanström and Palmstierna, *A Short History of Sweden*, pp. 338 *ff*.
[6] Karl XV promised 20,000 men if German troops invaded Holstein. *ibid*, p. 340. Many Swedish and Norwegian volunteers fought with the Danes, however. The Swedish Government could get no help from Great Britain or France with which to shield themselves against Russia, who had remained a fear in Swedish minds.
[7] This disappointment was vividly reflected in the lyrics of Henrik Ibsen. See Theodore Jorgenson, *Norway's Relation to Scandinavian Unionism 1815-1871*, pp. 345 *ff*.
[8] For the origin and nature of Norwegian nationalism see an article by Andreas Elviken in *Journal of Modern History*, Vol. III (September 1931), pp. 365-91, entitled "The Genesis of Norwegian Nationalism."
[9] For a compact statement of the Norwegian case see Dr Nansen's letter to *The Times* (London), in the issue of March 25, 1905. The files of *The Times* for 1905 furnish interesting reading for those interested in the details. See also Gjerset, *History of the Norwegian People*, Vol. II, pp. 561 *ff*. Compare Nordlund, *The Swedish-Norwegian Union Crisis* for the Swedish view.
[10] *The Times*, September 13, 1906; Geoffrey Pyke, *Fortnightly Review*, June 1916, pp. 35-6.

The bickerings and distrust between Norway and Sweden continued. The negotiation by Norway of the Treaty of 1907, by which Great Britain, France, Germany and Russia guaranteed the integrity of Norway, "appeared to rouse more bitterness than the dissolution of the Union itself."[11] Under the circumstances it was considered by Sweden as directed against herself. M. de Trolle, the Swedish Minister of Foreign Affairs, publicly emphasized that Swedish policy had not rendered necessary the guarantee sought by Norway.[12] But Norwegian opinion since the disruption of the Union had been suspicious of Swedish intentions with regard to her military reorganization. Five weeks after Haakon VII had taken the oath to observe the Norwegian Constitution and had entered upon his full exercise of rights as King (with the motto, "Alt for Norge"), the Swedish Ministerial Council had directed the General Staff to elaborate plans for the increase of the effectives of the army and navy.[13] Although the reorganization of the Swedish forces was a natural consequence of the new conditions which the discontinuance of the obligation of mutual defence and combined military action under the Union had entailed, it furnished a target for the Norwegian press, just as the Integrity Treaty of 1907 did for the Swedish press. Stockholm papers accused the Norwegian Government of inviting the Great Powers to dabble in Scandinavian affairs. They denied that Norway was menaced by the Swedish plans to increase her effectives, and argued that only by adequate preparation could neutrality in the North be guaranteed.[14] Perhaps the chief motive for strengthening the Swedish defences at this time arose from a recently revived fear of Russia, which by 1912 Fahlbeck and Sven Hedin were fanning with their passionate speeches. Like Damocles, Sweden could not forget the sword which was hanging over her head.[15]

[11] Svanström and Palmstierna, *op. cit.*, p. 350. See also Victor Mogens, "Norsk utenrikspolitikk gjennem 25 år," in *Vor Verden*, 1930, nr. 6, pp. 245 *ff*. Although the word "guaranty" is not used in the Treaty of 1907 (signed at Christiania on November 2), this was the effect of the treaty, as Article II shows. Compare Dickinson, *The Equality of States in International Law*, p. 251.

[12] *The Times*, November 4, 1907.

[13] *ibid.*, January 8, 1906.

[14] *ibid.*, October 17, 1907, and October 29, 1907.

[15] *American-Scandinavian Review*, Vol. II, March 1914, pp. 43-4. See the debate in the Swedish Riksdag, February 25 and 26, 1908, on the Baltic policy of Russia. Also Björkman, *op. cit.*, pp. 14-15. As one writer said, "From 1809, when Finland was

It would be unfair, however, to pass over the dissolution of the Union in 1905 without emphasizing the peaceful ways in which this separation of Norway and Sweden took place. Nationalistic states might well learn from this noteworthy episode that the maintenance of peace sometimes depends upon the ability to discipline one's sense of national pride, and even to make some sacrifice of interests. Sweden did not save the Union, but she saved the peace and prosperity of the Northern peoples. When agreement was reached at Karlstad for a final settlement between the sister nations, peace was strengthened by the creation of a permanent demilitarized neutral zone some fifteen kilometres broad on each side of the frontier. Fortifications were destroyed and a convention of arbitration was signed.

If the forces of divergency gained the ascendency in Scandinavia in the first decade of the twentieth century, there was a danger that they might have won an even greater victory in the next decade. The outbreak of the World War offered the possibility of ending the century of peace between the Scandinavian nations, for diverging sympathies towards the belligerents and opposing interests threatened conflict if it became a matter of choosing sides. Even if war should result from the act of one of the belligerents, there was no guarantee of a united front in Scandinavia.

What, precisely, was the danger to peace in the North? The only substantial agitation within Scandinavia for entering the War came from the so-called Activists in Sweden, "a small but trumpet-tongued minority," who wanted the country's destiny directed under the German aegis in order to strike a telling blow at Russia.[16] In Denmark, where hatred of Germany remained because of the loss of Schleswig,[17] a comparable movement for war did not exist because

---

lost by Sweden, every morning's sun had cast the threatening shadow of Russia across the Gulf of Bothnia and the Baltic Sea. This was the third time in less than a century that pieces of Swedish territory had been lost to Russia." Morris, *From an American Legation,* pp. 93-4. See also Charles H. Sherrill in *The Forum* (New York), Vol. 66: 339 (October 1921).

[16] E. J. Dillon, "Sweden and the Belligerents," *The Contemporary Review,* June 1916, p. 704. See also Lucien Maury, *Le Nationalisme suédois et la guerre 1914-1918,* Paris, 1918.

[17] According to Georg Brandes: "From the year 1848 Germany and everything German were regarded by Denmark as enemies, and this was particularly true after the second Slesvig war of 1864. . . ." *Foreign Affairs,* I (June 15, 1923), p. 34.

of an appreciation, even more real than in 1870, of the insanity of war against Germany.[18] Norway, only recently accepted into full status in the family of nations, had no wrong to redress, no ambition which war could achieve. But if she were to be forced into war it would be difficult in the extreme should she be required to fight against the Allies. As Dr Thommessen has written, "A war with Germany would bring fearful misfortune upon us, but a war with England would be suicide."[19]

So far as the sympathies of the three nations at the outbreak of the War were concerned, the situation as described by Björkman was as follows:

> The sympathies of Denmark are undoubtedly with the Allies, no reservation being made against Russia. The sympathies of Norway are in the main with England, though Norwegians view Russia with some apprehension. The sympathies of Sweden are to a large extent with Germany, although this implies no animosity toward England, and is coupled with a great deal of genuine love for France. The key to the situation is that Sweden does not love Germany so much as she fears, and for that reason hates, Russia.[20]

The War, however, as it happened, did not accentuate the division in Scandinavia.[21] When the peoples of the North reflected on the disastrous consequences which would undoubtedly follow their participation on either side or both, it was natural that they determined to relegate their differences to a position more compatible with their true importance. Many eyes in the North were opened for the first time to the value of Scandinavian cooperation. By standing together, the horrors of war might be escaped. Moreover, neutrality, on which the overwhelming majority in each country insisted, was the very policy—perhaps the only policy—through which agreement and cooperation could be achieved. The War cleared away irrelevant dif-

---

[18] P. Munch, *Le Projet danois de désarmement et la Société des Nations,* Paris, A. Pedone, Éditeur, Libraire de la Cour d'Appel et de l'Ordre des Avocats (1927), pp. 6-7.

[19] *Norges Utenrikspolitik,* p. 29. Quoted by Vigness, *op. cit.,* p. 94.

[20] *op. cit.,* pp. 12-13.

[21] See the excellent account by Eric Cyril Bellquist in *Some Aspects of the Recent Foreign Policy of Sweden,* Chapter I.

ferences and made manifest their true community of outlook and position, symbolized by neutrality.

The choice of neutrality did not come as a surprise. By 1914 in each of the three States this policy had been clothed in the honoured cloak of tradition. Decades of isolation from diplomatic entanglements in Europe was the basis for a policy which emphasized the common interests of the Scandinavian countries. The Peace Societies in Denmark, Norway and Sweden had for years agitated for neutrality as a permanent policy. As early as 1899, Frederik Bajer had launched his movement for "Pacigerance," which sought the alliance of States pledged to neutrality, in contrast with existing alliances whose object was the use of force to settle disputes.[22] Bjørnstjerne Bjørnson put the strength of his enthusiasm in an effort for a Scandinavian league for defence and neutrality. As the War clouds gathered over Europe in the decade before 1914, the Scandinavian Governments, of whatever political party, publicly emphasized their attachment to the policy of neutrality.[23] Whether from Right or Left, whether advocating increased or reduced military expenditure, the most widespread cry in the North was for neutrality.[24]

This common demand, coupled with the neighbouring geographic position, had already in 1912—despite lingering jealousies and misunderstanding—suggested the beginning of cooperation in regard to neutrality. According to a prominent Copenhagen newspaper, *Politiken,* "it is not a mere chance that the texts of the declarations of neutrality issued by the three Scandinavian countries are identical. On

[22] See *Nordisk Interparlamentarisk Forbunds Småskrifter,* No. 1, "Fredsførelse," by F. Bajer, 1913. Concerning the enthusiasm of Bjørnstjerne Bjørnson for a Scandinavian league of defence and neutrality see Oscar J. Falnes, *Norway and the Nobel Peace Prize,* New York (1938), pp. 22 ff.

[23] See the speech of the Swedish Foreign Minister, Count Ehrensvärd, who, on May 20, 1912, stated that, "no temptation shall induce us to forsake this policy (i.e. neutrality)," *The Times,* June 27, 1912 (5D). Also the Danish Foreign Minister's speech (Count Raben-Levetzau), in regard to the passage through The Belts and The Sound, *The Times,* April 16, 1907.

[24] The Social Democrat members of the Swedish Riksdag on May 20, 1912, introduced a bill providing for the permanent neutralization of Sweden. Although the bill was not accepted, members of the different political parties joined in supporting the traditional policy of neutrality. *The Times,* May 21, 1912. For the support of neutrality given by all political parties in Denmark, see Petersen and Nielsen, *Halvtreds Aars Fredsarbejde,* p. 42.

the contrary, it is due to a preliminary agreement between the three Governments," suggested by Sweden.[25]

The outbreak of the War led to more significant cooperation in the North. On August 8, 1914, the Riksdag and Storting were officially informed that the Swedish and Norwegian Governments had mutually declared their intention to maintain to the utmost of their ability their neutrality in relation to all the belligerent powers, and that the two Governments had exchanged binding assurances that the European War should, under no conditions, lead to hostile measures by either country against the other. The initiative in this joint action, which marks the *real* starting point of the common Scandinavian neutrality policy, was largely due to M. Wallenberg, the Swedish Foreign Minister.[26] In order to maintain the declared neutrality in the face of countless difficulties, the Governments deemed it essential to present to the belligerents a picture of firm solidarity in the North. King Gustaf V took the initiative by inviting Christian X of Denmark and Haakon VII of Norway to meet with him at Malmö, with their Foreign Ministers, in December 1914. This meeting, which was the first occasion at which the King of Norway had been present in Sweden since the separation in 1905, achieved more than a declaration of unity in a common effort for neutrality. The bitter feelings of the past were buried, as a new era of cooperation, characterized by ministerial consultation, arose in its stead. Another conference of the three Kings met in Christiania in November 1917, and, in addition, ministerial conferences in Copenhagen and Stockholm were held at intervals in 1916, 1917, and 1918. These conferences reaffirmed the common determination to maintain neutrality, and considered questions of economic and social, as well as of political or diplomatic character.[27]

[25] *The Peace Movement,* November 15, 1912 (Nos. 21-22), pp. 381-2. See "Declaration by Norway, Denmark and Sweden Relative to the Establishment of Uniform Rules of Neutrality" (December 21, 1912). *A.J.I.L. Suppl.,* Vol. 7 (1913), pp. 187-91.

[26] Christian L. Lange, "Scandinavian Cross-Currents," *Atlantic Monthly,* Vol. 121 (January 1918), p. 134; H. A. Larsen, "The Neutrality Alliance of Sweden and Norway," *American-Scandinavian Review,* November 1914, pp. 8-14.

[27] On the Malmö Conference see *American-Scandinavian Review,* March-April 1915, pp. 70-2; Bellquist, *op. cit.,* p. 257; Vigness, *op. cit.,* p. 169. On the Ministers' conferences see *The Times* (London), September 21, 1916; May 14, 1917; March 13, 1916; November 30, 1917; August 22, 1917; June 8, 1918; July 5, 1918; *American-Scandinavian Review,* 1917, p. 308.

The significance of the war-time cooperation in Scandinavia deserves emphasis. Herein the forces of unity and the forces of divergency were reconciled. Inter-Scandinavian cooperation furnished the compromise between nationalization and the old Pan-Scandinavianism. As in the experience of the Allied belligerents, the inter-state, not the super-state, principle was chosen for pursuing common ends.[28] From what has been said above, it is clear that such a choice by the Scandinavian States must have been nearly inevitable. When one remembers that only nine years had elapsed since the force of Norwegian nationalism had burst asunder the bonds of Union, can it be surprising that the peoples of the North in 1914 continued to "think and speak and act as Swedes, Norwegians or Danes, and not primarily as Scandinavians"? If Scandinavian cooperation did not attain the breadth of Inter-Allied cooperation, this must be attributed to the greater demands which belligerency claims upon the resources of peoples. The non-adoption of such a plan as that of the Danish jurist, M. Henrik Ussing, for regularizing and extending Scandinavian cooperation through the instrument of a Federal Council, may be accounted for along similar lines.[29] In conclusion, the use made of the technique of Ministers' conferences, however cautious, justified itself by the hearty approval with which it was received by public opinion in the three countries.[30] The basis was laid for continued collaboration when the problems of peace-time international organization arose.[31] Out of that collaboration was to come the crystallization of a common outlook towards international organization.

[28] Zimmern, *op. cit.*, p. 149.

[29] *American-Scandinavian Review*, 1915, p. 368.

[30] *The Times* correspondent from Copenhagen, following the Ministers' conference which met at the close of June 1918, wrote that, "the whole Scandinavian Press welcomes a sign of increased understanding." *The Times*, July 5, 1918 (5B). On the question of joint diplomatic action taken by the Danish, Norwegian and Swedish Governments during the War, see Vigness, *op. cit.*, pp. 96, 109. *The Times*, December 30, 1916; February 15, 1917.

[31] *The Times*, May 14, 1917; July 1, 1918. For a brief account of the growing cooperation among the Northern countries since 1864 see Louis de Geer, "Nordiskt Samförstånd," *Nordisk Tidskrift för Vetenskap, Konst, och Industri* (1925), pp. 318-29; also E. Hagerup Bull, "Det Nordiske Samarbejde i de sidste Halvhundrede År," *ibid.* (1928), pp. 1-11.

CHAPTER II

PRE-WAR ATTITUDE OF THE SCANDINAVIAN STATES

THE common attitude of Denmark, Norway and Sweden towards international organization took shape under the conditions of the pre-War European system. Between 1882 and 1885 peace societies were established in the Northern countries which were largely interested in assuring the aloofness of these countries from Power-politics.[1] The method employed was to agitate for the permanent neutralization of the North, and to urge disarmament and arbitration as supporting measures. As the Scandinavian outlook in the League of Nations was deeply influenced by the attitude developed towards neutrality, disarmament and arbitration, let us examine in turn these questions as they appeared in the period before 1914.

When the Danish Peace Society was founded in 1882, it was significantly named *Foreningen til Danmarks Neutralisering* (*The Society for the Neutralization of Denmark*).[2] Its founder, Frederik Bajer, was primarily interested in promoting the security of Denmark by effecting the isolation of Scandinavia from European politics. At that time the policy of neutrality made a wide appeal in the three countries, but it was not an assured policy recognized by international agreement, as in the case of Switzerland and Belgium.[3] At times during the nineteenth century the neutrality of the Scandinavian Kingdoms had been threatened by sections of opinion which desired a more active foreign policy.[4] But the peace societies considered that

---

[1] Beales, *A History of Peace*, p. 182. Petersen and Nielsen, *Halvtreds Aars Fredsarbejde*, pp. 36-8. Svenska Freds- och Skiljedomsföreningen, *Jubileumsskrift: 1883-1933*, pp. 11 *ff*. For the activities of the peace societies in Scandinavia, see also Niels Petersen, "Nordens Indsats i Fredsarbejdet," *Nordisk Tidsskrift for International Ret*, Vol. I (3), 1930, pp. 159 *ff*. See also Carl Sunblad, *Svenska Fredsrörelsens Historia Åren 1883-1919*. 3 vols. (Stockholm, 1903-1919).

[2] Petersen and Nielsen, *op. cit.*, p. 11.

[3] Hershey, *The Essentials of International Public Law and Organization*, p. 196.

[4] See Chapter I, pp. 5, 6, 7.

any resort to war by a Scandinavian State would, in view of the relative weakness of these States, constitute a real danger to their independence. Permanent neutralization, therefore, should be declared in order to assure the maintenance of aloofness in times of temptation or special risk. The argument of the Danish Peace Society came to this: since the rôle of Denmark as a "war-waging" Power had played out, any notion of *Alliancepolitik* must be abandoned, and neutrality must be made permanent.[5]

This idea gained adherents in the Northern countries.[6] In 1902 the Norwegian Storting (taking note of the motions concerning neutrality which had been introduced in the Swedish Riksdag in 1883, 1894 and 1899, and in the Danish Rigsdag in 1894) unanimously recommended that the Government consider the question of the declaration of the permanent neutrality of Norway and Sweden.[7] The Storting committee, however, which had studied the question had not been interested in a *guarantee* of Scandinavian neutrality, but thought it perhaps sufficient that other Powers declare their willingness to respect such neutrality.[8] Despite much talk in the peace societies, the political atmosphere in the Northern countries was not conducive to cooperative action, in view of the Union crisis of 1905 and the disliked Norwegian Integrity Treaty of 1907.[9] This treaty, however, did not provide for the neutralization of Norway, nor did Denmark or Sweden proceed to any arrangement for their own permanent neutrality. None the less, the successive Danish, Norwegian and Swedish Governments prior to the outbreak of the World War made it clear that neutrality would be the continuing policy of the Northern countries. In the following chapter the influence of Scandinavian neutrality will be considered as one of the paramount factors in the formulation of a Scandinavian plan for an "International Juridical Organization."

Disarmament, or anti-militarism, was a second question which figured in the discussions of the Northern peace societies prior to

[5] Petersen and Nielsen, *op. cit.*, p. 16.

[6] See the Draft Resolution of *Svenska Freds- och Skiljedomföreningen* at the Bern Peace Conference, August 1884, for the neutralization of the three Northern Kingdoms. Petersen and Nielsen, *op. cit.*, p. 21.

[7] Stortings Forhandlinger (1901-1902), Vol. 6a, *Indst. S. XXXXIII.*

[8] *ibid.*, pp. 6 *ff*.

[9] *British and Foreign State Papers,* Vol. 100, p. 536.

1914. There was considerable divergency of opinion on this subject; yet in general there was a conviction that "Europe suffered under the burden of armaments, which hampered progress *without safeguarding Peace.*"[10]

In Denmark, the movement for disarmament was an offspring of the desire for permanent neutralization. The Danish Peace Society, from its beginning, had founded its programme on the conception that "neutrality and preparation for war are absolutely incompatible, and that neutrality will only be a safeguard and security for preserving national independence when all fortifications are destroyed, and military effectives reduced to a police force to patrol the boundaries and territorial waters."[11]

This doctrine, known as "Defence Nihilism," won some adherents in Norway and Sweden,[12] but the proportion to the total electorate, even after the peaceful dissolution of the Union in 1905, was never so great as in Denmark. Before that time there was little inclination among the Norwegians to sacrifice their army, which might be needed if the quarrel with Sweden should unfortunately lead to rash action. Through a newly established Norwegian Peace Society (*Norges Fredsforening*), M. Paul Koht, one of its guiding spirits, prudently emphasized the need of retaining an adequate defence force.[13] Although "Defence Nihilism" gained ground in the North after the Treaty of Karlstad, it was checked in Sweden in February 1914, when King Gustaf V, at a tense moment, gave his influence to the parties advocating increased expenditure for national defence.[14] In Norway and Denmark, even during the War, disarmament remained a subject of much heated controversy. In 1909 the Danish Defence Law pro-

[10] These are the opening words of the First Peace Address of the Danish Peace Society to the King, Government and Rigsdag (October 14, 1892). See Petersen and Nielsen, *op. cit.*, p. 27. The italics are mine.

[11] From a speech of Niels Petersen made before the Sixth Scandinavian Peace Congress at Stockholm, 1910. Quoted in Petersen and Nielsen, *op. cit.*, p. 72.

[12] In 1912 the Swedish Social Democrats voted in the Riksdag for the abolition of the Army. See an article on "Försvarnihilism" in the *Morning Post* (London), January 25, 1919.

[13] Beales, *op. cit.*, pp. 212, 213. *Norges Fredsforening* was established July 31, 1895. Paul Koht and Bernhard Hansen were its early leaders. An earlier Peace Society, by the same name, founded by Konow, in February 1885, had agitated for military retrenchment before it finally expired in 1892.

[14] Bellquist, *op. cit.*, p. 253, and references.

vided for the future razing of the fortifications which protected Copenhagen from attack by land. In 1916 the Defence Nihilists sought to destroy the seaward fortifications of Copenhagen. Even the Government of Denmark, through its Minister of Defence, Dr Peter Munch, declared that its policy at that time was based on the recognition that the defence of Copenhagen (if it were attacked by the German navy) would be hopeless, no matter what steps were taken for its protection. In a later chapter we shall see how pacifism gained influence in the Danish Left (Socialist and Radical parties) after the War. In Norway the Defence Nihilists centered their discussion on army discipline during the War.[15]

Although the peace societies of the North were not agreed whether or not neutrality should be defended, their representatives which assembled at Stockholm for the Sixth Scandinavian Peace Congress in 1910 found a common front in the desire for a reduction of military expenditure. A resolution was adopted that "the three Scandinavian countries ought without delay to make important reductions in their military budgets, with the view of obtaining complete disarmament as soon as possible."[16] It is significant that the "friends of peace" were able to agree that *complete* disarmament should be their goal. Perhaps of more practical importance was their advocacy of a *substantial* reduction of armaments which was not to be conditional upon a similar action by other States. Regional limitation of armaments thereby became an immediate objective of the peace societies in Scandinavia. Many Scandinavians, especially Danes, were prepared to go further by advocating unilateral disarmament, but this extreme position met with opposition even within the peace societies.

At this same conference in 1910, the assembled Scandinavian "friends of peace" for the first time accepted the common view that the small States had "the right and obligation" to take the lead in the disarmament movement.[17] Two methods of action were possible. One was to urge their Governments to undertake a positive effort for an international agreement for the reduction of armaments. The other was to work for the reduction of their own national arma-

[15] See Munch, *Le Projet danois de désarmement et la Société des Nations*, pp. 6-7. *Morning Post*, January 25, 1919. *infra*, pp. 245 ff.

[16] Petersen and Nielsen, *op. cit.*, p. 72. See also Svenska Freds- och Skiljedomsförening, *Jubileumsskrift, 1883-1933*, pp. 37-8.

[17] Petersen and Nielsen, *op. cit.*, p. 73.

ments without awaiting a general reduction, in the hope thereby to win the world from militarism by example. Both alternatives had supporters. In view of the international situation, however, the possibilities for a general reduction of armaments in Europe were most discouraging. It was hard to visualize a small-State initiative which might successfully bring a halt to the armaments race between the rival Powers of Europe. Moreover, the peace societies faced a difficult task if they should attempt to persuade the "neutral" Scandinavian Governments to expose themselves to the risks of "meddling" in the international political arena.

The cautious policy of the Scandinavian Governments had already been demonstrated a few years before at The Hague Peace Conferences.[18] Their delegations had not made themselves conspicuous in the discussion concerning disarmament, but had chosen a modest rôle, commensurable with their position as small States.

Even the well established Danish Peace Society hesitated in 1910 to begin an effort for an *international* agreement for the reduction of armaments. When at a meeting of the Society in that year Pastor Kemp proposed that the Inter-Parliamentary Union should be requested to formulate a proposal for the international limitation of armaments, which should be submitted to a Third Hague Conference, there was no support. All the subsequent speakers agreed with Frederik Bajer, who emphasized the difficulties of achieving practical results along this line. The Danish Peace Society accepted the view of its founder that its guiding principle should be, "Let every country do what it can."[19] An "island of peace" in the North might

[18] Apparently no definite proposals for reduction of armaments were made by the Scandinavian Delegations. At the First Hague Conference an appeal was made to the Tsar of Russia to persevere in the work for peace. The First Delegate of Sweden and Norway, supported by the Danish delegation, declared that the Russian disarmament proposals were unacceptable, primarily because they made no distinction between armies that are adapted for attack and those of a merely defensive character. *Proceedings of The Hague Peace Conferences* (James Brown Scott, editor). *Conference of 1899*, pp. 316-17.

[19] Petersen and Nielsen, *op. cit.*, p. 77. In April 1914, however, the Executive Committee of the Inter-Parliamentary Union nominated a commission to study the question of a possible limitation of armaments. M. Neergaard, former Prime Minister of Denmark, Baron Palmstierna of Sweden, and Admiral Sparre, former Minister in Norway, were named on this commission, which did not meet because of the coming of the War. Hans Wehberg, *The Limitation of Armaments*, p. 96 (Pamphlet Series of the Carnegie Endowment for International Peace: Division of International Law, No. 46).

influence opinion in other countries, and in time lead to world disarmament.

If the traditional aloofness of the Scandinavian States to European politics was a barrier to a Scandinavian initiative for international disarmament prior to the War, still the policy of isolation was well adapted to encourage the growth of national disarmament movements in the North. Despite strong opposition, especially in Sweden, the campaign of the pacifists enlisted many converts for a counter-attack against the instruments of might, once dear to their Viking forefathers. Militarism had failed the North; the North perhaps would reject militarism. Despite differences in the geographical and political situations of the Northern countries, the emergence of a new *Scandinavian* attitude towards armaments was being prepared. Irrespective of the view entertained as to the requirements for national defence while powerful neighbours remained heavily armed, the threat which these weak countries were subjected to, even in times of peace, by the armaments of Great Powers argued in favour of the advocacy of a radical reduction of world armaments. The foundation was laid for their Geneva policy as the recognition of this truth became widespread.

In the Danish *Peace Advocates Catechism* of 1890 the doctrine of compulsory arbitration was stated in far-reaching terms, as follows :[20]

"We desire that arbitration be acknowledged as the only lawful means of settling disputes between States, the greater as well as the lesser." . . .

This was a bold doctrine to preach in 1890, and in Scandinavia as elsewhere many persons described it as visionary and as an example of misguided idealism. It was accepted, however, by the Danish Peace Society, and in time by the majority of the Northern peoples.[21] The

[20] Petersen and Nielsen, *op. cit.*, pp. 18 *ff*.

[21] There is no reason to suppose that Poul Sveistrup, who drafted the *Peace Advocates Catechism,* intended to exclude judicial settlement or conciliation procedure as proper means of settling disputes. Neither of these methods was then popularly known. Judicial settlement as distinct from arbitration was a later development. Sveistrup's use of the word "arbitration" really covered both arbitration and judicial settlement. Conciliation was also an unexplored field in 1890.

history of this doctrine, and of its development, furnishes a third element in the Scandinavian theory of international organization.

Agitation on behalf of international arbitration became very lively in Scandinavia after the signal success of the Alabama Case in 1872. Through an Englishman, Henry Richard, the arbitration movement, which owes much to the Anglo-Saxon peoples, was launched in Sweden. In 1874 Jonas Jonassen introduced a motion in the Swedish Riksdag requesting the King to support negotiations which foreign Powers might open with Sweden or with each other with reference to the creation of a tribunal of arbitration. This motion was adopted in the Lower House on March 21, 1874, but was rejected by the more conservative Upper House.[22] In Denmark, the farmers of Jutland went further in 1875 when they petitioned the Rigsdag to invite the Danish Government to take an initiative for the establishment of an International Tribunal of Arbitration. The Special Committee of the Folketing which considered this plea reported, however, that small countries like Denmark would find it difficult to lead the world in matters of international organization.[23] Searching for a more practical objective, Frederik Bajer, in a paper entitled "On the Prevention of War by Arbitration," suggested that Denmark should propose arbitration treaties to her neighbours, Norway and Sweden. Bajer argued that such treaties would furnish excellent moral support when it came to withstanding the attempts of Great Powers to entice or threaten them into participation in wars as Allies.[24]

In 1888 Bajer secured the adoption of a motion by the Danish Rigsdag advocating that all differences of whatever kind arising among the three Scandinavian Governments should in the future be settled by arbitration.[25] In 1890 and again in 1897 the Norwegian Storting decided to present Addresses to the King urging the conclusion of arbitration treaties between Norway and foreign powers. The Address of 1890, supported by the Left and a part of the Right, was adopted by a vote of 89 to 24 in the Storting. But it was rejected by the Swedish Foreign Minister, acting also for Norway. The second Address on arbitration, which was adopted unanimously in the

[22] K. P. Arnoldson, *Pax Mundi,* p. 15, and Beales, *op. cit.,* p. 147.

[23] Beales, *op. cit.,* p. 148.

[24] Arnoldson, *op. cit.,* pp. 17, 18.

[25] Beales, *op. cit.,* p. 183. This resolution was carried in the Folketing by 50 votes to 16. See *Herald of Peace* (1886), p. 71.

Storting, also came to naught when a Swedish controlled "Ministerial" Cabinet on February 15, 1899, "somewhat lamely" decided
not to act before seeing what The Hague Peace Conference would do
in the matter of arbitration.[26] The obstacle which thwarted the efforts
of the peace societies to secure any inter-Scandinavian arbitration
treaties was the dispute between Norway and Sweden over certain
constitutional questions concerning their Union. Norway wished to
proceed with arbitration treaties independently of Sweden, while
the Swedish Riksdag would not consent to separate action.[27] Although resolutions were adopted in the respective parliaments similar
to the recommendation for a threefold Scandinavian Arbitration
Treaty urged by the Third Scandinavian Peace Congress in 1895,
no arbitration treaties were concluded between the Scandinavian
States until the dissolution of the Union in 1905. Meanwhile, Denmark had turned elsewhere to negotiate the first "all-in" arbitration
treaty in European history.[28]

Before noting the treaties of arbitration which the Scandinavian
States made prior to the War, let us observe their arbitration policies
at The Hague Peace Conferences of 1899 and 1907. At the First
Conference their delegations were not active in the discussion concerning the draft convention for the Pacific Settlement of International Disputes, which, to be sure, they accepted. In the 1907 Conference their views were more fully expressed. All three delegations
declared in favour of the principle of obligatory arbitration, to which
certain States were opposed even in its most restricted form. The
position of Denmark was the most advanced of the Scandinavian
States. She had already under Governments of the Left (*Venstre*)
made conventions with the Netherlands, Italy and Portugal, the
so-called Deuntzer treaties, which required the submission of all
disputes of whatever character to compulsory arbitration.[29] The

[26] *Stortings Forhandlinger* (1890), Vol. 7, pp. 219-36; *ibid.* (1897), Vol. 7,
pp. 1163-72. See especially the account of these matters in Oscar J. Falnes, *Norway
and the Nobel Peace Prize,* pp. 117-25.

[27] Beales, *op. cit.,* p. 212.

[28] The Danish-Dutch treaty of February 12, 1904. See the letter of the Danish
Minister of Foreign Affairs to Theodore Marburg, October 6, 1916, available in
Marburg, *The Development of the League of Nations Idea,* Vol. I, p. 171. For the
text of the treaty see *British and Foreign State Papers,* Vol. 98: 454.

[29] *infra,* p. 22.

epoch-making convention with the Netherlands had provided, in Article IV, that that convention stood open for adherence by other States. When, therefore, the Danish delegation directed the attention of The Hague Conference to these conventions, it was equivalent to an expression of willingness to conclude with any State a compulsory arbitration treaty with absolutely no reservation.[30] This extreme position was equalled at the 1907 Conference only by that of the Dominican Republic.[31]

The Norwegian delegation also favoured a far-reaching obligation to accept compulsory arbitration. The delegation was instructed by the Michelson Government "to support in the Conference any effort tending to make international arbitration more obligatory and more extended."[32] Dr Christian L. Lange, whose services on behalf of world peace will be frequently referred to in this treatise, said that "The Norwegian delegation would perhaps be prepared to go farther than any of the propositions that have been submitted to the sub-commission."[33] He did not, however, express approval of the Danish-Dutch unrestricted arbitration treaty of 1904. In view of the attitude of nearly all Governments that the acceptance of an obligation for compulsory arbitration should not include disputes involving *vital interests,* M. Lange admitted that any possible convention must be of a quite limited scope. He urged that there should be no such reservation on questions involving the *honour* of States, for it was highly dishonourable for a State to invoke its honour to elude an obligation of the kind envisaged.[34] The Norwegian Government wished to confer on a court of arbitration the authority to determine, in case of doubt, whether or not disputes actually came within the field covered by a convention.[35]

The Swedish Government of the Right (Högern) held a more conservative view. M. H. L. Hammarskjöld explained that in the existing condition of the world, it would be asking too much to

30 "Declaration of the Danish Delegation" (James Brown Scott, editor). *The Proceedings of The Hague Peace Conferences, Conference of 1907,* Vol. II, p. 880.
31 *ibid.,* Vol. II, p. 412; also Annex 24, pp. 879 ff.
32 *ibid.,* Vol. II, p. 256.
33 *ibid.,* Vol. II, p. 257.
34 *ibid.,* Vol. II, p. 483.
35 *ibid.,* Vol. II, p. 258.

require matters of the highest interest to be submitted to compulsory arbitration.[36] His Government proposed that arbitration should be recognized as the most effective and equitable means of settling disputes of a legal nature, especially those involving the interpretation of treaties.[37] The obligation, however, to resort to arbitration should not include disputes involving the *independence* or *vital interests* of States. The Swedish proposition further provided that each party in dispute is its own judge of whether a difference involves its *independence or vital interests,* the only exception thereto being certain cases involving pecuniary claims.[38]

If the Swedish arbitration policy at the Second Hague Conference was more modest than that of Denmark and that of Norway, it was, nevertheless, more progressive than the Anglo-American project which made exception also of differences involving the *honour* of States. Yet despite the approval given the Anglo-American project by a large majority of delegations, no obligation to accept arbitration—except in cases involving a claim for the collection of contract debts—was recognized by the conference. The opposition of Germany to compulsory arbitration had been the chief hindrance.[39]

The attitude adopted by the Scandinavian delegations concerning the creation of a Permanent Court of Arbitral Justice was in some respects a forerunner of their policy expressed after the War, when efforts were finally successful in establishing a permanent court. In 1907, however, the Danish Government was not yet converted to the belief that such a court was desirable. M. Brun explained that his Government considered that the proposed Court of Arbitral Justice was "contrary to the very essence of the idea of international arbitration which would have the parties in dispute freely choose their arbitrators in each particular case."[40] This disapproval of centralization was really indicative of a profound distrust of the domi-

---

[36] *ibid.,* Vol. II, pp. 237-9.

[37] For the "Proposition of the Swedish Delegation" see *The Proceedings of The Hague Conferences, Conference of 1907,* Vol. II, Annex 22, p. 878. See also *ibid.,* pp. 416-17. Compare the view of Hj. L. Hammarskjöld in his article entitled "Internationella Skiljedomsaftal," *Nordisk Tidskrift för Vetenskap, Konst och Industri,* 1903, pp. 561-77.

[38] See Articles 17 and 18 of the Swedish Proposition.

[39] Compare Hershey, *op. cit.,* p. 470.

[40] *The Proceedings of The Hague Peace Conferences, Conference of 1907,* Vol. II, p. 147.

nation of international organization by the Great Powers. Although the Norwegian and Swedish delegations did not object to the establishment of a Permanent International Court, they insisted that the sole basis of composition of such a court must be "the absolute and unreserved recognition of the equality of all sovereign States."[41] Because of the disagreement between the large and small States on this important question of principle, it was not possible in 1907 to create a permanent court.

From this digression, let us turn to the practical achievements in the field of arbitration which Denmark, Norway and Sweden had made before the War.

No country could point to an advance comparable to that made by Denmark. Reference has already been made to the Danish arbitration treaty of February 12, 1904, with the Netherlands, the first in which two European States engaged to submit to arbitration all disputes without exception.[42] In the period before the War Denmark concluded arbitration conventions with twelve States,[43] of which those with Italy, Portugal and Brazil were of the same far-reaching type as the Danish-Dutch Convention. The convention with Brazil, however, made a reservation with respect to disputes which concerned certain constitutional questions. Of the other eight conventions concluded by Denmark, those with Great Britain, France, the United States and Belgium concerned only legal disputes; the last, however, also dealt with disputes concerning the amount of financial claims. All eight countries make exception of disputes which concern a party's *independence*, and all but the Danish-Norwegian Convention contain the corresponding reservation in regard to the *vital interests* of the States. Three, namely, the conventions with

[41] See the speech of M. Hagerup, the delegate of Norway, *ibid.*, Vol. II, p. 160. Also M. Brun's speech, *ibid.*, p. 147. The Norwegian delegation supported the British *voeu* for a permanent court, *ibid.*, p. 160.

[42] Brazil and the Argentine Republic have agreed to submit to arbitration all controversies in so far as they "do not turn upon questions involving constitutional rules of the one or the other of the two countries." *A.J.I.L., Supp.* Vol. III (1910), pp. 1-4, Art. 1. In 1902 the Argentine Republic and Chile bound themselves to submit all controversies except those affecting the Constitution of either country. *A.J.I.L.*, Vol. I (1908), p. 290. Cited in Hershey, *op. cit.*, p. 480

[43] The following description of Danish arbitration treaties before the War is taken from the Report of the Select Committee of the Folketing of February 13, 1930. *Rigsdagstidende* (1929-1930). *Tillæg* B., pp. 697-8.

France, Great Britain and the United States, have in addition made reservations concerning the *honour* of States and the *interests of third parties*. In the conventions with Norway and Belgium, all disputes concerning the interpretation of treaties are submitted to arbitration.[44]

The pre-War arbitration conventions of Sweden, on the whole, were less far-reaching than the Danish ones.[45] Thirteen conventions were made, none of which contained obligations for wholly unlimited arbitration. The treaties with Belgium, Great Britain, France, Portugal and the United States excepted from compulsory arbitration disputes involving a State's *honour, integrity* and *vital interests,* even in cases where, incontestably, only matters of law were involved. The convention with Brazil prescribed arbitration in disputes involving national interests, but made exception for the most important subjects, and with the right (as in the above five conventions) for the parties to define them for themselves. In the treaties with Switzerland and Spain certain legal disputes—such as the interpretation of treaties and the fixing of the amount of damages in disputes wherein the legal ground was clear—were to be submitted to arbitration no matter how vital the interests involved. In the most advanced Swedish treaties—those with Norway, Denmark and

[44] Following is a list of the general Danish arbitration conventions entered into prior to 1914:
1. The Netherlands, Convention of February 12, 1904 (unlimited).
2. Russia, Convention of March 1, 1905.
3. Belgium, Convention of April 26, 1905.
4. France, Conventions of September 15, 1905, and August 9, 1911.
5. Great Britain, Convention of October 25, 1905.
6. Spain, Convention of December 1, 1905.
7. Italy, Convention of December 16, 1905 (unlimited).
8. Portugal, Convention of March 20, 1907 (unlimited).
9. United States, Convention of May 18, 1908.
10. Sweden, Convention of July 17, 1908.
11. Norway, Convention of October 8, 1908.
12. Brazil, Convention of November 27, 1911 (unlimited, yet excepting constitutional matters).

See Axel Møller, *International Law in War and Peace,* Vol. 2, p. 14, for this list of treaties and for the list of eighteen arbitration treaties (seven of which are renewals) entered into by Denmark after the Great War.

[45] For this information see especially Löfgren, *De Nordiska Förliknings- och Skiljedomsavtalen deras Ställning till det Internationalla Rättssystem,* pp. 2-3. Compare Bellquist, *op. cit.,* pp. 323-4, who follows Löfgren closely, but not exactly.

Italy—disputes on non-legal (political) questions were also to be referred to arbitration, but with the usual reservation on *independence, integrity* and *vital interests*. The question of whether a dispute involved *vital interests,* moreover, should be decided by a court of arbitration. But the parties reserved the right of withholding from arbitration disputes in which either of them insisted that its *independence* or *integrity* was risked.[46]

The number of Norwegian arbitration conventions concluded before the War was comparable to that concluded by Denmark and Sweden.[47] Before the dissolution of the Union of Sweden and Norway in 1905, six conventions were entered into with foreign Powers

[46] Löfgren, *op. cit.,* pp. 2-3.

Møller, *op. cit.,* p. 15, notes 2 and 3.

Following is a list of Swedish arbitration conventions entered into prior to the Great War:

    (A) Conventions made before the Dissolution of the Union on behalf of Sweden and Norway:

        France, Convention of July 9, 1904.

        Great Britain, Convention of August 11, 1904.

        Belgium, Convention of November 30, 1904.

        Russia, Convention of December 9, 1904.

        Switzerland, Convention of December 17, 1904.

        Spain, Convention of January 23, 1905.

    (B) Conventions made by Sweden:

        Portugal, Convention of May 6, 1905.

        Norway, Convention of October 26, 1905.

        United States, Convention of May 2, 1908.

        Denmark, Convention of July 17, 1908.

        Brazil, Convention of December 14, 1909.

        Italy, Convention of April 13, 1911.

        Portugal, Convention of November 15, 1913.

[47] For the arbitration conventions concluded by Norway before the dissolution of the Union see *supra,* note 46.

Following is a list of arbitration treaties concluded by Norway independently prior to 1914 (renewals of conventions are not included):

    Sweden, Convention of October 26, 1905.

    United States, Convention of April 4, 1908.

    Denmark, Convention of October 8, 1908.

    Portugal, Convention of December 8, 1908.

    Brazil, Convention of July 13, 1909.

    Italy, Convention of December 4, 1910.

All of these conventions are printed in *British and Foreign State Papers* in French or English. See also the comment of the Storting's *Konstitutionskomiteen* on the development of arbitration in Norway between 1890 and 1910. *Stortings Forhandlinger* (1912), Vol. 6a, *Indst. S. XXXXIII.*

jointly by these two Kingdoms. The later Norwegian arbitration conventions are of the types already described above, with the exception of the most far-reaching Norwegian convention, that of December 4, 1910, with Italy. This convention provides for the submission of all disputes to arbitration with the exception of those involving the *independence* or *integrity* of the parties.[48]

In conclusion, it may be noted that the most advanced arbitration conventions of Denmark, Norway and Sweden show the following: Denmark was prepared to accept compulsory arbitration of all disputes without any reservation; Norway made exception of disputes involving the *independence* and *integrity* of the parties, but allowed them to be the judge of whether such questions were involved; Sweden, in addition to these reservations, also made exceptions of disputes involving *vital interests,* but she would permit an arbitral body to determine whether such interests (not, however, *independence* or *integrity*) were involved.

[48] *State Papers,* Vol. 103: 565. For the development of international arbitration prior to the World War see Lange, *L'arbitrage international en 1913.* Bruxelles (Union Interparlementaire), 1914.

CHAPTER III

SOME WAR-TIME PROPOSALS FOR INTERNATIONAL ORGANIZATION

Unofficial Plans Before March 1918

FROM 1914 to 1918 "the Northern European neutrals provided a clearing-house for pacific speculation"[1] out of which
crystallized certain proposals for the creation of a Society of
Nations. During these years hundreds of peace meetings were held
throughout Scandinavia, attended by thousands eager to testify to
the need for a new world order.[2] For the purpose of tracing the
development of the Scandinavian attitude towards international
organization, certain comments on the contribution of three or four
organizations will suffice.

The first of these to be considered is the Central Organization for
Durable Peace which, although not a Scandinavian organization,
was one in which individuals from the Northern countries played
a prominent part. The work of the Central Organization, which was
founded at The Hague in 1915, had an influence on the Scandinavian
attitude because some of the persons who participated in its discussions were the leading figures in Danish, Norwegian and Swedish
peace activity.[3] They were in a position, therefore, both to influence

---

[1] Beales, *op. cit.,* p. 301.

[2] B. de Jong van Beek en Donk, *Neutral Europe and the League of Nations,*
pp. 16-17. In Scandinavia and the Netherlands about 800 meetings were held in the
first days of August 1916, attended by 300,000 persons, who almost unanimously
applauded the resolutions taken by the Ford Neutral Conference. In Sweden,
106,000 persons adhered, within a short time to the "Minimum-Programme" while
in Norway 374 out of 674 Municipal Councils adhered to this programme and 918
Unions and Associations did likewise.

[3] On the work of the Central Organization for Durable Peace see Lange,
"Préparation de la Société des Nations" in Munch, *Les origines et L'œuvre de la
Société des Nations,* Vol. I, pp. 15-21. Lange, *Exposé des travaux de l'Organisa-
tion* (Organisation Centrale pour une Paix Durable), La Haye, 1917.

the lines upon which the "Minimum-Programme" was developed, and to direct the thinking of the Scandinavian peoples for the acceptance of a common programme. For instance, Baron Adelswärd, former Swedish Minister of Finance, presided over the commission created for the study of the principle of non-aggression.[4] Professor Halvdan Koht, who later became Norwegian Minister of Foreign Affairs, acted in a similar capacity for the commission which considered the problem of nationalities. The Scandinavians were inclined to stress that part of the "Minimum-Programme" based on the principle that if peace were to be lasting, it must be founded on justice between nations.

Perhaps the most valuable study for the guidance of the commissions later named by the three Scandinavian Governments to formulate proposals for an International Juridical Organization was that submitted by Dr Christian L. Lange of Norway and entitled "The Development of the Work of The Hague."[5] This report advised the continuation and extension of the principles and methods accepted at The Hague Peace Conferences of 1899 and 1907. Universality of membership, independence and equality of States, the progressive development of international law, and the exclusion of political and economic questions from periodic peace conferences were principles urged as the proper basis for the future international system.[6] Two recommendations in this report were important advances beyond the work of The Hague. The first was an intimation that the maintenance of peace in the future would require the abandonment of the old conception of neutrality. The second pointed to the need for the extension of international cooperation between technical groups, official and unofficial, in special fields of international concern.[7]

Although the "Minimum-Programme" received wide support in Scandinavia, it does not represent the Scandinavian point of view so well as the proposals made in 1918 by the conference of the Scan-

---

[4] For this and other reports of the organization see *Recueil de Rapports sur les différents Points du Programme-Minimum*, La Haye, 1917; *Problems of the International Settlement*, with an Introduction by Lowes Dickinson, London, 1918.

[5] *Rapport présenté par le Président de la Commission internationale d'Études No. IV, Développement de L'œuvre de la Haye*, La Haye, 1917.

[6] *ibid.*, pp. 7-24, 47.

[7] *ibid.*, p. 22.

dinavian Inter-Parliamentary Groups.[8] As early as November 1914, the Joint Council of these groups discussed the problem of a durable peace.[9] At Copenhagen in 1915 the conference of delegates from the Scandinavian groups considered the advisability of making a careful study of this question. The following year, when the annual conference met at Stockholm, Christian Lange, Secretary-General of the Inter-Parliamentary Union, having previously consulted the Swedish and Norwegian groups, submitted a complete programme for the organization of juridical and conciliation procedure, fortified by sanctions.[10] M. Lange took the view that arbitration, the sole procedure recommended for the peaceful settlement of disputes in the Danish Peace Advocates Catechism of 1890,[11] should be supplemented by the creation of a genuine Permanent Court of International Justice which would deal with questions of a clearly legal nature. A permanent court of trained judges constantly working together would contribute to the establishment of a real legal tradition and to the development of international law.[12] M. Lange called attention to the detailed scheme for a court which a special commission of the Inter-Parliamentary Union had drafted in 1914.[13]

His proposal for conciliation embodied the so-called "cooling-off" theory of the Bryan treaties of 1913 and 1914, which pledged the

[8] Since 1910 there have been annual meetings, or conferences, of delegates from the three Inter-Parliamentary Groups in Scandinavia. As the groups in these countries comprise the great majority of the national representatives in the Rigsdag, Riksdag and Storting, "the Scandinavian Congress represents truly the Parliaments of the three Kingdoms." At the 1916 Conference, there were nineteen delegates from each group. *Le Mouvement Pacifiste*, July-September 1915, p. 113. See also Falnes, *op. cit.*, pp. 115 ff.

[9] For an excellent summary of the activities of the Scandinavian Inter-Parliamentary Groups during the War, in regard to the organization of peace, see Lange, "Préparation de la Société des Nations," *op. cit.*, pp. 39-41.

[10] This plan was published by Lange in Norwegian under the title *Mellemfolkelige Retsmidler*, Kristiania, 1916. See also *Det Nordiska Interparlamentariska Förbundets Åttonde Delegerademöte, Stockholm, August 1916*, pp. 115-30.

[11] *infra*, Chapter II, pp. 17 ff.

[12] Lange, *Mellemfolkelige Retsmidler* (*Foredrag holdt i den Svenske og den Norske Interparlamentariske Gruppe*), p. 15. The citations here are from the edition published by Det Mallingske Bogtrykkeri, Kristiania, 1916.

[13] M. Henri la Fontaine was *rapporteur* of this commission. This draft statute was submitted to the Committee of Jurists appointed by the Council of the League of Nations in 1920 to elaborate plans for the Permanent Court of International Justice. See *Documents presented to the Advisory Committee of Jurists*, pp. 335-43.

parties not to go to war for a period of twelve months, while a dispute was under inquiry by an international commission. This moratorium for war was designed to give an opportunity for the mobilization of public opinion favourable to peaceful settlement. It should be noted that M. Lange proposed a single Institution of Inquiry and Conciliation, rather than bilateral and decentralized commissions of inquiry recommended by The Hague Conferences.[14]

These methods of achieving the peaceful settlement of international disputes were to be reinforced, if necessary, by sanctions. Aware of the difficulty of obtaining consent for coercive measures from some States, especially those in the North, M. Lange suggested that the obligation of members to employ sanctions should not be far-reaching. For this reason, he did not include in his proposals the demand of the French and intransigent pacifists for the obligatory arbitration of all disputes. This he deemed less important than the recognition of the principle of collective action in restricted cases.[15] When the application of sanctions was necessary, the action of the member States was to be coordinated by an International Executive Committee, which should institute penalties by stages, using military force only as a last resort. M. Lange remarked that the military measures "would, of course, be applied by the Great Powers."[16]

The proposals of the Secretary-General were in some respects too advanced for many of the politicians of the Northern countries, who calculated that public opinion would be sceptical of the dangers to traditional neutrality which acceptance would entail. When, therefore, the Scandinavian Inter-Parliamentary Groups adopted in 1918 a resolution favouring the creation of a society of nations, no provision for sanctions was included.[17] The Danish Peace Society had already at The Hague Conference of April 7-10, 1915, rejected the "Minimum-Programme" because it included military sanctions.[18] As

[14] *Mellemfolkelige Retsmidler,* pp. 12-13, 17-18. See also Zimmern, *op. cit.,* p. 343.
[15] Lange, "Préparation de la Société des Nations," *op. cit.,* p. 40, and *Mellemfolkelige Retsmidler,* pp. 19-20.
[16] *ibid.,* p. 20. The problem of sanctions had been discussed before the War at the Universal Peace Congress at Geneva in September 1912. *The Peace Movement,* Vol. I, Nos. 19/20, pp. 302-6.
[17] Lange, "Préparation de la Société des Nations," *op. cit.,* p. 41, and reference.
[18] Petersen and Nielsen, *op. cit.,* p. 87. M. Lange states that so far as he is aware only "The World Court League" and the "Société danoise de la Paix" (Dansk

Frederik Bajer, after a long life dedicated to the service of neutrality, wrote in the Danish periodical *Fredsbladet* in June 1918,
"the sacrifice would be too great if a little State went to war because
it was a Member of the League of Nations." He declared that Denmark must insist upon the retention of neutrality as a legal status in
the new order.[19]

The rejection of sanctions by the conference of the Scandinavian
Inter-Parliamentary Groups in 1918 did not signify that M. Lange
had no following on the question of sanctions. Many prominent persons in the Northern countries, especially among the Social Democrats, advocated the use of force against a disturber of the peace, after
mediation had failed. Baron E. Palmstierna, for example, although
he opposed any "World-Government or Trust of the Great Powers,"
expressed the view that an international police force should be established, supported by the small as well as the larger States.[20] He accepted the view of his compatriot M. Edward Wavrinsky that the
League of Nations should have an organ known as Public Prosecutor,
independent of individual States, which would have the duty to
watch for violations of international law, and, if necessary, to prose-
cute offending States. Such an arrangement, which was inspired by
a provision in the Swedish Constitution, would avoid the possibility
of a State that might be a party to the case taking the initiative in
mobilizing the political power of the League against a blameable
party.[21] This suggestion is characteristic of later Swedish policy at
Geneva when efforts were made to prevent the use of the League
machinery for achieving the political ends of individual members.

Fredsforening) wished to maintain the situation existing *before* the War—i.e., no
international application of sanctions. Lange, *op. cit.,* at p. 52.

[19] *Fredsbladet* (June 14, 1918), 27 Aarg. nr. 6, p. 46. Title of the article, "Skal
Neutraliteten ofres for Folkeforbundet?"

[20] Palmstierna, *An International Police Force* (International Congress for the
Study of the Principles of a Durable Peace, Berne, 1916), p. 17. This monograph
was published the same year in Stockholm in Swedish under the title, *En Interna-
tionell Ordningsmakt.* See Lange, *op. cit.,* p. 53. It may be of interest that Alfred
Nobel held the view that the most effective way of avoiding war was by means of
joint action against any State that broke the peace. In January 1893, he wrote, "All
States should bind themselves absolutely to take action against the first aggressor."
H. Schück and R. Sohlman, *The Life of Alfred Nobel,* p. 203.

[21] Palmstierna, *op. cit.,* pp. 17-19.

Profound differences of opinion at the 1918 conference of the Scandinavian Inter-Parliamentary Groups existed on the question of compulsory arbitration, even as they did on sanctions. The wide gap between the official Danish and Swedish positions at the Second Hague Conference has already been emphasized.[22] In 1918, it was not yet possible for the principle of the Deuntzer "all-in" arbitration treaties to be accepted generally in the North. The conference therefore chose an intermediate course by providing that only disputes of a justiciable character should be designated for compulsory arbitration. Such disputes should be referred to a Permanent Court of International Justice, or to the old Hague Court of Arbitration, whose decision or award would be binding upon the parties.[23]

All other disputes were to be submitted to permanent Commissions of Inquiry and Conciliation in which the parties to the dispute should be represented.[24] As there was no obligation to accept a recommendation of such commissions, all resort to war was not legally excluded in these Scandinavian proposals.

It is significant that great importance was now attached to conciliation procedure. At The Hague Conferences prior to the War little interest in this procedure had been manifested by the Scandinavian delegations.[25] Not until the Bryan treaties were negotiated in 1914 did conciliation gain much active support in the North, but during the War this procedure took its place by the side of arbitration as a major objective of Scandinavian peace-agitators.[26] At the conference of the Scandinavian Inter-Parliamentary Groups in 1918 the value of conciliation was given a prominent place in the suggested proposals.

The explanation for this new development in the Scandinavian peace movement lies in the challenge, offered by the War, of finding some peaceful means of settling every dispute which might arise between States. Arbitration or judicial settlement could not be rec-

[22] *supra,* Chapter II, pp. 19-21.

[23] Lange, "Préparation de la Société des Nations," *op. cit.,* p. 41.

[24] Lange's scheme for a Permanent Council of Inquiry and Conciliation was inserted, but it was only to serve as a plan for particular commissions.

[25] Apparently no declaration was made by the Danish, Norwegian and Swedish delegations on this subject at The Hague Conferences.

[26] "Bryan Treaties" were made between the United States and each of the Northern States. (Denmark, Treaty of April 17, 1914; Norway, Treaty of June 24, 1914; Sweden, October 13, 1914.) See *British and Foreign State Papers,* Vols. 107 and 108.

ommended for all disputes, as certain sections of opinion in the North were unwilling to accept arbitration for disputes involving vital interests. It was well known that in other countries there was even greater opposition to such a revolutionary step. Some practical method of dealing with political disputes, which States would be willing to employ and which offered possibilities of a solution acceptable to the parties, was needed. Compulsory resort to conciliation before an impartial commission in which the parties to a dispute were represented seemed to be the answer, for, unlike arbitration, no obligation rested upon the parties to accept the finding.

The resolutions adopted by the 1918 conference of the Scandinavian Inter-Parliamentary Groups were perhaps the most typical expression of the Scandinavian attitude toward international organization during the War. Certain other groups, however, preferred more ambitious undertakings. A radical segment of the Swedish pacifists, for example, met at Varberg in June 1915, and advocated Herr Carl Lindhagen's "Maximum-Programme" in preference to the "Minimum-Programme" of the Central Organization for Durable Peace.[27] This scheme included proposals for the creation of a world parliament, the suppression of national armies and of all war materials, and the acceptance of compulsory arbitration for all disputes.[28]

Another important conference was organized by the Comité Hollando-Scandinave Socialiste, which met at Stockholm in 1917 under the presidency of Hjalmar Branting, the leader of Swedish Social Democracy.[29] This committee also favoured the obligatory arbitration of all disputes, and general disarmament. It proposed the creation of permanent international machinery for the application of sanctions against States that should disregard their obligations to keep the peace. An extension of parliamentary control over foreign policy was deemed essential to rid the peoples of Europe of the "old diplomacy."

[27] de Jong van Beek en Donk, Neutral Europe and the League of Nations, pp. 17-18.
[28] For the Resolutions adopted by the General Swedish Congress in Favour of Peace (Varberg) see Le Mouvement Pacifiste (July-September 1915), pp. 72-5. See also Svenska Freds- och Skiljedomsföreningen, Jubileumsskrift: 1883-1933, pp. 44-5.
[29] For the following information see Lange, "Préparation de la Société des Nations," op. cit., pp. 27, 42; de Jong van Beek en Donk, op. cit., pp. 35-48; Beales, op. cit., p. 300. The report of the Comité Hollando-Scandinave Socialiste is available in "Stockholm," Comité organisateur de la Conference socialiste internationale de Stockholm, "Rapport général," pp. 411-521.

The unique character of this programme, however, lay in the far-reaching economic and social measures which were envisaged. Economic nationalism, including the use of protective tariffs and the denial of the "open door" in colonial areas, was condemned. International machinery, declared the report, should be created for the regulation of world economic relations in the interest of all peoples. In addition, international conventions for the protection of workers were suggested, thereby foreshadowing the International Labour Organization.

The committee pursued its work from May 1917 to January 1918; but it did not succeed in organizing the General Socialist Congress which it at first had contemplated. This programme indicated, however, the growing force of internationalism in Scandinavia, which, if in advance of the general thinking, was an important factor in the development of later Scandinavian policy in the League of Nations.[30]

Plan of the Scandinavian Official Commissions

Before 1910 the peace movement in the Scandinavian countries had been primarily absorbed in the problem of creating an "island of peace" in the North, which would stand high above the threatening billows of European conflict. But the consequences of the War, even for Scandinavia, indicated the urgency of placing greater emphasis on the problem of world peace. The proposals of the voluntary organizations just noted testify to this new direction in Scandinavian peace activity. Soon the Governments of the three countries were obliged to face the obvious need for a better international system.

Following a request of the Scandinavian Inter-Parliamentary Groups,[31] a decision was made by the Ministers' Meeting at Christiania, in November 1917, which led to the appointment of Commissions by the Danish, Norwegian and Swedish Governments to elaborate jointly a common plan for an international juridical or-

[30] The Congress of the National Organization of Swedish Syndicates (August 1917) in Stockholm adopted a resolution giving full adherence to the peace work of the Comité Hollando-Scandinave Socialiste. *Manchester Guardian,* August 22, 1917.

[31] The conference at Stockholm in 1916 voted a resolution requesting the Governments of the three Scandinavian States to take the initiative for a cooperation between the neutral States with the view of safeguarding "les intérêts des États neutres à la fin de la guerre." Lange, "Préparation de la Société des Nations pendant la Guerre," *op. cit.,* p. 40.

ganization. The Commissions met in Copenhagen, May 13-22, 1918, for preliminary considerations, and recommended to their Governments that a diplomatic conference of the neutral States be called for the purpose of safeguarding their interests after the War, and more particularly for the formulation of proposals for an international organization.[32]

The other European neutral States—the Netherlands, Spain, and Switzerland—were unofficially invited to participate in such a conference by the Swedish Government, with the approval of the Danish and Norwegian Governments; but each of them, although expressing sympathy for the undertaking of the proposed study, declined on the ground that it would be inopportune.[33] The Swiss Government pointed out that a Swiss Commission of Study had not completed enough of its work to justify Swiss participation at that time. The answers of the Governments of the Netherlands and of Spain, according to one member of the Swedish Commission, appeared to signify that "ils ne tenaient pas à s'exposer aux soupçons et aux désagrements qu'une action commune des États neutres risquait d'entrainer dans la situation internationale alors existante."[34]

The Danish, Norwegian and Swedish Commissions, however, were authorized to continue their study, which resulted, shortly after the Armistice in 1918, in their agreement on draft proposals for an "International Juridical Organization." It was hoped that this plan, which was communicated to the three Foreign Offices early in December, would be submitted to an international peace conference

[32] Bellquist, op. cit., pp. 266, 267 and notes.
[33] For an account of the proceedings of the Scandinavian Commissions see *Kungl. Maj:ts proposition* nr. 90, *Bihang till Riksdagens Protokoll* (1920), 1 Saml. 75 häft (nr. 90), hereinafter cited as *Proposition 90*; Utrikesdepartementet, *Betänkande Rörande En Internationell Rättsordning Avgivet av därtill av Kungl. Maj:ts utsedda kommitterada, jämte förslag till konvention utarbetat av Ovannämnde kommitterade i samarbete med motsvarande av danska ock norska regeringarna tillsatta kommiteér,* hereinafter cited as *Betänkande, Swedish Committee;* von Würtemberg, "L'Œuvre Commune des États Scandinaves," *Les origines et l'œuvre de la Société des Nations,* Vol. II; Bellquist, *Some Aspects of the Recent Foreign Policy of Sweden,* pp. 265-7. For the replies of the Swiss Government (October 2, 1918), the Government of the Netherlands (November 12, 1918), and the Spanish Government (November 25, 1918) see *Betänkande, Swedish Committee,* Bilag 6, 7, 8, pp. 110-12.
[34] von Würtemberg, op. cit., p. 209.

attended by all civilized States, and would there be considered as "matériel precieux" for the organization of lasting peace.[35]

The draft plan of the Scandinavian Commissions[36] should be viewed first of all in the light of the reasons which prompted the initiation of the study. It was not merely the humanitarian revulsion of the Scandinavian peoples to the horrors of war. By 1917 the loss and suffering which the Armageddon caused to these neutral States acted as a stimulus rousing the perplexed Governments to action. The fuel and food famine, the terrific toll on the high seas of lives and property—Norway, for example, losing nearly half of her great merchant fleet—the increased expense necessitated by the maintenance of neutrality, to say nothing of the constant and real fear of being forced into the War—all were obvious reasons why the Northern neutrals had a vital interest in accepting the challenge for the future organization of peace. True, the War brought pecuniary profits to some individuals, but on the whole it meant hardship, and material, as well as spiritual, loss for the Scandinavian peoples.[37]

Another important reason for appointing Commissions of Inquiry rested on the belief that in any case some new international system would be established after the conclusion of hostilities. By the time of the Ministers' Meeting which decided that such a study should be made, the establishment of a league for the maintenance of peace had already become a war aim of the Allied Powers, and had been endorsed by the Central Powers as well in their reply of August 16, 1917, to the Papal Note.[38] Prudence suggested, therefore, that the

[35] von Würtemberg, op. cit., p. 213.

[36] This proposed Convention is available in English as: "Draft of a Proposed Convention. Respecting an International Juridical Organization" in Permanent Court of International Justice, Advisory Committee of Jurists, Documents Presented to the Committee Relating to Existing Plans for the Establishment of a Permanent Court of International Justice, Annex 5, pp. 151-201. For the Swedish Draft see Betänkande Rörande En Internationell Rättsordning, op cit., Annex I, pp. 23-57. (Utkast till Konvention Rörande en Mellanfolklig Rättsordning Utarbetat av de Svenska, Danska ock Norska Regeringarna Tillsatta Kommittéer.) The French draft is printed in Annex II, pp. 58-85, of the same document. See also Norway, Utenriksdepartementet, St. prp. nr. 33 (1920), Bilag 1. (Utkast til internasjonal retsordning.) There are other publications also in Danish, French and English. See Florence Wilson, The Origins of the League Covenant.

[37] P. G. Vigness, Neutrality of Norway in the World War, p. 123. Eli F. Heckscher and Others, Sweden, Norway, Denmark and Iceland in the War.

[38] Felix Morley, Society of Nations, p. 7.

neutral States should investigate the character which the future organization should take, if it were to advance and safeguard their own, as well as general interests.

This was not all. The Governments in the North felt that a special rôle called for their acceptance. When the new organization was founded, it would be useful to hear the voice of States which had escaped the passions of war.[39] Especially among those actively engaged in the organized peace movement in Scandinavia, there was a conviction that the Scandinavian peoples had a real mission in the work for peace.[40] The Swedish Commission took note of the fact that eminent statesmen in belligerent countries had pointed to the special task of neutral States in preparing for the new internationalism—a special task because they were not so absorbed with the burdens of war.[41]

The distinguished personnel of the three Commissions is a tribute to the importance attached by the Governments to this study. The inclusion of some of the most outstanding and active political leaders was designed to procure a plan acceptable to public opinion and worthy of its support. From Sweden there were Branting and Trygger, the leaders of the Socialists and Conservatives, respectively; from Norway, Blehr, Minister of Justice, and Mowinckel, later Prime Minister; and from Denmark, Neergaard, a former Liberal Prime Minister, and Peter Munch, Radical Minister of Defence and advocate of unilateral disarmament. Diplomats, jurists, professors strengthened and broadened the outlook of the Commissions. Hagerup, Lange and Grieg had been Norwegian delegates to The Hague Conference of 1907. Lange was Secretary-General of the Inter-Parliamentary Union, and Adelswärd was president of the Swedish Group

[39] Munch, *La Politique du Danemark dans la Société des Nations*, pp. 7-8.

[40] At the General Swedish Conference in Favour of Peace, which met at Varberg, June 25-27, 1915, resolutions were adopted emphasizing the *mission* of the Scandinavian people in the work for peace, and stating that of all neutrals the Scandinavians "seem to have the greatest chance of having their point of view taken into consideration." *The Peace Movement*, July-September 1915, pp. 72-5. See also "The Mission of the Small States," by Fridtjof Nansen (An Authorized Interview) in *American-Scandinavian Review*, Vol. VI (January-February 1918), pp. 9-13.

[41] *Betänkande, Swedish Commission*, Annex 5, p. 99. "Memorandum" attached to the "Note Verbale" of the Swedish Government of September 7, 1918, communicated to the neutral Governments. See also Annex 3, "Letter of the Swedish Commission to the Swedish Minister of Foreign Affairs" (May 22, 1918).

of the same Union. These men, who served at various times on the Commissions of Inquiry, had already participated in the unofficial study of sundry groups, which had previously dealt with the peace problem. It was indeed a suitable body for the task assigned.[42]

Let us now turn to the official Scandinavian Plan and examine the main provisions which it included, especially in comparison with the earlier schemes which have been described and which were available for the Commission's study in 1918.

The hope was expressed that all States invited to The Hague Peace Conference of 1907 should be included as members of the organization. Any such society would be practically worthless unless adhered to by the larger Powers, the defeated as well as the victorious.[43] This desire for universality was the fundamental assumption of all plans which had previously been put forward in Scandinavia.

While it was recognized that not all international difficulties could be settled according to international law and justice, a great advance would be made by the general acceptance of obligations to submit every dispute, not settled by diplomatic means, either to judicial settlement, arbitration, or a procedure of inquiry and conciliation. In the first two cases the decision or award should be obligatory; but the procedure of conciliation, the recourse to which was obligatory in all other disputes, did not require acceptance of the report and proposals for settlement. It was desirable, moreover, that the principle of compulsory arbitration should be established as far as possible. If general agreements could not be reached as to the subjects to be submitted to arbitration, special agreements between States should be resorted to wherever possible.[44] These proposals for the peaceful settlement of international disputes were drawn from M. Lange's plan of 1916, later accepted by the Scandinavian Inter-

[42] von Würtemberg, *op. cit.*, p. 208, gives the names of those who served on the Commissions.

[43] The Commissions would not for the moment, at least, specify the States whose presence was deemed absolutely necessary. (See Articles 1 to 4.) A summary of the Scandinavian Draft Convention may be found in von Würtemberg, *op. cit.*, pp. 210-13.

[44] Articles 5 to 9 (General Obligations).

Parliamentary Groups. On the question of compulsory arbitration, there was an advance from the Swedish position at the time of the Second Hague Conference,[45] but the limit of the Deuntzer treaties was not attained.

Machinery appropriate for the fulfillment of these obligations was provided.

A Permanent International Court of Justice composed of a restricted number of competent judges should be set up to pronounce judicial decisions (in the strict sense of the word), while the Permanent Court of Arbitration, as well as Tribunals of Arbitration *ad hoc* were to continue for the consideration of disputes which could not be settled on strictly legal lines and in which political considerations must be taken into account. The aversion of the Danish delegation at the Second Hague Conference to a centralized Permanent Court found no expression in this draft of 1918. The plan gave no special consideration to the Great Powers, either in the composition of the Court, or in the method of election of judges. The election should be from a list nominated by the Governments and chosen by a special electoral body composed of the persons from each State heading the list of its judges in the Permanent Court of Arbitration. Thus the absolute equality of States was maintained as in 1907, and no real advance was made from the dilemma of finding a scheme acceptable both to great and small States.[46]

The Scandinavian Commissions rejected the proposal of the Lange Plan of 1916 for a Central Board of Inquiry and Conciliation in favour of special commissions which they recommended for each pair of States. The purpose of this decentralization was to allow the parties to a dispute to be represented directly and influentially on the organ whose duty it would be to prepare a solution.[47] Here was the basis for an important Swedish and Norwegian initiative at the First Assembly in 1920, which championed bilateral conciliation agreements and, if successful, would have relieved the Council, a centralized political body dominated by the Principal Allied Powers, of its unique rôle as conciliator of international disputes. The plan

[45] No reservations as to *vital interests* were made for disputes the character of which was incontestibly juridical.

[46] Articles 10 to 39 (International Court of Justice).

[47] Articles 48 and 49.

of the commissions entitled either party to a dispute to set the appropriate conciliation commission into action, and, if neither did so, an International Council was authorized to act.[48]

Conciliation was a useful and necessary expedient in international life, but the legal method for the settlement of disputes was a higher goal to be pursued. Justice through the rule of law has long been deeply ingrained in the mentality of the Northern folk. To facilitate this end the codification and development of international law would be useful. A recommendation was therefore made that a diplomatic conference, similar to The Hague Conference of 1907, should meet every five years for this purpose. Extraordinary conferences might be convened on the demand of a majority of the society's members. These conferences would prepare international conventions on all questions of general interest to the community of nations, the solution of which might contribute to the maintenance of peace. The delegation of each State was entitled to one vote.[49] This proposal for regularizing The Hague Conferences and for creating a permanent bureau as a preparatory and linking organ is readily recognized as a part of Lange's Plan of 1916. It was, of course, an essential feature of most War-time plans for a League of Nations.

One other organ was provided, namely, a permanent International Administrative Council of fifteen members, nationals of different States, but not governmental representatives.[50] Diplomats in active service were not to be eligible. The members of the Council were to be chosen for six years by an electoral Assembly composed of one person appointed by each State. This application of the theory of equality of States exposed the Great Powers, whose nationals were guaranteed no seats on the Council, to the possibility of being outvoted by the small States. Such an arrangement does not seem unreasonable when the very limited functions of the Council, nonpolitical as they were, are noted. These were as follows :[51]

1. To follow the development of international life in the sphere of politics and economics, and to submit to the Gov-

---

[48] Articles 48 to 72 (Commissions of Inquiry and Conciliation).
[49] Articles 73-88 (International Conference).
[50] Articles 40-47 (International Council).
[51] Article 40 (Duties of the Council).

ernments drafts of any international conventions which might be required.

2. To assure the continuity of the international peace or codi-fication conferences.

3. To register and publish treaties.

4. To serve as a central organization for the procedure of en-quiry and conciliation (although the Council itself was not to act as a Board of Conciliation).

5. To inform the signatory States of any cases of non-fulfil-ment of the obligations imposed on them by the present convention.[52]

It was further provided that the Council should reside at the seat of the organization, should fix its own rules, employ experts, and appoint commissions of investigation. No provision stated the neces-sary majority for decisions of the Council. The expenses of the organization and the work of the Council were to be borne in equal share by the signatory States. The Council would prepare the budget annually, and inform the States of the amount of their contribution.

The Scandinavian Plan as the Basis for a League of Nations

The Proposed Convention for an International Juridical Organ-ization has been examined in the light of its sources. Now let us look at this plan as a possible basis for that Society of Nations, which mil-lions of men and women were hopefully awaiting in December 1918. Although careful study has been devoted to many of the plans for a League of Nations drafted by statesmen and Foreign Offices in 1918 and 1919, little attention has been given to this Scandinavian plan. The reason for neglect is clear. This draft was of little utility for the commission of the Peace Conference which drafted the Covenant of June 28, 1919, which, indeed, seems never to have considered the plan.[53] Its supreme merit consists in the high measure of accuracy with which it portrays the "common denominator" of Scandinavian agreement on the question of international organization before the

[52] As an alternative to No. 5, it was proposed that the following addition be made: "It shall likewise propose the measures of an international character to which, in its opinion, such non-fulfilment should give rise."

[53] Munch, "Les États Neutres et le Pacte de la Société des Nations," in *Les origines et l'œuvre de la Société des Nations,* p. 162. von Würtemberg, *op. cit.,* p. 213.

Peace Conference began. The Danish, Swedish and Norwegian Commissions had made a painstaking inquiry of existing proposals. This fact, coupled with the responsible and representative character of the Commissions, suggests that their conclusions were the crystallization of the Scandinavian point of view. The plan was well received by the majority in the North when it was published in January 1919.[54]

The proposed convention, however, was deemed inadequate by a minority in Scandinavia which regretted certain serious omissions.[55] The plan would have found little support from the League of Nations's Commission of the Peace Conference. Viewed in terms of the needs of 1919, or compared with the variety of proposals which had previously been acclaimed in Scandinavia, the plan was disappointing. The "blue-prints" of a Society of Nations, even if well made, were obviously incomplete. Not that a solution should have been offered for all the political problems facing the statesmen who were to decide the terms of peace. The plan was incomplete because it dealt almost exclusively with the settlement of disputes along juridical lines and offered little for the elimination of the causes of war. It neither guaranteed the maintenance of peace as the French would have liked, nor emphasized, on the other hand, the necessity of developing international community spirit through a well defined system of cooperation. The questions of rights of nationalities, colonies, armaments, economic cooperation and sanctions were left untouched. It was, as the title significantly disclosed, merely an "International Juridical Organization."

The explanation for these serious omissions, of this wilful side-stepping, is not to be attributed so much to a lack of vision or lack of sense of reality in the North as it is to the special position of these States as small neutral Powers which had first to consider their own precarious situation. The Commissions of Study inevitably felt obliged to draft their proposals with respect to the interest their countries had in escaping entanglement with the political conflicts of Europe. Aloofness in that realm must be maintained, if possible, in

[54] von Würtemberg, *op. cit.,* p. 213.
[55] The ultra-pacifists objected that all war was not abolished. They thought that the absence of a central organ having political powers and the omission of a provision for sanctions took away much of its value. *ibid.*

the new era. It is understandable, therefore, that a Swedish commission would hesitate in May 1918, when millions were still fighting, to recommend any initiative by neutral States which concerned important controversial questions—questions which entailed serious international responsibilities dependent on the Great Powers for fulfilment.[56] To do so would possibly have exposed the neutrals to the charge of meddling, an action which undoubtedly would have been as unpopular in Scandinavia as among the belligerents.

Even after the question of a War-time diplomatic conference of the neutral European States had been abandoned and the Commissions were working towards a post-War Peace Conference, they were unprepared to tackle thorny political problems in which their countries had no immediate concern, especially since their influence in the solution of such problems would be inconsiderable. The force of the traditional outlook in *utrikespolitik* was too strong to allow Scandinavian official commissions to suggest the establishment of a political league, such as that created a few months later by the Paris Peace Conference.[57] Any commitments which would threaten the cornerstone of their neutrality policy could only be contemplated with the greatest apprehension and reluctance. The caution with which the question of sanctions was faced can best be understood by quoting at length from the "Explanatory Statement" made by the Swedish Commission in its report to the *Utrikesdepartement*:

> The Commissions have refrained from including in this scheme any provision for international sanctions to be applied to States which may offend against the Statute . . . because they consider that the initiative in this matter should not be taken by the smaller States. Such, at least, is the opinion of the Swedish delegates, an opinion in which their Government concurs. The question is closely connected with that of the international limitation of armaments. Small States would inevitably hesitate before binding themselves to join in international measures of coercion, as long as there is danger that such action might leave them opposed to a more powerful neighbour

[56] See Letter of May 22, 1918, signed by von Würtemberg, Adelswärd and Ewerlöf. *Betänkande, Swedish Commission,* Annex 3, pp. 86 ff. Also, "Memorandum," Annex 5, pp. 100-1.

[57] For a brief review of Swedish foreign policy since 1814 see an article by Rutger Essén, "Svensk Utrikespolitik," *Svensk Tidskrift* 19(3), 1929, pp. 205-18.

without immediate and adequate assistance. A general reduction of armaments would obviously modify such a case. But this is a subject in which small States should not take the initiative.[58]

Aside from the question of initiative, the Swedish comment made it clear that the Commission recognized the desirability of some restraining measures against offending States.

Even should there be no special provision for compelling . . . States to join in any collective action against the Power failing to carry out its engagements, it may be supposed that the violations of the Treaty would probably lead to some action by the other Members of the League, or at least some of them. *Moreover it is desirable that such should be the case,* whatever opinion may be held on the question of compelling by a Treaty participation in such action. . . .[59]

A final passage, however, will show that the Swedish Commission did not consider the Draft Scheme as an inadequate charter for the fresh start toward the organization of peace. The opinion was expressed that "the absence of provisions of international sanctions does not prevent its scheme from constituting, together with The Hague Convention of 1907, a whole which can be put into execution without the addition in question."[60]

Scheme of the Norwegian League of Nations Association

After the Scandinavian Governmental Commissions had formulated a proposed constitution for an "International Juridical Organization," the Council of the Norwegian League of Nations Association drafted its "Fourteen Points" for a League of Nations.[61]

[58] Permanent Court of International Justice (Advisory Committee of Jurists), *Documents Presented to the Committee* (1920), p. 167.

[59] My italics.

[60] Permanent Court of International Justice (Advisory Committee of Jurists), *Documents Presented to the Committee* (1920), p. 167.

[61] The Norwegian League of Nations Association [Publication No. 1], *Pronouncements Concerning the Principles of the League of Nations as Passed by the Council of the Association* (signed January 30, 1919) by F. Nansen, Kristine Bonnevie, Wilhelm Keilhau, Johan Castberg, Johan Bredal, Willy Gørrisen, S. C. Hammer, Ole O. Lian, and Arnold Raestad. The "Pronouncements" were based on the proposals of a committee under the chairmanship of Dr Keilhau, assisted by Dr M. H. Lie. Other members were Castberg and H. Løken.

The Norwegian Association was not hampered by the reticence which characterized the Governmental Commissions, but was imbued with the idealism and energy of its president, Dr. Fridtjof Nansen. In the pronouncements of the Norwegian Council all war was made illegal, and an obligation was placed on members to settle all international disputes by some peaceful method. In case of necessity the League was authorized to employ economic sanctions to ensure the enforcement of international engagements. Some members of the Council thought that, in addition, the use of military sanctions should be recognized.

Other gaps in the official plan were filled. A declaration of principle was made on the questions of compulsory military service, armaments, tariffs, labour conditions, minorities, and equality of commercial opportunity. In view of the important addition which these "Fourteen Points" add to an appreciation of the attitude of the Scandinavian peoples, a résumé is attached below stating the general principles which the Norwegian Association adopted as a desirable basis for a League of Nations.

> I. The aim of the League of Nations is to "preclude the possibility of war and to work for the improvement of the common interests of the Nations."
>
> II. An international judicial system shall be created with organs qualified for the development of international law and for ensuring the peaceful solution of all international disputes.
>
> III. "All civilized nations are entitled to join the League and to take part in the deliberations concerning its establishment and fundamental principles." Adhesion to the League must in all cases be approved by the national assembly or by plebiscite in the respective States.
>
> IV. Each State must be entirely sovereign in its internal affairs, unless express exception is made in the Fundamental Agreement.
>
> V. "All international disputes must be finally settled by conciliation, arbitration, or legal judgment. No nation of the League may resort to force."
>
> VI. Compulsory military service shall be abolished. National disarmament shall be effected according to rules and under supervision determined by the League.

The private manufacture of arms and materials of war shall be abolished. State manufacture shall be subject to international control.

VII. Tariff barriers shall gradually be removed. The equal economic standing of all members of the League shall be recognized.

VIII. All members shall engage to carry into effect a statutory maximum working day and other provisions for safeguarding workmen and seamen, provided that the League pass resolutions to this effect.

IX. Guarantees of national minorities shall be made by all members to allow their free development in accordance with principles fixed by the League.

X. Treaties shall be made public, and only then shall they become valid.

Organs of the League (There were suggested two alternatives; both had advocates on the Council of Association.)

First Alternative:

XI. "The supreme authority of the League shall be vested in a World Congress in which all Members of the League of Nations shall be represented in order of population and international importance, yet so that no nation shall have more than, *e.g.*, one-twelfth of the total number." The representatives shall be elected by the national assemblies.

The Congress may discuss all problems of international interest, but shall pass binding resolutions only in such international provinces as are subject to their authority according to the Fundamental Agreement.

XII. The Executive Power shall rest in an International Council of fifteen Members. No single Power shall have more than one national on the Council. The Members of the Council shall be elected by a majority vote of the electors, of whom one-half shall be nominated by the World Congress and the other half by the States with equal voting rights.

Second Alternative:

In addition to the organs provided in the first alternative, there shall be a Conference of States built on the foundation laid by The Hague Conferences (*i.e.*, retention of sovereignty by the States and equal representation of States).

The World Congress may discuss all questions of international interest, but shall pass binding resolutions only to such extent as may be determined in the Fundamental Agreement or by the Conference of States.

The International Council shall effect cooperation between the World Congress and the Conference of States.

XIII. Legal disputes between States shall be submitted[62] to a Permanent Court of International Justice for settlement. Disputes involving interests shall be submitted to conciliation. If, however, a dispute is not settled by this latter procedure, it shall be decided by permanently organized arbitration tribunals.

The conciliation and arbitration Boards shall be composed on the principle of the legal equality of States.

XIV. (The whole Council voted for the following) :

"The League bases itself on confidence in the people's sense of justice and world opinion being strong enough to ensure the enforcement of the rights of nations and the fulfilment of international engagements.

"In case of necessity the League may, however, sever international intercourse with a law-breaking nation, or resort to coercive means of an economic nature against it."

(Some of the Members of the Council, however, found it necessary to add that the use of *military* sanctions should be recognized. In their view an emergency force should be created to which all Members of the League "shall be bound according to rules fixed by the World Congress at the time being." Resolutions regarding the employment of sanctions should be passed by the International Council by a two-thirds vote.)

---

[62] Both parties must agree if a dispute is to be considered as a legal dispute.

CHAPTER IV

THE DRAFTING OF THE COVENANT AND THE SCANDINAVIAN STATES

THE Speech from the Throne to the Swedish Riksdag on January 11, 1919, stated that the Swedish Government, in conjunction with those of Denmark and Norway, was prepared to participate in a League of Nations for the preservation of peace and the defence of justice among nations, and expressed the hope that Sweden might be able to take part in this great international regeneration.[1] Unfortunately, the neutral States, some of which could claim the greatest impartiality to world political problems, were denied the privilege of sharing in the drafting of the Covenant.

Already in 1917, when the Governments of the Scandinavian States and of Switzerland[2] initiated the study of the problem of future international organization, there had been a widespread belief that the War would be followed by a general peace conference of belligerents and neutrals, victors and vanquished, as at the Congress of Vienna in 1814.[3] In December 1918, the Governments of Denmark, Norway and Sweden sent a note to the French Government calling attention to the importance of permitting all States, from the very outset, to participate in the work of establishing a League of Nations. The creation of the League would react upon the legal relations among States, and might affect their constitutional, economic and military organization.[4]

[1] *Bihang till Riksdagens Protokoll* (1919), 1 Saml. 16 Band.

[2] In October 1917, the Federal Council of Switzerland began the study of a vast programme embracing the principal questions which would arise at the making of peace. See W. E. Rappard, "L'Entrée de la Suisse dans la Société des Nations," in Munch, *op. cit.*, Vol. I, p. 367.

[3] Munch, *La Politique du Danemark dans la Société des Nations*, p. 8. Also Munch, *Norden og Folkenes Forbund*, p. 5.

[4] *St. prp.* nr. 33 (1920), p 2. *Proposition 90*, p. 13.

This appeal of the Scandinavian Governments was, however, un-successful and they were left unaware of what was being done at the Paris Peace Conference and of the status to be assigned the neutral States in the new organization.[5] Not until February 13, 1919, did the Commission on the League of Nations decide that other States, besides the Allied and Associated Powers, should be invited to join the League without being voted in by the Assembly.[6] The Draft Covenant of February 14, however, did not specify the States which should be included in the Annex to the Covenant. After the meeting of the sub-committee of the Commission on the League of Nations with the representatives of thirteen neutral States on March 20 and 21, it was decided to consider the States named in the Annex, whoever they might be, as original members of the League.[7]

The exclusion of the neutrals from the birth of the new order was a real disappointment to the Scandinavian States. This desire to contribute to the task of creating the League was emphasized in the speech of Dr Edén, the Swedish Prime Minister, at Örebro, on March 3, 1919.[8] One critic described the impression given the neutrals as that of "being compelled to wait at the doormat until the Great Powers, after some undefined period of approval, found them worthy of sharing the benefits of the League."[9] Some of the Scandinavian pique would probably have been removed if they had been made to understand earlier that, although it was necessary to exclude them from the drafting of the Covenant, they would be included among the original members of the League.

There was a more important reason, however, for the lack of enthusiasm, shown in Scandinavia, for the Draft Covenant of February 14, 1919. The Swedish Prime Minister stated publicly that "the scheme drawn up by the Peace Conference contains points which

[5] *Proposition 90*, p. 14.

[6] D. H. Miller, *Drafting of the Covenant*, Vol. II, p. 303. The opposition expressed by M. Bourgeois indicates the uncertainty of the position of neutrals before that time.

[7] At the Eleventh Meeting of the Commission, March 22, 1919. Even at that meeting, Cecil, who had been highly sympathetic with the neutrals, stated that the Annex "might contain the names of all the neutrals, some of the neutrals or no neutrals at all." Miller, *op. cit.*, Vol. II, p. 341.

[8] *The Times* (London), March 5, 1919 (9B).

[9] Vallentin in "What Sweden Thinks Today," *New Europe*, March 27, 1919, p. 254.

must arouse serious apprehension among all those who desire a real and permanent peace."[10] The disappointment of Norway with this "Power Alliance" can be deduced from her expressed desire for a League of Nations based on principles of law and "open to all civilized nations."[11] Baron Marks von Würtemberg even says that a sensation was caused in the neutral countries, notably in Scandinavia, by the Draft Covenant.[12] Contrary to the Scandinavian plan for an "International Juridical Organization," "the Covenant provided for a central organization, distinctly political, and foresaw economic and military sanctions as well as future arrangements on the subject of disarmament. It postponed, on the other hand, the important question of a permanent court and was silent on that of a procedure of conciliation."

Disappointed, apprehensive, critical, the Scandinavian Governments received, through their Ministers in Paris, Colonel House's letter of March 10, 1919, informing them that the Peace Conference desired, before the final adoption of the Covenant, to learn the opinions of the neutral States as to the provisions of the Draft of February 14. This letter explained that it would be impossible for the Commission on the League of Nations to receive them officially, as the conference was a meeting of the victorious Powers.[13] Representatives of the neutral States, however, were invited to a private discussion at Hotel Crillon on March 20.

Dr Peter Munch, one of the Danish representatives at that meeting, has written that in the neutral States this invitation caused little

[10] Örebro Speech, *The Times*, March 5, 1919 (9B).

[11] On February 3, 1919, the Norwegian Storting resolved to send a telegram to the Peace Conference stating that the Norwegian people would greet with favour a League of Nations based on principles of law and open to all civilized nations. M. H. Lie, "L'Entrée de la Norvège dans la Société des Nations," Munch, *op. cit.*, Vol. I, p. 345. C. A. Kluyver, *Document on the League of Nations,* p. 170.

[12] This information, and the following quotation are from von Würtemberg, "L'œuvre commune des Pays scandinaves relative à la Société des Nations," *op. cit.,* p. 213. Compare Bellquist, *op. cit.,* p. 270. See also a Danish critic, Severin Christensen's article, "Det Første Udkast til Folkenes Forbund," in *Retsstaten,* B.D. III (nr. 4), pp. 55 *ff.* (April 30, 1919).

[13] Munch, "Les États neutres et le Pacte de la Société des Nations," in Munch (ed.), *op. cit.,* Vol. I, p. 161.

satisfaction.[14] A private discussion of this kind was not a regular procedure.[15] The neutrals hesitated to assume responsibility for the provisions of the Covenant without being able to exercise any real influence upon them. Moreover, such short notice was given of the meeting that most of the States would not have time to send other representatives than their Ministers in Paris, who would have to rely upon telegraphic communication for their Government's point of view.[16] In any case, the discussion would be confined to the Draft of February 14, and only changes of detail could be hoped for. It would be impossible to set forth the plans elaborated by the official Commissions of Inquiry appointed in some of the neutral countries.

In spite of these objections each of the invited neutral States decided to take part in the meeting. To gain additional time for preparation, the Scandinavian and Dutch legations attempted, though unsuccessfully, to have the date of the meeting postponed.[17] As a result, the Norwegian, Swedish and other delegations failed to arrive in Paris in time for the sessions.[18] Sweden was accordingly represented by her Ministers at Paris and London, Count Ehrensvärd and Count Wrangel. Norway was represented by Baron Wedel Jarlsberg, Minister at Paris. Denmark, however, had a full delegation, which

[14] For the material in this paragraph see Munch, "Les États neutres et le Pacte de la Société des Nations," in Munch (ed.), op. cit., Vol. I, p. 162.

[15] The view of the Swedish Minister of Foreign Affairs was that "this manner of handling international affairs of general interest seemed little suitable, and constituted a departure from the methods which were formerly put into practice for the treatment of similar questions and which were founded on the principle of the legal equality of States." Proposition 90, p. 17.

[16] Even for Denmark, the Letter of Instructions of March 14 was received by the Danish Minister in Paris on March 19, "just in time for the meeting." Rigsdagstidenden (1919-1920), Tillæg A. II, p. 5395.

[17] Bellquist, op. cit., p. 271.

[18] How this interval was spent in the case of Norway may be noted as an evidence that it was indeed too short. On March 12, 1919, the Norwegian Foreign Minister received a telegram from the Norwegian Minister in Paris informing the Government of the invitation "to express their views." On March 14, the Norwegian Commission of Inquiry gave a translation of the Draft Covenant and its comment thereon, which was made the basis of the instructions given the Norwegian delegation, named by the Royal Resolution of March 17. The delegation arrived in London, March 21 and in Paris, March 22. The meeting for which they had come had already taken place. St. prp. nr. 33 (1920), p. 2. Johan Castberg, Nationernes Forbund og Den Norske Delegations Konferancer i Paris. (Den Norske Forening for Nationernes Liga, Skrift nr. 2), pp. 2, 6.

included, in addition to M. H. H. Bernhoft, Minister in Paris, two members of the Danish Commission of Inquiry which had collaborated with the Norwegian and Swedish Commissions.[19] These gentlemen, Dr Peter Munch, Minister of Defense, and M. H. Neergaard, Member of the Folketing, were already in Paris to express the Danish view on the Schleswig question.[20]

Meanwhile, on March 19, representatives of Switzerland, the Netherlands and the three Scandinavian States met to talk over possible amendments to the Covenant which they might offer jointly the following day. The discussion revealed the agreement of these neutral States on fundamental questions. Their interests and points of view were nearly identical, but opinion varied on the possibilities and manner of effecting the desires of the neutral States.[21] It was decided, therefore, that each State should present the amendments it desired, and that the representatives of the other States should support them, "in so far as they thought their instructions, general as they were, allowed."[22]

The Scandinavian States at Hotel Crillon, March 20-21, 1919

The six hours allotted for discussion of the Covenant with the representatives of the neutral States gave slight opportunity for them to deprive the Allied Powers of their desire to be the exclusive founders of the League of Nations. "None the less, the contributions made by a number of the neutral spokesmen at these meetings were of by no means negligible significance. Though they resulted in little further amendment of the Covenant, in several respects they closely foreshadowed the actual development of the League in

[19] Miller, op. cit., Vol. II, p. 621. The Norwegian delegation, as named, also included Beichmann, J. Castberg, and M. H. Lie, Dr A. Raestad acted as expert adviser to Baron Wedel Jarlsberg. Castberg, op. cit., p. 2. Baron von Würtemberg, Baron Adelswärd and Hjalmar Branting were named to represent Sweden. Proposition 90, p. 17.

[20] Munch, La Politique du Danemark dans la Société des Nations, p. 9.

[21] This is the view of the Swedish Foreign Ministry. Proposition 90, p. 19. Dr Munch further stresses the agreement of the neutrals, stating that they were not able to reach an accord on the form of the amendments because of lack of time. "Les États Neutres et le Pacte de la Société des Nations," p. 162. Also, Betænkning angaaende Danmarks Tiltræden af Folkenes Forbund. Afgiven af den af Regeringen Nedsatte Komité. Rigsdagstidenden (1919-1920), Tillæg A. II, p. 5395.

[22] Munch, op. cit., p. 163.

operation. . . . And the outspoken way in which a number of the smaller European neutrals refused to accept meekly certain of the arrangements approved by the Great Powers gave the first indication of the important rôle these little States were to play later in determining the League's constitutional development."[23] A glance at the minutes of these meetings shows that of the thirteen neutral States represented, only the six European neutrals and Chile took an active part in the discussion.

The League of Nations Commission was represented by Lord Robert Cecil (Chairman), M. Bourgeois, Colonel House, M. Venizelos, M. Hymans and M. Vesnitch. The decision was made to consider the Covenant of February 14, 1919, article by article, and to receive such amendments and critical remarks as the neutral representatives might care to offer. By supplementing the minutes of these meetings with the instructions given by the Danish, Norwegian and Swedish Governments to their representatives, it is possible to appreciate the changes which the Scandinavian States desired.[24] Let us follow, article by article, the proposals and discussions of these delegations.[25]

ARTICLE II

Norway proposed that "meetings of the Body of Delegates [*i.e.,* the Assembly] shall be held each year at a time determined in advance." Members of the League should be allowed to send five, in-

[23] Morley, *The Society of Nations,* p. 138.
[24] See D. H. Miller, *The Drafting of the Covenant,* Vol. II, pp. 592-645. (Document 25. Meeting with the neutral Powers March 20 and March 21, 1919, French and English texts.) Also Vol. I, Chapter 24, pp. 303-9.
      Denmark: *Instruktionsskrivelse af 14. Marts 1919 fra Udenrigsministeren til den danske Gensandt i Paris.* [Bilag 2 af *Forslag til Rigsdagsbeslutning angaaende Danmarks Tiltræden af Folkenes Forbund*] *Rigsdagstidenden* (1919-1920), *Tillæg* A. II, pp. 5443-52. See also, Bilag 3 and 4.
      Norway: *Uttalelse, avgitt 14. mars 1919 av den norske komité, etc.* (which suggests changes in the Draft Covenant of February 14). *St. prp.* nr. 33 (1920). Bilag 2, pp. 35-7. See also, Castberg, *op. cit.,* pp. 6 ff.
      Sweden: *Instruktion för Kungl. Maj:ts Minister i Paris och med honom adjungerade personer för officiösa överläggningar rörande frågan om nationernas förbund* [Bilag 3 of *Proposition 90*], pp. 156-62. The principal points are summarized in *Proposition 90,* p. 18. Compare Bellquist, *op. cit.,* p. 271.
[25] The Danish, Norwegian, and Swedish delegations express no comment on Articles I, IV, VI, X, XI, and XVII to XXV inclusive.

stead of three, delegates. Deliberations of the Body of Delegates should be public, unless special circumstances prevented. "It must be indisputably established that the Body of Delegates shall determine by special conventions the rule of conduct between States, as well as the rules of future International Law, subject to ratification by the States."[26]

Denmark and Sweden also wished to strengthen the authority of the Assembly, but offered no proposal for amending this Article.

ARTICLE III

Denmark proposed that the number of Lesser Powers on the Council be increased from four to eight, and that they be elected not by the entire Assembly but by all the Lesser Powers in that organ.[27] The principle in the Draft Covenant that the Great Powers should have a majority on the Council was maintained by providing for two representatives from each of the five Great Powers.

Sweden and Switzerland accepted the principle of the Danish proposition. Dr Munch explained: "ce n'est pas que l'on fut satisfait de cette règle, mais l'opinion générale était qu'il ne serait pas possible d'obtenir un changement à cet égard."[28] Nevertheless, Norway proposed an "increase in the number to at least fifteen."[29] Even after the admission of Germany and Russia to the Council under this arrangement a preponderance would be given to the Lesser Powers.[30]

[26] Miller, op. cit., Vol. II, p. 633.

[27] The Danish Instructions stressed the point that too much weight was given in the Draft Covenant to the Great Powers in the Council. It was most unfortunate that the four non-permanent members were not chosen by the Lesser Powers jointly. There was danger also that the non-permanent members might in fact become "somewhat fixed" on the Council. Rigsdagstidenden (1919-1920) Tillæg A. II, p. 5447.

[28] Munch, "Les États neutres et le Pacte de la Société des Nations," op. cit., p. 166. The Swedish desire concerning the composition of the Council was that "Stormakterna och de mindre staterna borde i rådet vara representerade med sammanlagt lika antal ombud." Proposition 90, p. 18.

[29] Miller, op. cit., Vol. II, p. 635.

[30] Johan Castberg, one of the Norwegian delegates who arrived in Paris after the meetings of March 20 and 21, says that it was especially Norway who raised the question of the representation of the smaller States on the Council. He states that Norway maintained that the small States should balance the Great Powers (this, no doubt, was a revised view, made necessary by the determination of the Powers not to change the principle of the composition of the Council embodied in the Draft of February 14). This principle should be maintained when in the future the permanent seats were increased from five to seven (with the entry of Germany and Russia). No

The Danish proposal, it was noted above, placed the non-permanent members of the Council in the position of representatives of the lesser Powers in the future Assembly. Sweden extended this idea, proposing that the Covenant itself should specify how the representatives of the secondary Powers should be nominated. Classes or groups of States ought to be established, based upon the geographical relations between them, their community of language, and their culture. If possible, these different groups should be successively represented on the Council.[31]

This idea, however, did not find expression in the Covenant, but was developed after Sweden entered the League of Nations.

ARTICLE V

Denmark proposed that the Secretary-General of the League should be chosen, not by the Council as had been provided, but by the Assembly on the motion of the Council.

Sweden, Switzerland and the Netherlands supported this motion.[32]

doubt the desire of Norway to have all the Great Powers in the League and the desire for the principle of an equal number of Great and Lesser States suggested the number fifteen as a reasonable size for the Council. Castberg, *op. cit.*, pp. 8-9.

[31] Castberg was strongly opposed to the proposal for the selection of Council Members from groups or blocs of States. He was pleased that Cecil, in private conversations on March 24, 1919, with the belated Norwegian delegation, should have stated that the plan of grouping for the election of non-permanent members was impractical. The difficulty of such arrangements is obvious. A Baltic group which would include both the Scandinavian States and the new Baltic States had no adequate basis for existence. Two blocs for these States seemed to raise unduly their strength in the Council, unless it were to be enlarged to a point beyond the desire of the Great Powers.

Castberg, however, was one of the extreme opponents of "Scandinavianism," which he once described as "a political conception as unreal as the old Atlantis." Castberg, *op. cit.*, pp. 10-11.

The Norwegian delegation on March 24, 1919, asked Cecil if the European small States could be definitely assured a minimum of four Council seats, and expressed the hope that the numerous non-European States would not be left in a position to exclude the European. Castberg, *op. cit.*, p. 9.

[32] Dr Munch states that the Danish motion was supported also by Norway. This is not mentioned in the official minutes. "Les États neutres et le Pacte de la Société des Nations," *op. cit.*, p. 166.

The Danish Instructions stated that, while it can be argued that the predominant influence of the Great Powers on the Council may be justified on the ground of their great responsibility in applying sanctions, there seems no justification for the provision in the Draft of February 14 for the election of the Secretary-General by the Council. *Rigsdagstidenden* (1919-1920), *Tillæg* A. II, pp. 5447-8.

ARTICLE VII

The question of eligibility for membership was raised by the Swiss delegation, whose proposal was supported by the Netherlands, Sweden and Norway. The Swiss, together with the other neutrals, desired to facilitate as much as possible the admission of the conquered States, but they recognized that it was necessary to accept the principles of the Draft Covenant.[33] The Swedish delegation, nevertheless, had been instructed to support the principle that "the period in which the number of the more important States should remain outside of the League should, in the interest of general peace, be made as short as possible."[34]

Norway proposed that admission to the League should be made as easy as possible, and therefore that a simple majority rather than a two-thirds majority should be deemed sufficient. The provision that "No State shall be admitted to the League unless it is able to *give effective guarantees of its sincere intention* to observe its international obligations. . . ." should be modified to permit "Every autonomous State" to become a member, provided always that such State *"have the intention and the ability* to meet the international obligations that fall on Members of the League."[35]

ARTICLE VIII

"The Danish and Norwegian Delegations expressed the pleasure of their Governments at the fact that the Covenant voiced the necessity of disarmament. The Danish Delegation, supported by those of Norway and Switzerland, thought that the private manufacture of munitions of war should be absolutely prohibited.

[33] Munch, *op. cit.*, p. 164. Munch herein states, contrary to the official minutes, that *Denmark* also supported the Swiss proposal.

[34] *Proposition 90*, p. 18.

[35] The italics above are mine.

On the subject of Norway's desire for universal membership, and the importance attached to it, see Castberg, *op. cit.*, pp. 6-7. When the Norwegian delegation on March 24, 1919, asked Cecil: "Can we consider it as promised that admission to the League will stand open for all fully self-governing countries under the conditions which are specified in the article, so that the League in principle will become a World League and not a League only of Allied and Neutral States?" Cecil replied, "Yes, most certainly."

"The Swedish Delegation expressed agreement with the general idea of the article, but thought that the control should be made stricter."[36]

ARTICLE IX

Denmark, supported by Sweden (and Norway, according to Dr Munch), proposed that the Permanent Military and Naval Commission should "control" the armaments of the several States [not merely "advise" the League] and should supervise the execution of the plan adopted for disarmament.

ARTICLES XII, XIII AND XV (CONCILIATION)

The Scandinavian States, the Netherlands and Switzerland proposed the creation of permanent machinery for conciliation which should always be employed before international disputes were submitted to the Council. Norway and Sweden called attention to the project of the official Scandinavian Commissions, which had considered the establishment of commissions of conciliation highly important.

Denmark's proposal concerning conciliation (found in the suggested amendment to Article XIV) specified that the machinery of conciliation be centralized.[37]

ARTICLES XIII AND XIV (ARBITRATION)

Among the neutral States the preponderant opinion was that obligatory arbitration ought to be proclaimed for all disputes of a juridical nature.[38] This idea had earlier been proposed in the Scandinavian Plan. Norway was more extreme, proposing that it would be desirable "to suppress every restriction, based on the nature or

[36] Miller, *op. cit.*, Vol. II, p. 626. The Swedish Instructions had urged that "The Covenant should include far-reaching agreements as to disarmament and international control over the continuation of the same." *Proposition 90*, p. 18.

[37] Norway and Sweden wished to provide for the organization of the conciliation procedure in the Covenant. Dr Munch in his article does not call attention to any difference between the Danish proposal for conciliation and that of the other four neutrals who met on March 19. It is clear, however, that the Norwegian and Swedish Governments attached greater emphasis to bilateral conciliation commissions than the more practical Danish Government. See "Les États neutres et le Pacte de la Société des Nations," *op. cit.*, pp. 170-1.

[38] Munch, *op. cit.*, p. 169.

origin of conflicts, limiting the obligation to submit to arbitration."[39]
Lord Robert Cecil, however, declared that the Commission on the
League of Nations had definitely rejected the entire principle of
obligatory arbitration.

In regard to a Permanent Court of International Justice, Denmark
proposed that the Council should be required to submit the plans
which it should formulate, to the Body of Delegates for approval. A
provision should be included that the Court shall be based on the
principle of the juridical equality of States.

Sweden preferred that the provisions concerning the creation and
working of a Permanent Court should be inserted in the Covenant.
If this were not expedient, Sweden would be content if the Danish
proposal for including the principle of the juridical equality of
States was accepted. In that event, the task of outlining the statute
of the Court should be entrusted to the Body of Delegates, and not
to the Council.

Norway also proposed an immediate attempt to establish the rules
concerning the functions of the Court.

ARTICLE XVI

Denmark, Norway and Sweden were agreed that the Covenant
should clearly specify that States whose cooperation with military

[39] Castberg, *op. cit.*, at p. 11, says that no other neutral State went so far as to
insist upon complete compulsory arbitration. Yet, as has been noted in Chapter II,
pp. 19-20, Denmark had in 1904 accepted this principle in bilateral treaties. Moreover,
Munch and Neergaard issued a memorandum in March 1919, in which they stated
that from the Danish point of view, it would have been desirable for the Draft
Convention of the Scandinavian Commissions (December 1918) to have gone further
with compulsory arbitration. *Rigsdagstidenden* (1919-1920), *Tillæg* A. II, p. 5453.
(This was the view of the Danish commission.) The Danish Instructions of March
14, 1919, also make clear Denmark's desire for compulsory arbitration without limit.
The Danish Foreign Minister, Erik Scavenius, therein stated that "first of all, from
the Danish viewpoint, it ought to be emphasized how important it is in the interests
of the smaller countries and especially Denmark . . . to institute a League of
Nations and to acknowledge the legal principle for the settlement of *all* international
disputes." And he pointed out that Denmark had "already for a long time attached
itself to the concept of unlimited obligatory arbitration." *Rigsdagstidenden* (1919-
1920), *Tillæg* A. II, p. 5444. Munch in *La Politique du Denmark dans la Société
des Nations,* p. 14, says that all five of the neutral States (which had met together on
March 14), declared themselves partisans of compulsory arbitration without reservation; but this seems doubtful.

or economic measures was desired should be invited to participate in any discussion and decision relative thereto.

The Swedish delegation thought it "both just and necessary that economic and military sanctions be employed in order to guarantee the performance of the principles of the League of Nations." There should be, however, "a consideration of the possibility of fixing the maximum military contribution which a State would have to make as a participant in joint action of the League."[40] The expediency of requiring the absolute prohibition of all financial and commercial relations, *immediately* against a State which has violated the Covenant, was doubted. It would be preferable to establish "definite economic measures which might be employed successively and according to a scale of increasing vigor." The Swedish delegation also asked if it were consistent with principles of law that States outside of the League should likewise be deprived of their connection with a State which has broken the Covenant.

The Norwegian representative thought that small States should not have to take military action against non-member States, and that they should regulate their armaments primarily with regard to their own defence. Military sanctions should be used only as a last resort.

Denmark, however, proposed even more far-reaching exceptions to the obligation for applying sanctions. "In designating the States who shall participate in military or economic measures, consideration should be given to peculiar difficulties which such participation in these measures will cause to States whose situation *in casu,* because of their military or geographic condition, might be more dangerous than that of certain other States." Moreover, "States which, because of their history and because of their political tradition of peace, offer firm guarantees of impartial conduct shall have the privilege of declaring themselves permanently neutral. It will follow that their territory shall not be violated," even by forces under the command of the League of Nations.[41]

----

[40] Miller, *op. cit.,* Vol. II, p. 643. The Danish proposals are at pp. 641-2, and the Norwegian at p. 642.

[41] The Danish Instructions state pointedly that the Great Powers have had an eye to their own interests in creating the League, while the position of the smaller countries has not been cared for to the same degree. One of the chief Danish anxieties, they continue, is that the Draft Covenant does not make it clear that small States can

ARTICLE XXVI

Norway wished to make it easier to amend the Covenant, and proposed that:

"An unanimous vote of the Executive Council should not be required as a condition precedent to changes in the Covenant. Just as in the Body of Delegates, a three-fourths majority in this Council should be sufficient."[42]

Result of the Discussion with the Neutrals

The common desire of the neutral States had been to give a more juridical character to the new international organization. Dr Peter Munch, the leading authority on Danish policy in the League of Nations, has written that if it had been possible to get such a change, a greater restriction on the sovereignty of States would have been accepted willingly. As the Great Powers deemed it necessary to maintain the political character of the League, the neutral States sought to accentuate the sovereignty of the members and to make as precise as possible the limits of the League's jurisdiction. Otherwise, they feared that the interests of the secondary States would be endangered by the predominance given to the Great Powers.[43]

hold themselves aloof from disputes between contending factions of the Great Powers. From the Danish standpoint, it was preferable to have an organization wherein access to neutrality would exist for those States not permanently neutral. (Munch, in *op. cit.,* pp. 174-5, states that the four representatives in the Danish delegation at Paris, representatives of the four chief parties in the Rigsdag, agreed that it ought to be provided in the Covenant that a State should have the right to declare its permanent neutrality. They differed, however, on the question of the advisability of Denmark making such a declaration. The Conservatives and Moderates were opposed; the Radicals and Socialists were in favour.)

The Instructions stated that if it were impossible to obtain recognition of the right of small countries to be free from the obligation of imposing sanctions, efforts should be made to introduce a system wherein participation of small countries would not be automatic, but only after special consideration by the League of the particular case in question.

In any event, the participation of small States in the application of sanctions could be only of secondary importance for the successful attainment of the task in question. Surely the Great Powers could accept the desire of the small States not to risk their very existence. *Instruktionskrivelse af 14. Marts 1919, Rigsdagstidenden* (1919-1920), *Tillæg* A. II, pp. 5445-7, 5451-2.

[42] Miller, *op. cit.,* Vol. II, p. 645. No comment was offered by Denmark and Sweden.

[43] Munch, "Les États neutres et la Pacte de la Société des Nations," *op. cit.,* pp. 184 *ff.*

The neutral States, however, as Prime Minister Stauning later remarked, obtained only to a slight degree an influence on the new world political *Sammenslutning*. It was the belligerent Powers' work.[44] Although the proposals of the neutral States were received with interest and good will, the draft of February 14 was not fundamentally changed along the suggested lines. The following points should be noted:[45]

Norway was unsuccessful in getting a definite provision for annual meetings of the Assembly. The proposal for permitting delegations of as many as five members was not accepted.[46] Yet at the First Assembly in 1920 the principle of annual meetings was recognized, and delegations (if alternates and experts are counted) became even larger. In like manner, publicity in Assembly meetings, although accepted in principle, was not included in the Covenant.

The composition of the Council remained as provided in the Draft of February 14. The number of the non-permanent seats was not increased; but, as the Swedish Government took occasion to note in its Proposition to the Riksdag for adherence to the League of Nations, "The possibility has been made to increase the representation of the smaller States in the Council."[47]

In Dr Munch's view, "perhaps the most important modification" was the new rule which assured States not Members of the Council the right to participate and vote in the Council on questions of particular interest to themselves.[48] By this provision and a new Article V, which stated precisely the necessity for unanimity, States were released from any obligation to participate in military sanctions or to take other positive action against their will.

[44] "Danmark og Folkenes Forbund" in *Folkeforbundets Første Tiaar*, p. 8.

[45] For the changes of particular importance to the Swedish Foreign Office, see *Proposition 90*, pp. 19-20. See also the remarks of the Select Committee of the Danish Government in its *Betænkning angaaende Danmarks Tiltræden af Folkenes Forbund, Rigsdagstidenden* (1919-1920), *Tillæg* A. II, pp. 5398-401. For the view of the Norwegian Foreign Office, see *Utenriksdepartementets Innstilling av 13. februar 1920, St. prp.* nr. 33 (1920) p. 6.

[46] Norway had wished to make it possible to have a representative in her delegation from each of the principal political parties.

[47] This was in accordance with the Swedish Instructions, paragraph 5. See *Proposition 90*, p. 19.

[48] "Les États neutres et le Pacte de la Société des Nations," p. 182.
See also, Swedish Instructions, paragraph 9.

The Danish proposal that the Secretary-General of the League be appointed by the Council *with the approval of the Assembly* was accepted.

The effort to make membership in the League more easily attainable was unsuccessful, mainly because of French opposition.[49] The British prevented the proposed international control of armaments, which the French as well as the Scandinavians desired.[50] Obligatory conciliation by permanent commissions was rejected on the ground that the authority of the Council ought not to be weakened. The Danish, Norwegian and Swedish Governments were obliged to seek consolation in the fact that the Covenant by no means excluded the optional use of bilateral conciliation.[51] The Covenant included no provision for compulsory arbitration and no guarantee that the Permanent Court should be based on the principle of equality of States. The Council, not the Assembly, was authorized to formulate plans for the Court. Nevertheless, the Swedish Government was able to state that "assurance had been given of the intention of setting up the Permanent Court as soon as possible. Provisions had been introduced with a view to accentuating the non-political and distinctly juridical character of the Court."[52]

One concession, "quite essential for the small States," was made which secured their independence of action in regard to military sanctions.[53] This, in M. Stauning's opinion, was the change of the word *"indiquer"* used in the French text of the Draft Covenant of February 14 to *"recommander."* By this alteration, it was made certain that the Council, in case a Member of the League should resort to war in disregard of its Covenants, would merely *recommend,* not *determine,* what military forces the Members should contribute. Other changes were made which seemed to make it clear that the

[49] See, for instance, the remarks of M. Larnaude, in the Ninth Meeting of the Commission on the League of Nations, February 13, 1919. Miller, *op. cit.,* Vol. II, p. 309.

[50] Munch, *op. cit.,* p. 182.

[51] *Rigsdagstidenden* (1919-1920), *Tillæg* A. II, p. 5409. *St. prp.* nr. 33 (1920), p. 6. *Proposition 90,* p. 20

[52] *Proposition 90,* p. 20. Presumably Article XIII, paragraph 2, is referred to. Therein a definition was given to the term "un différend susceptible à leur commune estimation, de solution arbitrale," used in the Draft of February 14, Article XIII.

[53] Stauning, "Danmark og Folkenes Forbund," *op. cit.,* p. 8.

Governments, not the Council, should take the decision on military sanctions.[54]

The failure of the Peace Conference to accept the other alterations suggested by the Scandinavian States in regard to the application of sanctions resulted in later action by the Assembly to modify the obligation of Article XVI.[55]

Norway's proposal that amendments to the Covenant should require only a three-fourths majority in the Council, as in the Assembly, failed. The Assembly prerequisite, however, was reduced to a simple majority.

[54] For instance the Dutch proposal was met by the insertion of the words, "au divers Gouvernements intéressés." Munch, *op. cit.*, p. 184.

[55] See the Resolutions adopted by the Assembly in 1921. *infra*, Chapter XII, pp. 218-19.

CHAPTER V

ACCESSION OF THE SCANDINAVIAN STATES TO THE COVENANT OF THE LEAGUE OF NATIONS

"I believe that we win more respect in the world, we win more self-respect, in case we wholly and completely and without reservations give our adherence to something which will be bettered, and which we wish to participate in bettering, but which we will not be able to better by remaining critical outsiders, but only by fully and wholly cooperating within the same."—Hjalmar Branting before the Northern Inter-Parliamentary Union, September 1919.[1]

THE thirteen neutral States which had met at Hotel Crillon on March 20 and 21, 1919, were invited to become original members of the League of Nations, on the condition that they accede without reservation, within two months of the coming into force of the Covenant.[2] The final draft of the Covenant was incorporated in Part I of the Treaty of Versailles of June 28, 1919, and went into effect January 10, 1920. Thus the neutral States had an interval of more than eight months in which to consider their attitude towards entry.[3] The decision, however, had to be taken before it was known exactly what States would adhere, thereby complicating the issue.

In the Scandinavian countries opinion was divided as to the value of a League founded upon the principles which had been chosen.[4] No section of opinion exhibited a real enthusiasm for the Covenant. All were agreed that the solution offered for world peace deserved criticism and alteration. On the practical question of whether to adhere, unconditionally and before March 10, 1920, as was stipulated, those who concerned themselves with the issue were not in agreement. As usual in democratic countries, public opinion first found expression in voluntary bodies, which marked the course for subsequent official action.

[1] Bellquist, op. cit., p. 265.
[2] See Article I, paragraph 1, and Annex to the Covenant.
[3] That is, from June 28, 1919, to March 10, 1920.
[4] On this subject, see von Würtemberg, op. cit., p. 214.

Two important inter-Scandinavian organizations declared themselves in September 1919, in favour of joining the League, and of working for its improvement. The Congress of the Scandinavian Inter-Parliamentary Groups in session at Stockholm adopted a resolution welcoming the possibility of founding through the League of Nations a new international organization of justice and cooperation in social, economic and cultural spheres. And it was hoped that the League *might develop so as to unite all States* in the safeguarding of a lasting peace and in the promotion of the highest interests of humanity.[5]

A resolution adopted by the somewhat less representative Scandinavian Peace Congress shows how far the Covenant fell short of the goal of the peace societies, and how much their point of view was determined by their pre-War attitude. The resolution, which commanded wide support especially from the Centre and Left parties in the three countries, was as follows :[6]

> The Scandinavian Peace Congress in Stockholm acknowledges the work which the Paris Peace Conference has accomplished for creating a League of Nations.
> The Congress thinks that the Scandinavian States should join the League of Nations with the aim of getting the Covenant improved and expanded, in such a manner,
> (1) That the League may embrace all civilized peoples everywhere ;
> (2) That the League's representative organs may be so developed in a democratic direction that the Assembly may become a real "parliament of man";
> (3) That compulsory arbitration may be stipulated for all future conflicts between States, and that the "right of war" may be abolished ;
> (4) That universal military service may be abolished ;
> (5) That individual States shall have a right, so long as war is not prohibited as a means of settling international disputes, to declare themselves permanently neutral.[7]

[5] Bellquist, *op. cit.*, p. 273.

[6] Petersen and Nielsen, *Halvtreds Aars Fredsarbejde*, pp. 99-100.

[7] Only one of the twenty-five representatives of the Dansk Fredsforening voted against the resolution. Olaf Forchhammer opposed it on the ground that acceptance

The official discussion of the question of adherence to the Covenant can be more conveniently followed by considering each country separately.

Denmark's Accession to the Covenant

Of the five European neutral States which had collaborated at Paris prior to the meeting at Hotel Crillon—Denmark, Norway, Sweden, the Netherlands, and Switzerland—Denmark was the one which showed the least hesitation in joining the League of Nations.[8] Not one vote was cast in either House of the Danish Rigsdag against the Government's proposal for admission. There was, in fact, very little discussion in Denmark on the question of entry into the League.[9]

Although some few persons regarded the League of Nations as a new Holy Alliance, designed to perpetuate the submission of Germany, the great majority of the Danes considered adherence as a natural consequence of the situation after the War. The enthusiasm with which the idea of a League of Nations had been greeted at the time of the Armistice had grown perceptibly weaker, but the newly created League was regarded as an important beginning for an international organization. In political circles all were agreed on the advisability of adhesion.[10]

The question of Denmark's accession to the Covenant was submitted to the committee which had been set up by the Government to study the interests of the neutral States at the conclusion of the War. In January 1920, this committee made a report advising the entry of Denmark into the League before March 10 following.[11] A careful

of the Covenant implied a surrender of Denmark's position as a neutral State. *ibid.*

For the neutral view as stated unofficially by Hjalmar Branting see an authorized review entitled "The League of Nations" in *The American-Scandinavian Review,* September-October 1919, pp. 343-4.

[8] Munch, *La Politique du Danemark dans la Société des Nations,* p. 14. Also, Petersen and Nielsen, *op. cit.,* p. 101.

[9] On the question of Denmark's accession to the Covenant, see especially *Forslag til Rigsdagsbeslutning angaaende Danmarks Tiltræden af Folkenes Forbund* (Anmeldt den 11. Februar 1920), *Rigsdagstidenden* (1919-1920), *Tillæg* A. II, pp. 5321-500. Also, Munch, "Les États neutres et le Pacte de la Société des Nations," *op. cit.,* pp. 186-7; Stauning, "Danmark og Folkenes Forbund," *op. cit.,* p. 9.

[10] Munch, *op. cit.,* p. 186.

[11] *Betænkning angaaende Danmarks Tiltræden af Folkenes Forbund. Afgiven*

analysis of the provisions of the Covenant was included, and the criticisms which had been offered to the Draft Covenant of February 14 were, for the most part, repeated. But much of the harshness contained in Foreign Minister Scavenius' Instructions to the Danish delegation at the Paris meeting in the previous March had been erased. The committee was disposed to recognize the good points of the Covenant wherever possible, and even answered objections which some of their number had previously raised. It was stressed that the principle of equality was maintained in the Assembly, and that this body ought to be considered the supreme organ of the League of Nations. The Assembly was clearly not doomed to a rôle of unimportance, if the British official commentary on the Covenant could be relied upon.[12]

The preponderant influence of the Great Powers in the Council was acceptable, since the Council had been assigned functions which ought largely to fall upon those States. Indeed, the criticism to be made of the Covenant was that it failed to take sufficient notice of the decided and undeniable difference between small and great States. The Great Powers demanded for themselves a decisive influence on world politics, an influence which the small States had renounced. The obligations of States therefore should not be uniform. Moreover, the secondary States wished to be assured in the future as hitherto, that their part in international life, especially in the application of sanctions, would not involve them in warlike complications. Such entanglements were too great a risk for small States, for war would nearly always be more disastrous for them than for the Great Powers.[13]

What were the obligations which might endanger the neutrality of Denmark?[14] The committee stated clearly that military sanctions were not obligatory, and that the pledge to allow passage of the

af den af Regeringen nedsatte Komité (Januar 1920). Rigsdagstidenden (1919-1920), Tillæg A. II, pp. 5394-430. This report is signed by P. Munch, N. Neergaard, O. C. Scavenius, J. Clan, and Georg Cohn.

[12] This commentary, which was laid before Parliament in June 1919, was a document of which each of the Scandinavian Governments took special notice. For the reference cited above see ibid., p. 5404.

[13] Rigsdagstidenden (1919-1920), Tillæg A. II, pp. 5422-3.

[14] ibid., pp. 5412-17.

League's forces through a member's territory could be recognized only on condition of prior assent of the member concerned. The obligation of members "to take the necessary steps to afford passage through their territory" should be deemed to have been fulfilled if, restricted by a constitutional provision in its right to grant passage, a government should institute the necessary steps—for example, before the national legislature—to obtain this authority. Cooperation, however, in the automatic economic sanctions of Article XVI, paragraph 1, might subject a State to very great hardship and risks, and could be accepted only with the greatest hesitation by a small State. After entry into the League, Denmark with the other small countries should work to modify this obligation to permit consideration of the special circumstances of exposed States.

The committee concluded, however, that despite the imperfections of the Covenant, especially of Article XVI and its effect upon neutrality, the position of the small States would be far better in the League than out of it.[15] Moreover, the entry of the neutral States would in itself alter the partial character of the League and afford the possibility of cooperation in the League for the amelioration of international legal relations. It would be especially difficult for Denmark, which had been one of the first and most active advocates of obligatory arbitration, to hold itself aloof from an organization which aimed at the maintenance of justice and the preservation of peace.

On February 11, 1920, the Danish Government submitted to the Rigsdag at Christiansborg a proposal for the adherence of Denmark to the Covenant of the League of Nations.[16] The Explanatory Statement (*Bemærkninger*) of the Government seconded the conclusions of the committee whose report has just been examined. The question of adherence had been previously discussed at a meeting of the Prime Ministers and Foreign Ministers of Denmark, Norway and Sweden in Christiania, where agreement was expressed on their conception of the obligations of the Covenant.[17]

[15] *Rigsdagstidenden* (1919-1920), *Tillæg* A. II, p. 5427.

[16] *Forslag til Rigsdagsbeslutning angaaende Danmarks Tiltræden af Folkenes Forbund. Rigsdagstidenden* (1919-1920), pp. 5321 ff.

[17] *St. prp.* nr. 33 (1920), p. 17. (For the full title of this document, see *infra*, note 32.) *The Times*, February 2 and 7, 1920.

The *Bemærkninger* stated that "the reduction of national armaments to the lowest point consistent with national safety and the enforcement by common action of international obligations, provided in Article VIII, signified that the Covenant intended to combat armaments, and not to impose upon the members of the League the obligation of maintaining a certain minimum below which it would not be permitted to reduce armaments. But the Covenant assumes that the several States have something of a military organization."[18] The Government, like the committee, stressed the importance of the reduction of armaments as one of the League's essential functions.

On the question of sanctions, the comment of the Government is of sufficient importance to be quoted at length:[19]

> The obligation found in Article XVI, paragraph 1, to take part in economic sanctions should be understood to imply that this participation can only be demanded in the cases expressly indicated in Articles XVI and XVII. The stipulations of Article XVI, paragraph 2, relative to military sanctions do not signify that participation of the various States can be demanded in the military contingents. The Council has only the right to submit to the various States proposals which the States themselves have the right to accept or reject. There is nowhere in the Covenant the obligation on States to participate in military action. The obligation contained in Article XVI, paragraph 3, to take the necessary steps to afford passage through its territory concerns only the cases expressly indicated in Articles XVI and XVII. The provision ought to be understood in the sense that passage, in such event, can only be demanded after a resolution of the Council, adopted at a meeting wherein the interested State has been invited in conformity with Article IV, paragraph 5, or after consultation and agreement with the States concerned as to the conditions of passage. In this connection, it should be emphasized that the principle of neutrality is not incompatible with accession to the Covenant. In wars which, according to the Covenant, do not involve a breach of its provisions, States have the right to remain neutral under the same conditions heretofore recognized by International Law.

[18] *Rigsdagstidenden* (1919-1920), *Tillæg* A. II, p. 5389-90.
[19] *ibid.*, pp. 5389-90 ff.

Only one other point from the comment of the Government will be noted: the fundamental conception of the League demanded that membership be made available to all European States in the near future.

The debate on the Government's proposition for adhesion to the Covenant was opened in the Folketing on February 18 by M. Neergaard, who announced the support of Venstre (The Left), the largest party in the Rigsdag.[20] Spokesmen of the other three parties made similar declarations on behalf of their parties. Contrary to the position in the Norwegian Storting and in the Swedish Riksdag, no party opposed entry into the League. M. Borgbjerg, an outstanding Socialist, explained that the Covenant was by no means as far-reaching as the programme of the Social Democrat Party, which desired compulsory arbitration in all disputes and complete disarmament. Nevertheless, as this "First League Covenant" was a move in the right direction, it would receive the vote of his party.[21] For the Conservative Party, Dr Axel Møller, on the following day, advocated adherence. Although he thought that the advantages of membership outweighed the objections, this distinguished authority on international law stressed the dangers which Article XVI might entail for Danish neutrality. He pointed to the practical difficulty of refusing passage to League forces, if it were demanded. Dr Møller had the support of all parties when he urged a genuine cooperation of the small States in Europe, especially the Scandinavian States, the Netherlands and Switzerland, for the development through the League of Nations of *Retsprincippet* as a substitute for *Magtprincippet*.[22]

On February 27, the Folketing unanimously approved the Government's proposition for adherence with 77 affirmative votes.[23] On March 4, after a short debate in which the leaders of the different parties in the Landsting expressed approval of the proposition, the Upper House also gave a unanimous vote of 42 ballots.[24]

[20] *Rigsdagstidenden* (1919-1920) *Folketinget* II, pp. 3816 ff.
[21] *ibid.*, p. 3821.
[22] *ibid.*, pp. 3852 ff.
[23] *ibid.*, p. 4099.
[24] *Rigsdagstidenden* (1919-1920), *Landstinget*, p. 1211.

What did the lack of opposition in Denmark to the entry of the country into the League really mean? In the view of one Danish official of the League Secretariat later events have certainly shown that, while there can be no doubt about the sympathy felt practically everywhere in Denmark with international cooperation and peace in general, there was not sufficient understanding of the real objects or structure of the League as set up in 1919-1920. The cynicism as regards the development of the League and superficial criticism of its activity, or lack of activity, has since then definitely shown that real understanding of international problems and difficulties is indeed limited to a small circle in Denmark (as probably in most other countries). Moreover, it is reasonable to believe that the restoration of North Schleswig to Denmark, made possible by the Allied victory, was a factor of some importance in securing a unanimous vote. Under the circumstances, it would not have been advisable for Denmark to spurn membership in an organization sponsored by those who had made possible the realization of this long-standing desire of the Danish people. The figures of the votes cast in the two Houses, however, show that there must have been a considerable number of members absent or abstaining.

Norway's Accession to the Covenant

As early as September 1919, a Norwegian Committee of Examination submitted a report advising Norway's entry into the League of Nations.[25] A comparison of this report with that of the Danish committee already examined reveals a marked similarity of attitude on most questions. Certain of the Norwegian comments, however, deserve emphasis.

The League of Nations was not a super-State with authority to enact legislation binding on its members. Its existence rested especially on the idea of justice between nations, an idea which made a special appeal to the Norwegian people. The entry of Norway into the

[25] *Betenkning angående spørsmålet om Norges tiltredelse til Folkenes Forbund. Avgitt 22 September 1919 av den til sakens utredning nedsatte komité. St. prp.* nr. 33 (1920), Bilag 4.

On the whole subject of Norway's adherence to the League see M. H. Lie, "L'entrée de la Norvège dans la Société des Nations," in Munch, *Les Origines, etc.,* Vol. I, pp. 345-60. The members of the committee were: O. Blehr, J. L. Mowinckel, J. Grieg, Chr. L. Lange, and M. H. Lie.

League would make possible an acceleration of the efforts for arbitration. By working to extend the recognition of this principle for the settlement of all conflicts which could not be solved otherwise, the small States might succeed in restraining the authority of the Council to intervene in disputes.[26]

The committee looked with much disfavour on a great part of Europe being out of the League. This increased the danger of two blocs of hostile States being formed in Europe. The committee, however, did not have serious reasons to fear development in this direction, for it seemed likely that Germany and Austria would have their wish satisfied in regard to League membership.[27]

Like the Danish committee, the Norwegian committee deemed it just that the Great Powers should have a majority on the Council. Even greater stress was laid on the desirability of increasing the importance of the Assembly. By making it into a Parliament of Peoples, public opinion which it could mobilize would exercise a kind of parliamentary pressure on the Council. It was a League of democratic nations which Norway should help to create.

It was recognized that the acceptance of the Covenant altered the status of neutrality in the future. The War, however, had already made it clear that neutrality was in reality changed.[28] The Integrity Treaty of 1907 ought to be considered abrogated by the entry of Norway into the League by virtue of Articles X and XX of the Covenant. On the questions of sanctions and disarmament there was the same general attitude as that expressed by the Danish committee. Once again a strong appeal for adherence was made on the ground that Norway, like other small States which remained neutral in the World War, had a special mission to perform in the establishment of international life on an equitable and stable basis.

This report of the committee was based on the assumption that the five principal Allied and Associated Powers would accept the Covenant. On January 31, 1920, the day before the meeting of the

[26] See the objection raised by the Neutral States to the Council's mediatory functions, *supra,* Chapter IV, p. 56.

[27] *St. prp.* nr. 33 (1920), p. 7. According to M. Johan Castberg the Norwegian delegation had been given assurance on this point by Cecil on March 25, 1919.

[28] A large part of the security which neutrality made possible in the past had vanished during the World War. The committee was prepared to recommend the reconstruction of the status of neutrality in the light of recent experience.

Scandinavian Ministers' Conference in Christiania, after thirty-two of the victorious Powers had ratified the Treaty of Versailles, the Norwegian committee in a supplementary declaration advised entry even if the United States remained outside. M. Mowinckel, however, did not concur in this recommendation.[29]

Other opinion, private and official, was declared in favour of adherence. In a letter dated October 1, 1919, signed by Professor Nansen, the Norwegian Society for the League of Nations advised the Government to accept the Covenant without condition. The weaknesses of the League system were naturally acknowledged by an organization which, only a few months before, had pleaded for a League founded on considerably different principles. But now, rather than lose any opportunity for the promotion of international understanding, Norway should speedily join the new association and assist in its proper development. Never had a comparable effort been made to organize all the democracies of the world in a fight against war.[30]

The Norwegian Department of Defence, although it pointed out the serious risks which membership would entail from a military point of view, was prepared to recommend adhesion in the event that Denmark and Sweden also adhered.[31]

On February 13, 1920, the Council of Ministers accepted unanimously the proposal of M. Ihlen, the Foreign Secretary, for the submission of a resolution of adherence to the Storting for approval.[32] The Royal Resolution of that date was accordingly laid before the parliament in *Karl Johans gate,* and because of its importance

---

[29] Lie, *op. cit.*, p. 349. In Mowinckel's view, the presence of the United States was necessary to prevent the formation of an opposing group of Powers outside the League. See also the view of Branting on this point, *infra*, p. 92, note 33.

[30] *St. prp.* nr. 33 (1920), p. 16.

[31] *St. prp.* nr. 33 (1920), pp. 10-12. The General Staff pointed out that no Scandinavian State was then represented in the Council, and that the other small States thus represented were "very far from us in temperament, character and general outlook." *ibid.*, p. 11. The General Staff, however, agreed with M. Castberg that the suggestion of having one representative on the Council as a representative of the Scandinavian bloc ought not to be considered.

[32] *St. prp.* nr. 33 (1920). *Om innhentelse av Stortingets samtykke til at Norge tiltrer den for Folkenes Forbund vedtatte Pakt som inneholdes i Versailles-traktaten av 28. juni 1919* (Utenriksdepartementets innstilling av 13. februar 1920, som er bifalt ved kongelig resolusjon av samme dag).

referred to the augmented standing Committee on Foreign Affairs (*Forsterkede Konstitutions-komité*). The Committee examined the arguments of the proposal of the Foreign Minister, and on February 25 made its report to the Storting.[33] The Committee was divided on the question of the policy which Norway should adopt. The majority of nine, all members of the bourgeois parties, advised acceptance of the Royal Resolution, emphasizing the essential advantages of a political and economic nature which the League assures to its members. "There is every reason to be fully aware of the precarious and difficult position in which Norway would find herself, if she remained outside of the League."[34] In this connection, the position which Denmark and Sweden take towards the League will be of importance. In the majority's view, Norway, despite the weak points in the Covenant, should avail herself of the opportunity to work for the avoidance of war and help build a safer and more just foundation for international collaboration.

M. Enge and M. Gjøstein, members of the Social Democrat Party, in a minority report, opposed the entry of Norway into the League. They stated that it would be inconsistent with the aims of their party to advocate adherence to a League which did not provide for disarmament. It was highly regrettable that the Covenant was linked to the Treaty, for thereby the League was attached to one of the sorest spots in the life of the defeated Powers. A feeling of mutual confidence could not be established under such an arrangement. The League was therefore doomed to failure. It was stated that "nothing would be dearer for the minority than the collaboration of Norway for the creation of a real international peace organization. But this must be built on the free consent of all peoples and have as its basis the principle that war is not approved as a means for the settlement of international disputes. . . ."[35]

[33] *Stortings Forhandlinger* (1920), Vol. 6a, II, *Indst. S. XXXVIII*. The Committee was increased by the addition of J. Castberg, Johan Gjøstein, O. B. Halvorsen, and Ivar Tveiten.

[34] *Stortings Forhandlinger* (1920), Vol. 6a, II, *Indst. S. XXXVIII*, p. 6. *Angaaende Norges tiltredelse av Folkenes Forbund.*

The majority were: Castberg, Halvorsen, Hegge, Ivarsson, Skaar, Stolt-Nielsen, Stousland, Tveiten and Tronrud. Michelet, *formand og ordfører,* also favoured the majority report.

[35] *Innst. S. XXXVIII* (1920), pp. 8-9.

The report of the Committee on Foreign Affairs was debated in the Storting, March 3 and 4, 1920.[36] The Socialists bitterly opposed acceptance of the Covenant. The League was described by M. Lian as a mere caricature created by the conquerors in their imperialism and arrogance in face of the vanquished. M. Gjøstein said that the League contained the germ of its own death, or to readapt a figure of Henrik Ibsen: The League ship even when launched, sets sail with "a corpse in the cargo." It was an ill omen that the possibility of war was retained in the Covenant. It could even be said that war had been guaranteed by the Covenant, and the great sinews of war, armaments, were maintained.[37]

As a substitute to the Government's proposition, the Socialists introduced the following resolution:[38]

> The Storting cannot give its consent to Norway's adhesion to the Covenant of the League of Nations in its present form.
>
> But the Storting declares that Norway is ready to collaborate in the creation of a League of Nations founded on the following principles:
>
> (1) That all States be able to adhere without hindrance and become members of the League.
>
> (2) That war be abolished as a means of settling international conflicts. All conflicts which cannot be settled by direct negotiation between the parties or by some other means through the mediation of the League, ought to be settled ultimately by a permanent international court of arbitration.
>
> (3) Compulsory military service ought to be abolished and general disarmament ought to be proceeded to.

This motion received the votes of only the Socialist Party, and was defeated by a majority of 103 to 17.[39]

In addition to the opposition of the extreme Left, a few members of the bourgeois parties opposed the Royal Resolution. The most outstanding of this number was Carl J. Hambro, a rising young Conservative, who later became one of Norway's most active

---

[36] *Stortings Forhandlinger* (1920), Vol. 7a, *Tidende S.,* pp. 423 *ff.*

[37] Lie, *op. cit.,* p. 352. But see the reply of Blehr, at p. 355.
Gjøstein said: "Naar denne skute seiler ivei, saa seiler den 'med lik i lasten.'"
Stortings Forhandlinger (1920), Vol. 7a, p. 430.

[38] *ibid.,* pp. 359-60. *Innst. S. XXXVIII* (1920), pp. 9-10.

[39] *Stortings Forhandlinger* (1920), Vol. 7a, pp. 544-5 (March 4).

representatives at Geneva. The future President of the Storting emphasized the difference between the League created by the Covenant and the League visualized in President Wilson's Fourteen Points.[40] Why, asked Hambro, had the Covenant not aroused enthusiasm among the various political groups? Why had no small State shown enthusiasm? It was because the Covenant did not contain a single word as to the equality of the small nations with the great ones. It was silent on the sovereignty of States as well as upon justice as a fundamental principle. The defeated Powers had been excluded. It was unwise to accept an obligation to maintain the independence, territorial integrity and historic rights of States and nations, some of which could not be found on any map and others of which had uncertain boundaries.

The critics from the two extreme wings of the Storting were answered by a number of speakers from the bourgeois parties. Several members of Venstre, the party in control of the Government, spoke in favour of entry.[41] M. Michelet, a Conservative, who as chairman of the Storting's committee played an exceptionally important rôle, was among those most willing to admit the deficiencies of the Covenant. He agreed with the opposition that the principal objection to adherence was that Norway would be forced into a position of abandoning the old concept of neutrality. This was indeed a grave objection. With regard to the connection of the Covenant with the Peace Treaties, he stated that by adhering to the League, Norway would give no guarantee, either morally or juridically, for the other provisions of the Treaties. The belligerent Powers must look to their execution.

M. Michelet agreed that the League ought to include Germany, Russia and all other excluded States. But he argued that if the neutral States should remain out of the League, other States would not have an easier time coming in.

[40] Lie, *op. cit.*, pp. 358-9.
[41] These include Gunnar Knudsen, Prime Minister; O. Blehr, Minister of Justice and President of the Royal Commission which had collaborated with the other Scandinavian commissions on League questions; Foreign Minister Ihlen; and Herr Skaar.
See also the speeches of Konow (*Frisindede venstre*) and Castberg (*Radikale folkeparti*).

After two days' debate, the Storting on March 4 adopted the following resolution:[42]

> The Storting, declaring that
> In conformity with its traditions, it rallies to the great conception on which the League of Nations is founded, and seeing in this institution the most important attempt which has yet been made to establish justice between peoples,
> And declaring moreover,
> That the future of the League depends in principle on an evolution of the basis of admission to include all civilized peoples, on a general reduction of armaments and on a pacific settlement of all international disputes as a means of avoiding war—
> —The Storting gives consent to the adherence of Norway to the Covenant of the League of Nations. . . .

One hundred votes were cast in favour of the resolution and twenty against. The opposition was composed of three Conservatives, one member of Venstre, and sixteen Socialists. One member of the Labour Party, M. Gausdal, voted with the majority.[43]

Swedish Accession to the Covenant

The accession of Denmark, Norway and Sweden to the Covenant of the League of Nations affords an excellent measuring-rod of the agreement in Scandinavia concerning the organization of peace. The collaborations of the three Royal Commissions in 1918 and 1919, the discussion of the delegations at Paris, and subsequent meetings of Scandinavian Ministers, produced a common policy towards the League of Nations which is attested to by the respective Royal Propositions for adherence. The lengthy report of M. John Hellner, the Swedish Foreign Minister, attached to His Swedish Majesty's Proposition of February 14, 1920, interprets the provisions of the Covenant, and recognizes its shortcomings in a spirit comparable to

[42] Lie, *op. cit.*, p. 360. *Stortings Forhandlinger* (1920), Vol. 7a, p. 437.
[43] As a result of this vote, M. Gausdal, one of Norway's ablest Socialist parliamentarians, was expelled from the Labour Party by a decision of the National Party Executive. *Morning Post,* September 22, 1920. MM. Hambro, Mohr, Sollie and Belland were the bourgeois members in question, *ibid.*, p. 545.

the corresponding Danish and Norwegian reports.[44] It is not an exaggeration to say that the *Genève- or folkförbundspolitik* of the Scandinavian States had already been initiated when the Christiania Conference adjourned on February 4, 1920.

If, however, the Liberal Governments in the Scandinavian States were in substantial agreement, the same was not true of all the corresponding official and political groups. The Chiefs of Staff of the Swedish Army and Navy were opposed to the entry of Sweden into the League. In their reports to the Government the view was expressed that Sweden's danger of becoming involved in war would be greater if she adhered to the Covenant than otherwise. With Germany and Russia outside the League, it would be safer for Sweden not to bind herself to commitments which might impair her neutrality. The compulsory economic sanctions of Article XVI might easily lead to war. These advisers seemed to fear that Sweden's entry into the League would be used as an argument for the reduction of armaments. The Chief of Staff of the Navy emphasized that in any case the geographical position of the country demanded the maintenance of Sweden's defence forces. The policy of armed neutrality was one which had served Sweden well during the War, and ought not to be abandoned.[45]

In the Riksdag the opponents of the League were considerably stronger than in the Storting. While in Norway the chief opposition came from the Labour Party, in Sweden it was the Right (Högern) which fought most bitterly against adherence, and cast the largest negative vote. The Swedish Social Democratic Party, the largest single party in the Riksdag, led by Hjalmar Branting, combined with the Liberals to secure the ratification of the Royal Proposition. In both Chambers, however, the Conservatives were strongly entrenched, and throughout the Kingdom occupied a large proportion of the higher posts in the civil and military services, in industry, finance and the Church. It was, therefore, a real misfortune for the League that it made so little appeal to this prominent element of the Swedish nation. It was as if in the Parliament at Westminster the Covenant

---

[44] *Kungl. Maj:ts Proposition* nr. 90, *Bihang till Riksdagens Protokoll* (1920), 1 Saml. 10 Band.
[45] *Proposition 90*, pp. 98-105. *Yttrande av chefen för generalstaben till Konungen*, Bilag 8, pp. 202-11. See Bellquist, *op. cit.*, pp. 274-6.

should have been submitted in 1920 to a vote, and had won the support of only the Liberal and Labour Parties. Although the Conservative Party in the Riksdag was somewhat less numerous than either of the two Government parties, it was a group accustomed to holding office and one which might readily be returned to power, as indeed it was a few years later. Its vote against acceptance of the Covenant, therefore, was of greater significance than the opposition of the Labour Party in Norway.

Högern did not furnish the sole opposition to the Covenant in the Swedish national legislature. When the debate on the Royal Proposition for adherence began in the Upper House on February 18, 1920, M. Trygger, leader of the Conservatives (Nationella parti), had as an ally a small party of Left Wing Socialists (Socialdemokratiska Vänster Gruppen). This group was a Swedish "Independent Labour Party," which in 1917 had grown impatient with the moderation of Branting's leadership and had created its own organization under the guidance of M. Carl Lindhagen.[46]

The objections offered to the Covenant by these widely separated parties were similar to those which were made in the Norwegian Storting. The Right could not consent because to do so would be a deviation from the sound principles of Swedish foreign policy long tested. Trygger complained that the Covenant was a part of an unduly severe treaty imposed by the victors upon a conquered nation. It failed to voice the wishes of the neutrals and entailed a substantial impairment of the sovereign equality of those States with the favoured Allied and Associated Powers. The time given for consideration of the Covenant was too limited and adherence was required before it was known whether or not the peace treaty would be ratified. It was galling to be placed in an inferior position to that of such communities as Cuba, Equador, Haiti, Liberia, Siam. The over-

[46] A useful reference for the contemporary history and organization of Swedish political parties is available in Edvard Thermaenius, *Sveriges Politiska Partier,* Uppsala, 1933.

There is no official party in Sweden called Högern (the Right), but in daily speech the term is generally used to refer to the two Riksdag parties of the Right: Nationella parti in the Upper House (Första Kammaren) and Lantmanna- och Borgarepartiet in the Lower House (Andra Kammaren). Sweden is apparently unique in having a Lower House entitled (literally) "The Second Chamber." The best translation, therefore, is not "First Chamber" and "Second Chamber," but "Upper Chamber" and "Lower Chamber."

balanced position of the Council was a great objection, as mere membership in the Assembly would not be of great advantage.[47]

M. Lindhagen, an insistent pacifist whose radical "Maximum-Programme" has already been noted, thought that the League was "opposed to both divine and human law as there had not yet been a change in the ways of thinking."[48] Some sort of *rapprochement* must take place between the nations before such an institution could be made to function successfully. The League still had the old spirit of militarism behind it. "A League of Nations without Germany and Russia was a mere babe in swaddling clothes, a weak creation walking on crutches. A League without disarmament and abolishment of compulsory military training was but a threat against peace and humanity."[49]

The Government's proposition following the preliminary debate in both Houses was referred to a Special Committee of twenty-four, presided over by M. Branting, leader of the largest party in the Riksdag and member of the Coalition Government. Fifteen members of the committee gave approval to "Proposition 90," but stressed that the following aims ought to be sought by Sweden after her entry into the League: "admission as soon as possible of the uninvited States to the League; the effecting of a more satisfactory arrangement for the representation of the secondary States in the Council of the League; a more precise regulation of the meeting and functions of the Assembly and of the mutual competence of the League's organs; organization as soon as possible of the Permanent Court of International Justice, provided for in the Covenant, and a greater precision and wider development of the mediation and arbitration procedure of the Covenant; lastly, but not least, that the work for a universal and effective limitation of national armaments, which is promised in Article VIII of the Covenant, be set in motion immediately and pursued with real vigour."[50]

[47] *Första Kammarens Protokoll*, 1920, nr. 19, p. 13. Compare Bellquist, *op. cit.*, pp. 278-9.

[48] *supra*, Chapter III, p. 32. Bellquist, *op. cit.*, p. 279.

[49] *Första Kammarens Protokoll*, 1920, nr. 20.

[50] *Bihang till Riksdagens Protokoll* (1920), 14 Saml. 2 Band. *Riksdagens Skrivelse* [nr. 53] *till Konungen i anledning av Kungl. Maj:ts proposition angående Sveriges anslutning till Nationernas förbund. (Särskilda utskottets utlåtande* nr. 1), pp. 7-8.

One member of the committee proposed that action be delayed until the United States had made its decision. The other eight members dissented from the majority's recommendation, chiefly on the ground that adherence to the Covenant would endanger the venerable policy of neutrality. Six of these members, the Conservatives including Trygger, gave a minority declaration which especially emphasized that by entry Sweden would risk her independence of action and even subject herself to the service of foreign Powers. This degradation would result from the exclusion from the Council of all the small European neutrals, who were among the most civilized and most pacific of the nations of the world. This left the all-powerful Council nothing more than a dictatorial alliance of the victorious Powers, which had been substituted for the pre-War system of balance. Where was the international juridical régime to which the Scandinavian States had looked forward? If there were risks to be faced outside the League as the Government had stated, let Sweden face them with open eyes and maintain her own honour.[51]

The discussion of the committee's report began in both Houses on March 3 where the arguments pro and con were repeated. On the following day, the same in which the Norwegian Storting and the Danish Landsting gave approval to the adherence of their countries, both Houses of the Riksdag accepted the Government's proposition. In the Second Chamber, where the Right was less militant, the poll was 152 to 67. In the First Chamber, traditionally more conservative, 86 members supported and 47 dissented.[52]

[51] This report is also available in Trygger, *op. cit.*, pp. 434-9. The minority's position had already been answered by the *Utrikesdepartement* in its comment on Article IV of the Covenant, *Proposition 90*, pp. 30 ff. Therein the preponderant "Great Power" representation in the Council was explained by reason of the Council's functions concerning the execution of military sanctions. The *Utrikesdepartement* declared that it would be highly exceptional for the grouping of interests to be such as to unite on one side all the Great Powers against the smaller States. The much more likely division of interests (between the Great Powers) would increase the opportunity for the smaller States successfully to maintain their points of view.

[52] *Första Kammarens Protokoll*, II (1920), nr. 20, 60-1. *Andra Kammarens Protokoll*, II (1920), nr. 24, 81.

II. ORGANIZATION OF THE LEAGUE'S MACHINERY

INTRODUCTION TO PART II

THE great importance which the Scandinavian peoples attached to the cause of peace is evidenced by the praiseworthy manner in which their Governments have accepted the responsibilities of membership in the League of Nations. It was not to be expected that much enthusiasm should have been displayed for an organization which, to a marked degree, departed from their own conception of what the League ought to be. Disappointment, however, was not accompanied by despair or littleness of spirit. The faith of men like Branting and Nansen in the idea of a Society of Nations which would assure international peace and justice remained firm. They insisted that the League, despite its shortcomings and weaknesses, must be supported by the Northern peoples. With their cooperation and leadership the League might develop in time as an institution more in keeping with the Scandinavian ideal.

Therefore, if the delegations from the North came to the First Assembly at Geneva in the capacity of critics and reformers, they did so primarily in behalf of the true League which they visualized and desired. In the Swedish delegation was M. Trygger, who had led the opposition to Sweden's adherence to the Covenant. Because of "the largeness of his views and of the considerable authority which he enjoyed," the Conservative Party, once adherence had been decided upon, acknowledged the responsibility of Sweden to work for the development of the League.[1] Only in Norway did a political party of importance remain recalcitrant to participation in the League. Not until 1935 did the Norwegian Labour Party (*Arbeiderpartiet*) abandon its yearly effort to effect the withdrawal of Norway from the League.[2]

To appreciate the activities of the Scandinavian States in the League of Nations it is essential to understand the strength of the determination of their representatives to alter the League as created

[1] von Würtemberg, *op. cit.*, p. 220.
[2] *American-Scandinavian Review*, June 1935, p. 173.

by the Covenant. Different from some of the small States, the Viking breed had a well-conceived programme for which to fight at Geneva. It was based upon the principles which had already been enunciated in 1919 and early 1920 by the Royal commissions and parliaments in Scandinavia.[3] After entry into the League had been voted, these commissions were authorized to suggest amendments to the Covenant, which the Scandinavian Governments might submit to the League. In the summer of 1920 the Royal commissions agreed upon changes in four Articles of the Covenant which should be recommended for consideration by the First Assembly.[4] Certain chapters which follow will deal with these proposed amendments.

[3] See Chapters III and IV.
[4] von Würtemberg, *op. cit.*, p. 220.

CHAPTER VI

ADMISSION OF NEW MEMBERS

THE view that "all civilized States" should be entitled to membership in the League had been advocated in 1919 by the Norwegian Storting in a telegram to the Peace Conference.[1] Subject to different interpretations of the expression "civilized States," this view was quite generally held in the North. In any event, universality was the goal which it was thought the League should strive to achieve. Time and again in the parliaments at Copenhagen, Oslo and Stockholm, as well as at the Geneva Assembly, Scandinavian orators expressed their conviction that a League of Nations not founded on the principle of universality could hardly achieve its high calling.

One of the most disturbing provisions of the Covenant, objected to by all parties in the North, was the demarcation of victors, neutrals and vanquished into separate categories. Although the neutral States were invited to become original members, special conditions were imposed upon them.[2] Still greater discrimination was provided in the case of the defeated Powers and the other fully self-governing States, Dominions and Colonies which were not admitted as original members. According to Article I, paragraph 2, of the Covenant, any such political unit "might become a member of the League if its admission was agreed to by two-thirds of the Assembly, provided that it should give effective guarantees of its sincere intention to observe its international obligations, and should accept such regulations as might be prescribed by the League in regard to its military, naval and air forces and armaments."[3]

If the Scandinavian States objected to this classification of States and if the principle of universality was the acknowledged goal which

---

[1] See *supra,* Chapter IV, p. 49, note 11, and Chapter III, p. 44.

[2] Article I, paragraph 1, stated that these States must accede without reservation to the Covenant, within two months of its coming into force.

[3] The tense of the verbs are herein changed.

they desired for League membership, why was it that no alteration of Article I of the Covenant was proposed by these States? Why was it that the Scandinavian delegations did not support the proposal of the Argentine for effecting universal membership in the League? The second question will be answered first.

At the 1920 Assembly the Argentine delegation introduced a proposal "that all Sovereign States recognized by the community of nations be admitted to join the League of Nations in such a manner that if they do not become members of the League, this can only be the result of a voluntary decision on their part."[4] When this motion for automatic admission of all States was discussed in the Second Assembly, the Danish delegate, M. Herluf Zahle, declared that it was absolutely unacceptable in its present form. He referred to the difficulty of the official recognition of sovereign States by the "Community of Nations." There were some States the independence of which was so doubtful that they could not be admitted.[5] Although the representatives of Chile, Persia and other States supported the Argentine amendment, and M. Motta of Switzerland favoured it "in substance," no such declarations were made by any of the Scandinavian representatives.[6] The Norwegian and Swedish delegations were significantly silent. By a vote of 29 to 5, a proposal amounting to disapproval in principle was adopted by the First Committee.

In the discussion Professor Gilbert Murray, delegate of South Africa, said that there were two possible theories as to League membership: (a) That all States ought, *ipso facto,* to be members of the League; (b) that the League of Nations was an association of law-abiding and stable States, and that some examination was necessary before a State became a member. There is little doubt that the Scandinavian Governments adhered to the second theory. They could not, therefore, support the Argentine amendment. Yet the silence of the Norwegian and Swedish members was possibly due to a reticence to speak against any proposal which aimed at universal membership. To do so might cause misunderstanding at home, and lead to attack by men like Herr Carl Lindhagen, the Left Socialist,

---

[4] *1A.P.,* 261. For the abbreviations used in this treatise see the explanation given, p. ii.

[5] *2A.1C.,* 8.

[6] *2A.1C.,* 6-13.

who introduced more than one motion in the Riksdag urging that the doors of the League be flung open for all comers.[7]

The answer to the other question is quickly given. The Scandinavian States did not propose an amendment to Article I of the Covenant because they were more interested in the practical question of securing the admission of the defeated Powers than they were in doing homage to the principle of universality. The admission of these States could be effected by a two-thirds vote of the Assembly. Hence an amendment was not really necessary.[8]

The Scandinavian policy was more realistic than that of the Argentine. It was the entry of Germany into the League which the Northern neutrals especially desired. In 1918, the Scandinavian commissions had emphasized that a future international organization would be "practically worthless unless adhered to by all the larger Powers."[9] When the League was created, it was generally believed in the Northern countries that its success as a permanent institution for peace depended largely on the admission of Germany and the other defeated Powers. Self-interest reinforced this belief. From the standpoint of traditional neutrality, the Scandinavians were inclined to feel uncomfortable in a League dominated by one Power-group and excluding the other, shattered though it was for the moment. Accordingly, they, like the other European neutrals, regretted that Germany's request to the Peace Conference for admission had been denied.[10]

At the First Assembly, the influence of the Scandinavian delegations, unlike that of some States, was cast in favour of early German entry. Although the French delegate, M. Viviani, eloquently expressed the desire of France for universality, he insisted that it must be in accordance with the spirit and letter of Article I of the

[7] See, for instance, *Riksdagens Protokoll* (1924), *F.K.,* 19: 29 *ff.* (*Motion* nr. 148) where he moved that the Riksdag request the Government to work for an amendment which would strike out paragraph 2 of Article I of the Covenant, "thereby facilitating universal adherence to the League." The motion was defeated in both Houses on March 12, 1924. *A.K.* 18: 59 *ff.*

[8] When Lindhagen's motion for Swedish initiative for an amendment to the Covenant [see note 7] was referred to the Constitution Committee of the Riksdag, it reported that such an amendment was unnecessary. Sweden ought to work through the Assembly for the realization of the principle of universality. *Riksdagens Protokoll* (1924), Saml. 5 nr. 11.

[9] *supra,* Chapter III, p. 37.

[10] See the speech of M. Motta (Switzerland) in the First Assembly. *1A.P.,* 572-3.

Covenant. "It would be an outrage which would revolt the judgment of history and the conscience of the world . . . if a State were to be admitted which had neither fulfilled its obligations nor given, in accordance with the Covenant, adequate guarantees of its sincere intentions." And, he continued, "it is now two years since the Armistice was signed, and . . . we still await adequate guarantees of sincere intentions from Germany."[11] This led Dr Nansen, the first delegate of Norway, to say that there was a great majority in the Assembly who were hoping (with due respect for the principles laid down by M. Viviani) to be able to welcome Germany as a member of the Assembly as soon as possible.[12] The famous Norwegian explorer expressed the conviction held in many countries,[13] but nowhere more widespread than in Scandinavia, when he added that the League could not be perfect until all the Great Powers of Europe were members. Hardly a year passed in which spokesmen from the North did not reiterate their desire of welcoming Germany into the League as soon as possible. In 1922 M. Trygger stressed that the League could not hope to deal with the important questions of international life as long as it remained a partial association. The League could not hope to be of "great value" unless the distinction between victors, vanquished and neutrals was forgotten.[14]

When in 1924 the question of Germany's admission into the League became actual, occasion arose for Sweden, then a member of the Council, to make clear its attitude in regard to the conditions of Germany's entry. In reply to a query of "the Wilhelmstrasse," the Swedish Government wrote:[15]

> It is a matter of extreme satisfaction to the Swedish Govern-
> ment to learn that the German Government desires to become
> a member of the League of Nations. On several occasions since
> the foundation of the League, the Swedish Government has

[11] *IA.P.*, 576.

[12] *IA.P.*, 577.

[13] See, for instance, the British view expressed by Mr Barnes. *IA.P.*, 152.

[14] *3A.P.*, 78-9. See also the Instructions given to the Norwegian delegation to the Third Assembly. *St. med.* nr. 8 (1923), p. 7.

[15] Note of the Swedish Government (November 22, 1924) to the German Government. *L.N.O.J.*, VI, 3, p. 326. [Doc. C, 32, M, 1925, VII.]
See also Utrikesdepartementet, *Nationernas Förbundsråds Verksamhet under år 1925*, pp. 12-13.

urged that the League of Nations should aim at universality. In agreement with public opinion in Sweden, it considers it specially important that Germany should become a member of the League.

The Royal Government considers that, once she has been admitted as a member of the League of Nations, Germany should be given the same place in the organization of the League as is held by the other Great Powers members of the League. She should therefore be granted a permanent place on the Council. . . .

Despite the keen desire of the Swedish Government to have Germany a member of the League, it was not prepared to accept the German request for special reservation concerning the obligations of Article XVI, and in the same note informed the German Government to that effect. In short, Sweden insisted on a "standard for membership" which ought to be applied generally.

The important rôle which Sweden played in the embarrassing situation which arose in 1926 over the admission of Germany and the reorganization of the Council will be considered in connection with the latter question.

Attention must now be turned to the other defeated Powers. The request of Austria[16] for admission to the League was granted in 1920 without opposition and that of Hungary in 1922, both with Scandinavian approval.[17] When objection to the admission of Bulgaria was expressed in the Fifth Committee of the First Assembly, M. Branting and Dr Nansen both came to the defence of this Balkan Power. After Nansen had argued that the prestige of the League would be weakened if Bulgaria were excluded for the reasons advanced by her Balkan neighbours, these States reversed their attitude and Bulgaria was admitted to membership.[18] The Turkish Republic was not admitted until the Special Assembly of July 1932, when a Draft Resolution proposing her entry and sponsored by twenty-nine delega-

[16] See Branting's speech, *1A.5C.*, 168.

[17] *St. med.* nr. 8 (1923), p. 7.

[18] *1A.5C.*, 179. See especially Dr Nansen's objection to the conclusions drawn by M. Politis that Bulgaria did not desire to fulfil her obligations. *1A.5C.*, 170.

tions was adopted. Denmark and Sweden, but not Norway, were among the proposers.[19]

Clearly the Scandinavian States had wished no discrimination against the defeated Powers. They did not hesitate, however, to oppose certain other applications for admission. All three delegations voted against the request of Liechtenstein, juridically a sovereign State and recognized *de jure* by several States, but so small in size that it had contracted with neighbouring States for the control of its customs and diplomatic representation.[20] Azerbaidjan and the Ukraine received negative votes from the Scandinavian States because they had not been recognized *de jure* by any States.[21] Even in the case of more stable communities, Esthonia and Latvia, the Scandinavian delegations in 1920 opposed their applications, while Denmark and Norway voted against the admission of Lithuania as well.[22] M. Branting explained the opposition of Sweden to the admission of the Baltic States on the ground that no Great Power had given them *de jure* recognition.[28] It was doubtful business to assume the obligations of Article X in behalf of States thus exposed to Russia, then in the grip of anarchy. At the Second Assembly, however, the Scandinavian delegations expressed pleasure that the situation had so changed that their Baltic neighbours could now be welcomed into the League.[24] It was a Scandinavian interest to support these small States

[19] *Records of the Special Session of the Assembly* (*1932*), Vol. II, p. 9. Dr Chr. L. Lange has written me that Norway abstained from signing the invitation on grounds of principle. She objected to the creation of a precedent which might subsequently prove awkward for the Assembly. Such a situation actually arose in 1934 when Russia refused to apply for membership, invoking the precedents of Turkey and Mexico.

[20] See an article by Lilian M. Friedlander, "The Admission of States to the League of Nations," *B.Y.I.L.*, 1928, pp. 89 *ff.*

[21] *1A.P.*, 651-2.

[22] Sweden merely abstained from voting on the application of Lithuania. *1A. P.*, 627, 630.

[23] *1A.5C.*, 187, 196.

[24] *2A.C.* (*II*), 518, 519, 520, 532. Before the Second Assembly, the Great Powers led the way with *de jure* recognition of Esthonia, and the Scandinavian States followed. Latvia had been recognized *de jure* by 21 States, Esthonia by 20 States, and Lithuania by only 7 States. *Monthly Summary*, Vol. I, p. 122.

and Finland,[25] which served as a buffer to Soviet Russia, provided they did not have to accept grave commitments in their behalf.

Although the Scandinavian States were agreed with Professor Murray that the League should be an association of law-abiding and stable States, they differed somewhat from one another in the application of that theory. For example, Sweden abstained from voting on the request of Albania, which Denmark and Norway supported.[26] On the application of Georgia, Norway voted yes, Denmark no, and Sweden abstained.[27] It was Dr Nansen's great sympathy for the destitute peoples of Eastern Europe which led the Norwegian delegation to support the application of a community whose possession of a stable government was highly doubtful.[28] One writer says that Dr Nansen was motivated by a desire to stem the tide of Bolshevism, but that it was just this fear of Bolshevism which prevented the Assembly from seriously considering the proposals.[29]

Yet Norway, whose efforts had been directed in March 1919 to making admission to the League as easy as possible, definitely subscribed to the maintenance of certain standards for entry. When the request of Abyssinia was discussed in 1923, Norway was one of four States which expressed doubts in the Sixth Committee of the Assembly as to the advisability of granting immediate admission. Dr Nansen, like M. Motta of Switzerland, desired assurance that the Ethiopian Government did, in fact, possess the power, in all parts of its Empire, to carry out the engagements which it was prepared to undertake against slavery.[30]

The failure of the United States to join the League was a great disappointment to the Scandinavian States. In the summer of 1919 M. Branting stated that the attempt of the nations to create a world

[25] Finland had been unanimously admitted by the First Assembly (*1A.P.*, 585) with Nansen's support (*1A.5C.*, 185).

[26] *1A.P.*, 651.

[27] *1A.P.*, 630-1, 633-4.

[28] Nansen's influence on Norwegian policy at Geneva was considerable. On the whole, the Norwegian delegation in the first years of the League maintained a large degree of independence from control by the Storting. See C. J. Hambro's annual complaint (1920-1926) in the Storting that the Norwegian delegation improperly represented that body as well as public opinion in Norway.

[29] Lilian M. Friedlander, *op. cit.*, p. 91.

[30] *4A.6C.*, 16. The States were, in addition to Norway and Switzerland, Great Britain and Australia.

order based on justice would be doomed to failure if the United States did not participate. "A League of Nations without the United States would be no League of Nations."[31] The importance attached to the decision which the United States might adopt towards entry into the League has already been noted. The delay in submitting to the Northern parliaments for debate the question of adherence to the Covenant was largely due to the desire of first knowing what action the great democracy of the West would adopt.[32]

Although Scandinavian opinion regretted America's aloofness,[33] there was a greater understanding of it than in other countries which did not share a common suspicion of European politics. This was especially true of some of the opponents of adherence. M. Hambro, for example, asked how American entry could be expected unless the League should rise above the old game of European diplomacy and rivalry. When he opposed Norway's adherence to the Covenant, he was looking forward to the creation of a "free and moral" League, which the United States and the European neutrals should originate and into which other States would feel obliged to enter because of its strong moral position.[34] The impracticability of this suggestion was so obvious that it never received serious consideration even in the North.

Since it became clear that the United States would not enter the League, at least in the near future, the Scandinavian, as indeed

[31] In an "Authorized Interview" to the *American-Scandinavian Review,* September-October, 1919, p. 344.

[32] *supra,* Chapter V, pp. 71-2. Bellquist, *op. cit.,* p. 277.

[33] See Moltesen's speech, *8A.P.,* 53 (Danish delegate.). Branting, however, had less patience with America's reactionary policy. In a lecture given in June 1922, in fulfilment of the obligation as Nobel Prize winner, he emphasized that the absence of the United States, Russia, and Germany greatly curtailed the efficiency of the League, and said: "No nation is so great that it can permanently remain outside of a more or less universal League of Nations." Branting, "The Peace Movement After the War," *American-Scandinavian Review,* September 1922, p. 534. On January 26, 1923, M. Lindhagen introduced a motion in the Upper House of the Riksdag that the Government be instructed to take the initiative for an appeal to the United States to enter the League. But his motion was rejected on April 7 by a vote of 83 to 16. Such an appeal, it was felt, would not be effectual. *Riksdagens Protokoll* (1923) *F.K.,* 4 : 7; *F. K.,* 24 : 58 *ff.*

[34] Hambro, "Folkeforbundet Idag," *Nordisk Tidskrift för Vetenskap, Konst, och Industri,* 1934, Årg. 10, p. 75. See also, his speeches in the Storting, June 12, 1923. *Stortingets Forhandlinger* (1923), Vol. 7b, p. 2190.

general, policy was to welcome the increasing cooperation of the United States in the League's activities. M. Mowinckel, the Norwegian Prime Minister, spoke to that effect when, as President of the Council, he opened the Assembly in 1933.[35]

Despite the aversion of the overwhelming majority of the Northern people to Bolshevism, the attitude of intelligent opinion in Scandinavia from the outset favoured the entry of Russia into the League. Even an outstanding Conservative leader, M. Michelet, declared to the Storting in 1919 that Russia ought to be a party to the League.[36] When the question of Russia's admission to the League was acted upon by the Assembly in 1934, the Scandinavian States did not join company with the Netherlands, Portugal and Switzerland in opposing entry. Nor did they abstain from voting, as did seven other States.[37] In a speech at the ancient university town of Uppsala shortly after Russia's entry to the League, M. Rickard Sandler, the Swedish Minister for Foreign Affairs, said:

> As to the desirability of the Soviet Union's entry to the League of Nations I entertain no doubt. Cooperation in a tolerable form between States is nowadays a necessity on our little planet. . . . Up to now no better form of cooperation has been brought into being than the League of Nations affords. There should be given within that institution room for all, even for diametrically opposed political régimes. Whether or not Germany has a Nazi régime, it is desirable that she take part in the League's work. The same applies to Russia, whether it have a Soviet régime or not. . . . For us, this point of view must be fundamental.[38]

[35] *14A.P.*, 29.

[36] Lie, "L'entrée de la Norvège dans la Société des Nations" in Munch (ed.), *op. cit.*, Vol. I, p. 354. See also *supra*, p. 75.

[37] See the Letter from the First Delegate of Sweden to the President of the Council, September 15, 1934, stating that the Governments of Denmark, Finland, Norway and Sweden had that day confirmed to the Soviet Government their decision to vote in favour of the admission of the U.S.S.R. to the League. *15A.6C.*, 97. The delegations of these four States "would have been authorized to associate themselves with an invitation to that effect had such an invitation been issued by the Assembly itself."—i.e. rather than by thirty Governments. *ibid.*

[38] *Mellanfolkligt Samarbete*, December, 1934, Årgang 4, p. 321. (Speech of December 14, 1934.)

If the League could not be an association of democratic States, still, in the Scandinavian view, it must retain its character as an association of law-abiding and stable States. The withdrawal of Germany from the League was deeply regretted in the North, because "a League without Germany would be weak." But there was little disposition to argue that members should be held in the League at any cost. In 1926 when Spain threatened commercial retaliation against Sweden because of Sweden's legitimate refusal to support the Spanish claim for a permanent seat in the Council, there was considerable Swedish feeling that if Spain could not play according to the rules, she might fittingly withdraw from the League.[39] As for Japan, who violated the Covenant and other solemn engagements in 1931-1932, the Scandinavian attitude was less regretful for her later withdrawal than it was indignant at her wanton disregard for the peace of the world.[40] Yet the day is looked forward to when universality, the fundamental principle of the League, may be realized.[41]

[39] See an article in *Berlingske Tidende* for March 12, 1926, referred to by *The Times* correspondent in *The Times* (London), March 13, 1926 [12A].

[40] *infra*, Chapter XIII, pp. 256 *ff*.

[41] *15A.P.*, 84-5. (Speech of M. Sandler in the 1934 Assembly.)

CHAPTER VII

ORGANIZATION AND PROCEDURE OF THE ASSEMBLY

SINCE the days of William the Silent the small States have repeatedly assailed the Great Powers for injustices heaped upon them.[1] In the nineteenth century complaint was levelled against the Concert of Powers for excluding interested States from international congresses dealing with important political questions. In defence of their interests the lesser Powers seized upon the theory of Pufendorf (developed by Burlamaqui, Calvo and others) that States are naturally equal.[2] It was not surprising that the Scandinavian States were among those adhering to a theory which offered equality of right irrespective of "population, extent of territory, and military power."[3] At The Hague Conference of 1907, their delegates and those of other small Powers defended the principle of equality of States.[4] If, however, their hope for a greater voice in international affairs was raised in 1907, the Paris Peace Conference must have been disappointing in the extreme. The Great Powers dictated the Peace; equality was denied, and in the newly created League of Nations the Great Powers were given a preeminent status.

The composition and jurisdiction assigned by the Covenant to the Council and Assembly foreordained that the Council should become the instrument of the Great Powers and the Assembly an important forum for the smaller States. Only in the Assembly were all of the members of the League granted permanent representation. In this organ the lesser Powers were entitled to send delegates on a basis of equality with those of the British Empire, France, Italy and Japan.[5] Although the Council had been given special functions

---

[1] Figgis, *Gerson to Grotius,* p. 242.
[2] Dickinson, *The Equality of States in International Law,* pp. 81 *ff.*
[3] *ibid.,* pp. 100-1.
[4] *supra,* Chapter II, p. 22.
[5] *Annals of the American Academy,* 96, p. 19.

which the Assembly did not share, Article III, paragraph 3, made possible a legitimate claim for the extension of the Assembly's authority beyond that intended by some of its founders. There it was provided that "The Assembly may deal at its meetings with any matter within the sphere of action of the League or affecting the peace of the world."

To men of the outlook and temper of Nansen, Branting and Motta, an opportunity was presented for strengthening the Assembly and asserting its preeminence. Throughout the League's history no members have been more active and determined in their loyalty to the Assembly than the Scandinavian States. To safeguard the rights of this body and to affect its constitutional supremacy over the work of the League have been a foundation-stone of Scandinavian policy.

As we examine the activity of the Scandinavian States in regard to constitutional questions affecting the Assembly, three basic principles should be kept in mind: First, that the League of Nations should be strengthened and made an effective instrument for world peace and cooperation; second, that the Assembly should be recognized as the supreme organ of the League; and third, that within the Assembly, the principle of equality should be safeguarded. Let us begin with the Scandinavian effort to assure annual meetings of the Assembly.

Meetings of the Assembly

Although the Covenant provided that the Council should meet "at least once a year," the Assembly received no similar guarantee.[6] Article III, paragraph 2, reads that "The Assembly shall meet at stated intervals and from time to time as occasion may require. . . ." The rejection of the Norwegian proposal,[7] made at the conference with the neutrals in Paris in 1919, to specify annual meetings of the Assembly was in keeping with the British Foreign Office idea that the Assembly should meet quadrennially on the analogy of the British Imperial Conference.[8] Fearful lest some such arrangement be followed, the Scandinavian Commissions recommended to their respective Governments in 1920 that an amendment be offered to Article

[6] Article IV, paragraph 3.
[7] *supra*, Chapter IV, p. 52.
[8] Alfred Zimmern, *op. cit.*, pp. 207, 458.

III of the Covenant stipulating annual meetings.[9] Amendments differing only in detail were then submitted by the Scandinavian Governments to the Secretariat and incorporated in the agenda of the First Assembly. The Danish and Norwegian amendments stated that "The Assembly shall meet *each year at the time fixed by its rules of procedure*. . . ." The Swedish draft definitely fixed the time as the *"second Monday in September"* each year. The Swedish Government's comment was that the Assembly should be strengthened and "should possess all the requisite power if the League is to maintain permanently the authority which it needs for the accomplishment of its lofty and important mission."[10]

Although the Scandinavian amendments to Article III were not accepted, the principle of annual meetings of the Assembly was recognized by the incorporation of a provision to that effect in the Rules of Procedure adopted by the First Assembly.[11] A decade later, Mr. Arthur Sweetser, an able student of the League, described this decision as "almost certainly the most important taken in League development . . . since the War."[12]

The importance attached by the Swedish Government to safeguarding the regular meeting of the Assembly is illustrated by the objection raised by M. Sandler to the postponement of the Assembly's opening in 1933. He insisted that it would be dangerous to create a precedent which would make it possible to postpone the Assembly of any year for reasons of expediency. "If it is desired to avoid difficulties in connection with other international conferences, it is to these conferences, rather than the Assembly, that these reasons of

---

[9] von Würtemberg, *op. cit.*, pp. 221-2.

[10] For the draft amendments to the Covenant proposed by the Danish, Norwegian and Swedish Governments, respectively, see *L.N.O.J.*, I, 6, pp. 353-6. For the comment by the Swedish Government, *ibid.*, pp. 356-7.

[11] *1A.P.*, 236 (Rule 1) The sub-committee of the First Committee of the 1921 Assembly gave two reasons for not recommending acceptance of the Scandinavian amendments to Article III: First, because the purpose of these amendments had been satisfied by the adoption of the Rules of Procedure; second, it was not thought desirable to be too specific in setting the time of the Assembly meetings. *2A.1C.*, 148. Because of the first of these reasons, the Scandinavian Governments withdrew their proposed amendments to Article III at the Second Assembly. *2A.P.*, 822.

[12] "The First Ten Years of the League of Nations," *International Conciliation Pamphlet*, no. 256, p. 13. See also Dr Benjamin Gerig's statement quoted in Morley, *op. cit.*, p. 510.

expediency should be applied . . . it is upon the League and its organs that we wish to confer the highest degree of stability.

"It has been felt necessary to make use of organizations other than the League because the League is not sufficiently universal. Since, however, the League is the only one of them that imposes clearly specified obligations on its members, the task of those other international conferences will inevitably fall upon the League, if the methods of working outside the League machinery prove unsuccessful."[13]

In the Scandinavian draft amendments to Article III, it was also proposed that "On the demand of ten Members of the League, the Secretary-General shall immediately summon a meeting of the Assembly." Although the Covenant's provision that the Assembly should meet "from time to time as occasion may require" was never amended, the Scandinavian initiative served the useful purpose of directing attention to the need for a specific rule on the question of extraordinary meetings of the Assembly. The Rules of Procedure as actually adopted in 1920, however, provided that a majority of the League members—not ten as the Scandinavians desired—must concur in a request by a member for a special meeting of the Assembly.[14]

One final point in regard to Assembly meetings illustrates the Scandinavian determination to assure the appropriate influence of the larger League organ. In 1926 Dr Nansen opposed the fixing of a date for closing the Assembly at a time when the general debate had not yet been completed. He warned against the mistakes which might result from undue haste, especially since the whole work of the League during the ensuing year depended in a great measure upon decisions taken by the Assembly.[15]

Delegates to the Assembly

The frequent visits of the Foreign Ministers of the Great Powers to Geneva in recent years should not be allowed to blur the memory of those days when the League was taken less seriously by Whitehall and the Quai d'Orsay. In contrast with the Principal Allied Powers,

[13] *14A.P.*, 43.
[14] See also, Draft Amendments to the Rules of Procedure for the Assembly proposed by the Representative of Sweden. *1A.1C.*, 59-60.
[15] *7A.P.*, 64.

from the beginning the Scandinavian and certain other small States wanted the League's machinery to be used as the instrument for arriving at important international decisions. It was thought that not only the Council, but also the more representative organ of the League should be endowed with this function. Accordingly greater emphasis was attached by these States than by the Great Powers to the importance of sending Foreign Ministers and other responsible statesmen to League meetings. Sweden especially deserves mention for representation by her Prime Minister at the First Assembly. Throughout the history of the League Sweden and Denmark have splendid records for sending Prime Ministers or Foreign Ministers to the Assembly, and since 1925 there has been only one Assembly at which the Prime Minister or Foreign Minister of each of the three Scandinavian States did not attend the Assembly.

At the time of the establishment of the League there was much support in the North for the theory that the Assembly should be a "parliament of peoples," as distinct from a diplomatic conference of Governments.[16] When a "League of States" was created by the Covenant rather than a "parliament of peoples," the practice of the Northern Powers was brought in line with the accepted system. But in two important ways their general practice of representation has differed from that commonly employed at pre-War diplomatic conferences. The first of these was definitely to restrict the number of professional diplomats in the delegations which they sent to Geneva. The Scandinavian States wished for general acceptance of this view. Accordingly, in the Eighth Assembly, M. Hambro expressed regret that the proportion of the delegates to the Assembly which was composed of active politicians and statesmen was not so strong as it had been at the first Assemblies. The Norwegian Storting had also commented on the strength of the diplomatic element at Geneva.[17]

As a practical suggestion to relieve far-away States of the necessity of sending as delegates diplomatic representatives to a European (usually Great Power) capital, M. Hambro suggested in the 1929 Assembly that the travelling expenses to Geneva of three delegates

[16] See Chapter III, pp. 32, 41. As late as September 27, 1921, Hambro said in the Storting that it was really the Storting and not the Government which should be represented at Geneva. *Stortings Forhandlinger* (1921), Vol. 7b, p. 3444.
[17] *8A.P.*, 57.

from each Member State should be met annually by the budget of the League. Nothing, however, came of this suggestion.

In order to reconcile the desire for a "parliament of peoples" with the need for a conference of responsible members of Governments who could make decisions which would be accepted by these Governments, the Danes adopted a system of sending a delegate from each of the four principal political parties in the Rigsdag, usually headed by the Foreign Minister.[18] In Denmark, Norway and Sweden the practice of sending a one-party or partisan delegation was avoided from the very first Assembly. M. Hambro, for instance, has represented Norway at Geneva "under a Conservative Government, a Liberal Government, the Farmers' Party and a Socialist Government."[19] There is naturally more continuity of policy in these States than in those whose delegations are constantly changing. This practice is easier to utilize in the North than in some States because of the fundamental agreement of the parties concerning League policy.[20]

In Norway less attention has been given to the selection of delegations with the view of giving representation to political parties. Not that party delegations were sent. The guiding principle which seems to have been followed from the beginning was, as Prime Minister Mowinckel said, that of choosing the men of distinguished character and high international reputation and training who could exercise real influence at Geneva.[21] Until M. Hambro was sent to the Assembly as a member of the Norwegian delegation in September 1926, he repeatedly attacked the Government for sending delegations so little representative of the Storting and, as he said, of public

[18] For the party representation of the Danish delegations see the speech of Moltesen (Venstre), October 24, 1922. *Rigsdagstidenden* (1922-1923), *Folketing*, I, p. 529. It is usual for the members of the opposition parties in the Rigsdag to speak in the Government's name at Geneva. If a delegate cannot agree with the Government's instructions, he must speak only in his own name. See also P. Munch, *La Politique du Danemark dans la Société des Nations*, pp. 19-20.

[19] *International Affairs*, Vol. XV, nr. 2 (March-April 1936), pp. 170-1.

[20] The failure of the Norwegian Labour Party to cooperate with the bourgeois parties in the League's work meant, of course, that they were not represented in the delegations. See Mowinckel's speech contrasting the cooperative spirit of Right and Left (i.e. Social Democrats) in Sweden and Denmark with that in Norway on questions of foreign policy. *Stortings Forhandlinger* (1927), Vol. 7b, pp. 1513 *ff*. (May 21, 1927).

[21] See the debate in the Storting, June 12, 1923. *Stortings Forhandlinger*, Vol. 7b, pp. 2189 *ff*. (Esp. at pp. 2195-6.)

opinion in Norway.[22] He succeeded in getting the Storting's Committee of Foreign Affairs to back up his annual complaint against the non-representative character of the delegations. In 1923 this committee reported to the Storting that so far as it was aware, Norway was the only State in the League whose National Assembly had not been represented at the Geneva meetings.[23] In the Storting, M. Mowinckel's defence was that Dr Lange, Dr Lie and Mlle Bonnevie were sent because of their special qualifications; other delegates, M. Michelet and M. Blehr, had been out of the Storting but a short while.[24] He would be glad to send an active member of the Storting but he was not prepared to drop members of previous delegations in order to find a place for a *Stortingsmann*.[25]

From this discussion of Scandinavian practice in regard to the choosing of delegations for the Assembly, let us turn to one other qualification which was asked for by the Norwegians. M. Hambro said in 1929 that it was important that the members of the League should be represented by governmental delegates and not by nationals of those States who were in the employment of the Secretariat.[26] This view was held because of the desire to have "political" as contrasted with "technical" representatives at the Assembly, as well as to safeguard the international character of the League's civil service.

Officers and Committees of the Assembly

The guiding principle which the Northern States have followed on the detailed questions concerning the organization and direction of the Assembly is that the position of various delegations should be equalized. This had been one reason for suggesting that the Assembly should pay the expenses of three delegates from each Member State. Another application of this principle was Nansen's proposal in 1920 that three of the six Vice-Presidents of the Assembly should be nationals of non-European States.[27]

---

[22] See, for instance, *Stortings Tidende* (November 16, 1920), p. 3628; (September 27, 1921), p. 3443; (June 12, 1923), p. 2192; (July 17, 1925), p. 2905.

[23] *Stortings Forhandlinger* (1923), Vol. 6a (II), *Innst. S. LIV.*, p. 5.

[24] *supra*, note 21.

[25] *Stortings Forhandlinger* (1925), Vol. 7b, pp. 2907-8 (July 17).

[26] *10A.4C.*, 51. See also *infra*, p. 151.

[27] *1A.P.*, 70, 72.

Norway has taken a strong line on the question of the proper basis of election of the Assembly's officers. It was insisted that "individuals" and not "States" should be elected to the Vice-Presidencies. M. Hambro, the leading Norwegian critic of constitutional procedure in the League, warmly supported the stand taken by M. van Karnebeck of the Netherlands, who as President of the Second Assembly objected to a practice resorted to by some of the nationals of Great Powers. This practice was that of sending a colleague as a substitute chairman of an Assembly committee when the elected chairman was not present. Vice-Presidents should be chosen because of their personal qualifications and not for other reasons. M. Hambro has also pointed out the inconvenience that has sometimes resulted from the tendency of the Assembly to choose diplomats rather than parliamentarians as its Presidents.[28]

A Swedish proposal introduced at the First Assembly indicated apprehension lest the Great Powers exercise too great an influence over the personnel of committees which the Assembly might set up. The Provisional Rules of Procedure, under which the 1920 Assembly began work, provided that the nomination of such committees should be made by the President assisted by the General Committee of the Assembly. As it was probable that the Great Powers and some of their satellites would control a committee limited to twelve members, the Swedish Government proposed that the General Committee be supplemented by nine other members elected by the Assembly.[29] For administrative reasons, however, the Swedish proposal was unacceptable.

An insight on the mentality of the Scandinavian Governments is admirably given in the instructions of the Norwegian delegation to the Ninth Assembly "to work for the election of at least two representatives in the General Committee of the Assembly that come from States quite independent of leading Great Powers and who, because of their personality, will be able to take care of the smaller

[28] See especially C. J. Hambro, *Folkeforbundet og Dets Arbeide,* pp. 34-40, in his chapter, "Konstitutionel og ukonstitutionel praksis." At the Second Assembly, a motion by Branting was carried which called for the election of the chairmen of the six committees of the Assembly *before* the election of the other Vice-Presidents so that "we shall not be voting in the dark." *2A.P.,* 30, 31, 32. See Zahle to the same effect, *3A.1C.,* 33.

[29] Draft amendments to the Rules of Procedure for the Assembly proposed by the representative of Sweden. *1A.1C. (I),* 60.

States' interests, especially their interests in seeing every matter treated according to the stipulations of the Covenant and the Rules of Procedure."[30]

In 1929 when the question of Assembly supremacy over the other League's organs was a very live one, M. Hambro wrote in a letter to *The Times* (London) that, "It is one of the constitutional weaknesses of the League that there are no permanent committees elected by the Assembly."[31] It should be noted, however, that in the early years of the League the Scandinavian delegations did not officially suggest the creation of permanent committees chosen by the Assembly. Indeed, when the Swiss delegation introduced a resolution to this effect at the 1920 Assembly, neither the Danish, Norwegian nor Swedish delegates in the First Committee offered any support.[32] The outspoken opposition of the British and French members doomed it to failure, a failure which was not erased until the full tide of small State opposition was marshalled by M. Hambro in 1928.[33]

The Unanimity Rule

For purposes of convenience the Scandinavian attitude towards the unanimity rule in the Assembly and Council will be considered together. Article V, paragraph 1, of the Covenant clearly specified that, "Except where otherwise expressly provided in this Covenant or by the terms of the present Treaty, decisions at any meetings of the Assembly or of the Council shall require the agreement of all the members of the League represented at the meeting." Questions of procedure necessarily had to be excepted.

The provision for unanimity was regarded as a great safeguard by the Scandinavian States in 1920, for they were anxious to retain as far as possible their liberty of action in regard to sanctions and other obligations which might affect their status of neutrality.[34] In the Committee on the Composition of the Council in 1926, M. Sjöborg, of Sweden, argued against enlargement of the Council on the ground that such action would increase the difficulty of obtaining

[30] *St. med.* nr. 3 (1929), p. 8.
[31] *The Times,* September 4, 1929 [11A].
[32] *1A.1C. (I),* 11-14, 99.
[33] *infra,* p. 158.
[34] *supra,* Chapter IV, pp. 57-8, 59.

unanimity, and would endanger maintenance of the rule. To surrender the unanimity rule, he added, would be to run the risk of dismembering the League.[35]

As the League gained strength and as its popularity in the North increased, thoughtful advocates became more impressed with the difficulty of achieving positive results as long as agreement among fifty-odd nations was necessary. When preparation was being made for the 1930 Conference for the Codification of International Law, M. Lange urged that if agreement could not be reached by all States in the process of treaty-making, arrangements should be made for effecting agreement among a smaller number of States. It was, of course, not proposed that new convention-law should be binding on States which did not accept it.[36] To interpret the unanimity rule to mean that one or a few Powers could place an absolute veto on any action by other States at a conference was declared intolerable.

The serious problem arose within the Council of the League. The question was given prominence when, in December 1933, the Grand Fascist Council sharply criticized the existing structure of the League, advocating restriction of the privileges of the small States and the abandonment of the unanimity rule. A directorate of the Great Powers was urged.[37] Although no official proposal to this effect was made at Geneva, the question of League reform became an important topic for discussion. M. Sandler, the Swedish Foreign Minister, took occasion to speak of his Government's attitude in a radio address on April 4, 1934.[38] The rule of unanimity, he said, was a clear-cut corollary of the principle of legal equality of States, which was anchored in the Covenant. It was true, however, that the Covenant did not consider unanimity so fundamental as it did legal equality. There were exceptions which necessity compelled, as on questions of procedure, which the Swedish Government readily recognized. But where, asked M. Sandler, was the dividing line between questions of principle and questions of procedure? The United

[35] *L. of N. Doc.*, C. 299, M. 139, 1926, V, p. 18. See Munch, *5A.3C.*, 57.
[36] *8A.1C.*, 17-18.
[37] *The Times* (London), December 7, 1933 [14A]. For the reaction in the Scandinavian press to the criticism of the Grand Fascist Council, see *The Times,* January 10, 1934.
[38] This speech is printed in a volume of collected speeches. See Rickard Sandler, *Ett Utrikespolitisk Program,* Stockholm, 1934, pp. 74-86.

States had been invited to the Council table at the time of the Man-churian crisis, and this action had been considered as a matter of procedure. Although M. Sandler recognized the importance of the question, he refrained from drawing the line. But he defined the Swedish position—and incidentally the Danish and Norwegian—when he said that eventual modifications of the rule of unanimity must refer to closely delimited and quite precise instances. More particularly, M. Sandler stressed that his Government would "think more than twice" before it consented to any alteration which would allow majority decisions to bind Sweden to participate in conflicts in which she was unwilling to take sides. For, he added, "the situation in the world and the security furnished at present by the collective system through the League of Nations are not such that we can surrender in advance the right to pursue the path of neutrality."[39]

In the Storting on March 8, 1930, M. Hambro compared the American Articles of Confederation of 1777 with the League Cov-enant, pointing to the serious hindrance the unanimity rule caused in both instances. Although he flatly said that "Unanimity makes the Assembly and the Council unsuitable as political instruments," it is clear that neither his country nor others were ready to abandon the unanimity rule on matters of prime importance.[40] Nevertheless, the Scandinavians have asked for some alleviation from the disheartening interpretation given to Article XI of the Covenant in the Sino-Japanese conflict of 1931-1933. The Swedish Government declared in 1936 that it would favour an interpretation which would deny votes to the parties involved when the Council, acting under Article XI, should recommend measures to prevent the aggravation of a dispute. Moreover, unanimity is not required, according to the view of the Scandinavian Governments, for a decision of the Council to ask, when examining a dispute, for an advisory opinion from the Permanent Court of International Justice.[41]

[39] *Ett Utrikespolitisk Program*, p. 82.
[40] *Stortings Forhandlinger* (1930), Vol. 7b, pp. 1555 *ff.* (*Tidende S.*, March 8, 1930). In M. Hambro's article, "Folkeforbundet Idag," *op. cit.*, p. 77, the author refers to the unanimity rule as a real stumbling-block when States which are in arrears in the payment of their dues to the League are allowed to veto measures.
[41] *L. of N. Doc.*, C. 357, M. 233, 1936, VII; *L. of N. Doc.*, C. 543, M. 351, 1936, V, 9.

CHAPTER VIII

ORGANIZATION AND PROCEDURE OF THE COUNCIL

Composition of the Council

THE reform of the League demanded by the Fascist Grand Council in 1933, like certain Italian adventures of a more recent date, had its British precedent. Fascist Italy complained of a democratic League which hindered the working of the Concert of Europe.[1] In 1919 Lord Robert Cecil had advocated a Council limited to the Great Powers.[2] Both disregarded the interests of the smaller Powers. Both were vigorously objected to by the Scandinavian States.

At the Paris Peace Conference the smaller States, supported by French sympathy, obtained a provision for representation on the Council, only after a struggle. The Draft Covenant of February 14 called for an international executive of representatives of the Principal Allied and Associated Powers and of four other members of the League. This victory was won before the meeting was held with representatives of the neutral States, who were not, however, entirely satisfied with this arrangement. At the Hotel Crillon meeting the Scandinavian spokesmen proposed a further enlargement of the Council. They did not oppose in principle permanent seats for the Great Powers, but they wished to obtain a wider representation of the secondary States. In this, however, they were unsuccessful at Paris.[3]

When the question of adherence to the Covenant was debated in the parliaments of the North, objections were offered to the overwhelming preponderance of the Great Powers in the Council. Much of this criticism would have been spared if all of the Great Powers,

[1] *supra,* p. 104.
[2] Miller, *op. cit.,* Vol. I, p. 53. "He thought that the Great Powers must run the League and that it was just as well to recognize it flatly as not."
[3] *supra,* Chapter IV, pp. 53-4.

Germany included, had been named as permanent members of the Council. But even so, the Scandinavian conception was not that of the British Foreign Office or of the Italian Grand Fascist Council. In the League's Council, the various small-State groups should be represented. There was no justification for the Great Powers to assume the entire responsibility for managing world affairs. This feeling was stronger in Sweden, still conscious of her one-time greatness, than in Denmark and Norway. In order to make the preponderance of the Great Powers in the Council more palatable to public opinion, the Scandinavian Governments called attention to the unpleasant duties which members of the Council might have to perform.[4] Especially if the League did not include the defeated Powers, the responsibilities of Council membership might endanger traditional Scandinavian impartiality before the rival Powers.

Following this line of thought the Scandinavian Governments agreed upon an amendment to Article IV, which they introduced at the First Assembly. It is significant to note what the amendment did *not* provide. There was no attempt to return to the principles which the official Scandinavian commissions had selected in 1918. The scheme of those commissions contemplated a Council of non-government representatives chosen by an electoral college in which state-equality was recognized.[5] Such a Council was forgotten when a League of Nations was created on lines quite different from those of their proposed "International Juridical Organization." Still another change had come in the Scandinavian attitude. Less importance was now attached to the enlargement of the Council, so much so that no proposal for its enlargement was introduced at the First Assembly. The abandonment of the advocacy of a large Council calls for an explanation. Was it merely that efforts to increase the number of the secondary Powers on the Council seemed futile? Or were there other reasons? It is not characteristic of the Scandinavian temper to be easily discouraged by difficulty. Moreover, the enlargement of the Council as early as 1922 would suggest that the difficulty of getting the Great Powers to agree to such a step was not insurmountable. The truth seems to be that the Scandinavians had no desire to destroy the

[4] *supra*, Chapter V, p. 66.
[5] *supra*, Chapter III, p. 39.

effectiveness of the Council by flooding it with a large number of minor States. The Scandinavians were primarily interested in the success of the League as a working institution for world peace. Now that the Covenant had prescribed for the Council an important rôle in the execution of the League's will, the need for a small, workable Council where decisions could be arrived at expeditiously seemed reasonable. The presence of Germany, the United States and Russia on the Council could not be effected by any proposal they might make, for these Powers were not yet members of the League. The refusal of the American Senate to ratify the Treaty put the existing ratio of large to small States on the Council at four to four. It was not so much a question of increasing the number of small States as it was of arranging for the better representation of small-State interests. At least, so it appeared to the prevailing counsel at the meeting of the Danish, Norwegian and Swedish Commissions in the summer of 1920.

The amendments offered by the Scandinavian States to Article IV sought recognition of the principle that "a large number of States should be successively represented on the Council, while, at the same time, a certain continuity should be maintained. In order to achieve this double aim, and to obviate all discussion at the time of the elections," it was proposed that non-permanent members be elected for terms of four years and not permitted to succeed themselves. Of the four non-permanent members, one should retire each year, thus producing a Council on which there would never be more than one new member.[6]

The underlying reason for introducing this amendment seems to be this: precaution should be taken that Belgium, Brazil, Spain and Greece, the Powers named in the Covenant as the first non-permanent members, should have no temptation to retain indefinitely their Council seats.[7] In the Riksdag the previous March, fears had been expressed that the unanimity rule might be applied to the election by the Assembly of the non-permanent members, thereby resulting in

---

[6] The quotation is from the comment by the Swedish Government on the Swedish Amendment to Article IV of the Covenant. *L.N.O.J.*, I, 6, p. 356. The draft amendments of the Danish, Norwegian and Swedish Governments did not differ in principle. See *L.N.O.J.*, I, 6, pp. 353 ff.

[7] Compare Morley, *op. cit.*, pp. 350-1.

a "permanent" seat for the first occupants who might refuse to vote themselves out.[8] The Scandinavian statesmen correctly anticipated the extreme reluctance members would have in stepping down from the Council unless this were automatically provided for. Another reason for the proposed system of rotation arose from a desire to minimize the use of the Council for the special interests of the Great Powers. It might be unusually difficult to unseat their satellites, such as Belgium and Greece, if the Great Powers used their influence, as no doubt they would, to retain their presence.

If rotation would eliminate the possibility of embarrassment at the rejection of a candidate whose re-election was sponsored by a Great Power, the second aim, continuity, was more consciously designed to check Great Power domination of the Council. A four-year term for non-permanent members, and the retirement of only one State a year from the Council would permit members to become accustomed to their duties and would partially offset the natural advantage which Great Powers possess over small States in international bodies. In any event it would be difficult enough for representatives of small States in the Council to express their convictions in an outspoken fashion.[9] The proposed system, however, would serve to maintain their influence at a higher level than in the case of one-year terms.

There can be no hesitation to stress the importance of what may be called the "small-State complex" as the motivating force behind most Scandinavian initiative in the first years of the League. There was an ever-present tendency to criticize freely the Great Powers. At times it was even rumoured about Geneva that some Scandinavians had interpreted the right of criticism as the joy of critcism. But it was generally the sort of criticism which could not be lightly ignored, for it rang true to many persons anxious to strengthen the League and to make of it a real force for international justice.

[8] The minority report of the Riksdag's Special Committee stated that it was not clear whether a unanimous vote would be required for the election of the non-permanent members of the Council. In such case, it would be difficult to modify the "first" Council as named by the Covenant. See Trygger, *op. cit.*, p. 436.

[9] See the speech of M. Sjöborg, May 12, 1926, in the Committee on the Composition of the Council. *L. of N. Doc.*, C. 299, M. 139, 1926, V, p. 42, and Viscount Cecil's speech, at p. 41.

What success did the Scandinavian States have in introducing a proposal for rotation? Although the First Committee of the 1920 Assembly decided not to submit to the Assembly proposals which would constitute amendments to the Covenant,[10] the Swiss delegation was of the opinion that the fundamental question raised by the Scandinavian amendments had not been prejudiced.[11] The Swiss proposed, therefore, that there be inserted in the Assembly's Rules of Procedure a provision for the selection of one member of the Council each year.[12] But as the constitutionality of such a rule was doubtful, in view of Article IV of the Covenant, the Swiss proposal was discarded.[13]

At the Second Assembly the logic of the Scandinavian proposal made sufficient appeal to carry a resolution "that the non-permanent members of the Council should, in future, be elected according to a system of rotation for a fixed period." This resolution was "noted" at the request of M. Zahle of Denmark, who presented the Report of the First Committee to the Assembly. On the same day, October 5, 1921, an amendment to the Covenant was unanimously adopted declaring that: "The Assembly shall fix by a two-thirds majority the rules dealing with the election of the non-permanent members of the Council, and particularly such regulations as relate to their term of office and the conditions of reeligibility."[14]

But this amendment which would have afforded a "rational, impartial, simple and early solution of the Council problem" was not ratified by France and Spain, "the only members of the Council

[10] On November 22, 1920, the committee decided by a vote of 20 to 8 against consideration of the Scandinavian amendments by the Assembly. With the Scandinavian States voted Argentina, Cuba, the Netherlands, Panama and Siam. *1A.1C.*, 9-10.

[11] Swiss Proposal (November 23, 1920) for the Selection of Four Non-Permanent Members of the Council. *1A.1C.*, 100-2.

[12] Marks von Würtemberg spoke in favour of the Swiss proposal since the amendments of the Scandinavian States were rejected.

[13] On this constitutional problem, see the Swiss argument in the *Explanatory Statement* to its proposal. *ibid.* Also Morley, *op. cit.*, pp. 352-3. The French text was even stronger.

[14] The quotations of this paragraph are from *2A.P.*, 892-3. For the comment of Zahle on the conclusions adopted by the Committee on Amendments at London, see *2A.1C.*, 34.

which of intention" failed to do so.[15] It was not, therefore, until 1926, when the crisis of Germany's entry into the League arose, that the Scandinavian initiative for rotation finally bore fruit. In the interval a Swedish suggestion had been made that the Permanent Court of International Justice might be asked for an advisory opinion on the question of whether or not an amendment to the Covenant was necessary for instituting a system of rotation.[16]

Sweden's attitude after she was elected to the Council was in marked contrast to that of some of the other non-permanent Council members who clung tenaciously to their seats. In the Sixth Assembly, M. Eliel Löfgren urged rotation, arguing that such a system would strengthen the position and influence of the Council in the face of public opinion.[17] No legitimate argument could be found to refute the logic of an arrangement which would give all members of the League "an opportunity of participating in turn in the important work of the Council."[18] In the first seven years of the League "just two nations—Greece and China—had vacated their seats on the Council, in each case as the result of a profound domestic upheaval."[19]

Meanwhile the pressure of the non-Council members led to other action. In the Second Assembly, M. Rolin of Belgium proposed an increase of the non-permanent members of the Council from four to six.[20] This was not agreed to unanimously by the Council, as was necessary according to the Covenant. Dr Lie states that there are reasons for believing that this addition was opposed by Brazil and Spain.[21] The following year, however, at the instigation of the British and French, the Council voted unanimously to increase its membership by two seats. In the Assembly, where a majority vote

[15] Morley, *op. cit.*, p. 355. This amendment and others adopted by the 1921 Assembly were quickly ratified by the Scandinavian States, and were described in the *Folketing* on June 28, 1922, by Dr P. Munch as a move in the direction of the Scandinavian point of view developed in 1919. *Rigsdagstidenden* (1921-1922) *Folketinget*, III, pp. 8932-4.

[16] *L. of N. Doc.*, C. 299, M. 139, 1926, V, pp. 17-18 (Minutes of the Committee on the Composition of the Council).

[17] *6A.P.*, 111.

[18] Mowinckel's speech, *6A.P.*, 45.

[19] Morley, *op. cit.*, p. 356.

[20] *St. med.* nr. 5 (1922), p. 11.

[21] *St. med.* nr. 5 (1922), p. 11 (*Om Folkenes Forbunds annet delegertmøte i Genf september-oktober 1921*).

was required to carry the proposal, only the delegation of the Netherlands were in opposition. The Dutch argued that if the Council were enlarged the Great Powers would not consider the League of Nations as the central organ for international intercourse.[22] The Swiss also expressed doubt as to the advisability of such a change, but did not vote against the position taken by the majority.[23] Denmark, Norway and Sweden quietly approved. They did not state their reasons. The official reports submitted to the Scandinavian parliaments did not consider the delegations' position.[24] It would seem that they preferred rotation rather than enlargement, but did not vote against enlargement as it was not considerable, and as it was probable that one of the new seats would fall to one of their number. As it turned out, Sweden, the largest and wealthiest of the Scandinavian States, was elected by the Third Assembly to one of the newly created seats.[25] A few weeks later M. Holger Andersen, one of the Danish delegates to the Assembly, expressed pleasure that the non-permanent members of the Council had been increased from four to six. "There will certainly be aroused in Denmark general satisfaction that one of the new non-permanent seats . . . for the coming year falls to our neighbour Sweden."[26]

Germany's Entry into the League

The question of Scandinavian attitude towards the composition of the Council is closely connected with the intricate negotiations which preceded Germany's admission to the League. Emphasis has already been laid upon the importance which the Northern neutrals attached to Germany's entry. In the midst of the Fifth Assembly Dr Nansen, the First Delegate of Norway, hurried off from Geneva to Berlin on a private mission which sought to persuade Germany to apply for

[22] 3A.P., 223.
[23] St. med. nr. 8 (1923). Om Folkenes Forbunds 3dje forsamling i Genf i 1922, p. 27; 3A.1C., 37-8, 39.
[24] Om Folkenes Forbunds 3dje forsamling i Genf i 1922. St. med. nr. 8 (1923), pp. 27-8; U. N. F. (1922), pp. 31-2. On March 24, 1926, in the Lower House of the Riksdag, Dr Undén, the Foreign Minister, said that when the increase in the Council membership took place in 1922, it occurred "without opposition from Sweden." U.N.F. (1926), p. 14.
[25] 3A.P. (I), 383.
[26] Folketing (1922-1923), I, pp. 552-3.

League membership.[27] In the same month (September 1924) the German Government decided to consider the question of Germany's adherence in the near future.[28]

After the European political atmosphere had been improved by the Locarno Agreements of October 1925, the German Government made application for admission to the League in its letter of February 8, 1926, to the Secretary-General.[29] In the following March, special sessions of the Council and Assembly met for the purpose of effecting Germany's entrance, but the hopes for immediate admission were thwarted. As the Swedish Foreign Minister said to the closing meeting of a disappointed Assembly:[30]

> Unfortunately Germany's admission was brought into relation with other and irrelevant issues. National claims were advanced in various quarters; individual interests came into conflict with the general interest, the common good of the League.

These "national claims" to which Dr Undén referred were demands of Spain, Brazil and Poland for permanent seats on the Council. This was not the first occasion when second-class Powers sought the status assigned by the drafters of the Covenant to the Great Powers alone. At the 1921 Assembly the Chilean delegation had proposed that Brazil and Spain be given permanent seats.[31] This proposal was objected to by the Scandinavians and won little support in any quarter. A similar effort failed in 1923. When the Council met on March 8, 1926, the "status-climbers" included Poland and China as well. Since Germany would not enter the League until guaranteed a permanent seat on the Council[32] and since any single member of the Council had the power to prevent its increase, Spain and Brazil were in a position to delay the entry of Germany into the League, and to demand permanent seats for themselves. The shameful affair was complicated by the backing which France was giving Poland and the

---

[27] *New York Times*, September 20, 1924 (3: 6).

[28] *L.N.O.J.*, VI, pp. 323-5.

[29] *L.N.O.J.*, VII, p. 867.

[30] *Records of the Special Assembly*, March 1926, p. 28.

[31] See Professor Undén's review made in the Lower Chamber of the Swedish Riksdag, March 24, 1926, conveniently reproduced in *U.N.F.*, 1926, p. 12.

[32] See the German note of February 8, 1926, quoted by Morley, *op. cit.*, p. 357.

promise of support which Great Britain had made Spain. Moreover, France was willing to support Spain and Brazil in order to neutralize the effect of Germany's entrance into the Council.[33]

As Sweden was a member of the Council in 1926, she played a more important rôle than Denmark and Norway in counteracting this attempt to distort the original conception of the Council. The instructions of the Swedish Government were drawn up after the meeting of the Riksdag Committee on Foreign Affairs on February 12, in which all political parties were represented.[34] The nature of these instructions is revealed in a speech of Dr Undén, the Foreign Secretary, in the Lower House of the Riksdag on March 24, 1926, which in part was as follows:[35]

> The Government shares the opinion expressed in the Assembly in 1923 and which at that time seemed to find general acceptance. An increase of the permanent members—over and above the entrance of the Great Powers—should in the opinion of the Government, meet with the strongest hesitation. From the Swedish viewpoint, it has always been held that the relation of the Assembly to the Council would be considerably weakened by such an increase. Added to that comes the difficulty, if not impossibility, of finding a principle upon which some states might obtain the same advantageous position as the Great Powers and be given permanent seats. The question in regard to the composition of the Council, which from the Swedish point of view needed a solution, was not an increase in the number of permanent seats, but rather the method of choosing the non-permanent seats. . . . The point of view taken on these matters should be entirely with the interest of the League in mind rather than the particular interests of special parties. In any case, the Government is of the opinion that, should the question of the reorganization of the Council come up at the meeting in March, it should be referred to a future Ordinary Assembly. . . . *The Government has in accordance herewith instructed the Swedish delegates to oppose any agreements of a positive char-*

[33] On this subject see especially Morley, *op. cit.*, pp. 356-61; John Spencer Bassett, *The League of Nations*, pp. 304 ff. George Scelle, *Une Crise de la Société des Nations*; Jean Ray, *Commentaire du Pacte de la Société des Nations*, pp. 178 ff.
[34] *U.N.F.* (1926), p. 14. *American-Scandinavian Review*, XIV (1926), p. 365.
[35] Bellquist, *op. cit.*, p. 348. The italics are his.

acter regarding the reorganization of the Council, except the establishing of a permanent seat for Germany, as well as, above all, not now binding itself to any certain solution of this complicated and important problem.

Acting on these instructions Dr Undén proved an effective barrier to the plans of other Governments to enlarge the Council. As the deadlock continued, frequent appeals were made to obtain modification of the Swedish position. An American historian described the rôle of the Swedish Minister of Foreign Affairs as follows:[36]

> Mr Unden remained quietly in his hotel. He was instructed to oppose Poland's demand as contrary to the spirit of the League, and he never wavered from his instructions. One suggestion after another was taken to him: he rejected them all. Pressure was brought to bear on him, but he resisted it. One country threatened to annul a contract it had to buy Swedish-made telephones unless he yielded: he did not budge. Spain threatened to renounce a commercial treaty she had with Sweden; it availed nothing.[37] In the Junta circle Unden was pronounced narrow and stubborn, but he paid no heed. A newspaper correspondent described him as the "least active and the most effective of the men holding the centre of the stage at Geneva."

In his refusal to vote for the enlargement of the permanent membership of the Council, Dr Undén not only had the support of all the parties in the Swedish Riksdag; Denmark, Norway and the Netherlands, although not members of the Council, approved this firm

[36] J. S. Bassett, *The League of Nations,* p. 314. Bellquist, *op. cit.,* p. 351.

[37] Scandinavian solidarity on the question of opposition to enlargement of the Council is evidenced by a leading article in the Conservative Copenhagen paper, *Berlingske Tidende,* of March 12, 1926. It was there declared unwise for Sweden to yield to threats. If members of the League were to behave as Spain, all ideas of cooperation on equal terms would disappear, and sooner or later the League would be destroyed. The view of this journal was that if Spain wished to leave the League, the League could exist without her. If Brazil wished to prevent Germany from entering the League, Brazil must take the responsibility for the exclusion. The League of Nations could only operate successfully if the "rules of the game" were observed. *The Times,* March 13, 1926 (12A.B).

stand.[38] The representatives of Belgium and Uruguay also declared their opposition in principle to any increase in the number of permanent members.[39] But it was primarily a victory won by the determination of Sweden. As Mr Felix Morley said: "The little neutrals of North Europe had for the first time broken the dominance of France and the British Empire, hitherto all-powerful in the League."[40] Later, in the Riksdag, Dr Undén related the story of how Sweden had won her chief resolve in regard to the composition of the Council.[41] On March 12 the principal Great Powers were compelled to abandon the plan for new permanent seats, which in the Swedish view was fraught with such momentous consequences for the League. The decisive opposition had been directed partly from Germany, because of Germany's special interests, and partly from Sweden, because of her concern for the interests of the League of Nations.[42]

It was not, however, a complete victory. Germany was still out of the League. There was "fear that France might obliquely prevent Germany's entry rather than abandon the claims of Poland."[43] Already Germany had refused to accept a compromise proposal, drafted by M. Vandervelde and supported by French, British and Italian representatives, to create one temporary non-permanent seat to be filled by Poland. In this dilemma the Swedish delegation agreed to surrender Sweden's non-permanent seat to the disposal of the Assembly (to accommodate Poland) on the understanding that one of the allies of France on the Council would retire simultaneously in favour of a *bona fide* neutral. This the Swedish Government was

---

[38] The Copenhagen correspondent of *The Times* in an article, March 1, 1926 (14B) states that the Danish Government had been kept informed by the Swedish Government of the measures it was taking in opposition to the proposed extension of the Council.

[39] Bellquist, *op. cit.*, p. 350.

[40] *The Society of Nations*, p. 359.

[41] Interpellation of the Minister of Foreign Affairs in *Andra Kammaren*, March 24, 1926.

[42] Undén said: "Det avgörande motstandet har bjudits dels från tysk sida, ur Tysklands speciella synpunkter, dels från svensk sida, ur inre folkförbundssynpunkter." *U.N.F.* (1926), pp. 15-16.

[43] Morley, *op. cit.*, pp. 359-60.

prepared to consent to in order to get a settlement which would bring Germany into the League.[44]

In the Riksdag Dr Undén stated that "at no occasion did there occur even the slightest intimation of pressure on the Swedish delegate" in respect to Sweden's departure from the Council.[45] The idea of the withdrawal of Sweden was not mentioned in Council circles until after the Swedish-German discussions of the question. One State, however, prevented the solution of the problem by this arrangement. Brazil, whose attitude from the beginning was a serious hindrance, would not surrender her demand for a permanent seat.[46] As a result the Assembly was compelled to postpone the question and to adjourn midst general disappointment. At the final session of the Special Assembly, M. Zahle, the chief Danish delegate, although agreeing with M. Motta, of Switzerland, that the time had not come to "apportion responsibility for the present state of affairs," said that it was only right to proclaim that, at any rate, responsibility did not rest upon the Assembly.[47]

The action of the Swedish Foreign Minister at Geneva led to criticism in much of the Swedish press. Regret was expressed that the offer of withdrawal from the Council should have been made by Dr Undén. There should have been no compromise of the principle defended from the beginning of the League by Sweden, namely, "the principle of safeguarding the independence of the League against a special combination of political interests."[48] There was a clamour from the Conservative press for a full explanation of the reasons which led to this change of policy, especially since "Brazilian persistence in claiming immediate admission to a permanent seat seemed to render the Swedish concession useless."[49]

On March 24, 1926, an exciting debate was held in the Second Chamber of the Riksdag in connection with an interpellation of the

[44] *U.N.F.* (1926), pp. 17-18.
[45] *ibid.*, p. 19.
[46] See José Carlos de Macedo Soares, *Brazil and the League of Nations,* Chapters III and IV, pp. 87-143, for the Brazilian case in regard to the organization of the Council. See also E. Montarroyos, *Le Brésil et la Crise de la Société des Nations en 1926.* Genève, 1926.
[47] *Sp.A.,* 1926, p. 32.
[48] Stockholm correspondent. *The Times,* March 17, 1926 [14B].
[49] *ibid.,* March 18, 1926 [16C].

Foreign Minister. Admiral Lindman, leader of the Conservative opposition, severely criticized the offer of the Social Democrat Government to resign from the Council. This proposal, he said, was entirely at variance with the delegation's original instructions, which had been formally approved by all parties in the Riksdag.[50] One critic observed that it was the Conservatives, who previously had manifested no warm support for the League and who were sceptical of its value to Sweden, who now argued that it would have been more to the credit of Sweden and more to the benefit of the League if she had clung to her original attitude and had defended the League against improper intrigues.[51]

The Foreign Minister gave an able defence of his action at Geneva. He emphasized the positive obligation of the Swedish delegation to work for the entry of Germany to the League.[52] The delegation could hardly have achieved its mission if it had not sought to make this possible, and if it had remained quite passive during the negotiations which were necessary. Some action seemed imperative as the German delegation was about to retire. The Swedish offer, therefore, was designed to save the League from a most embarrassing situation. It prevented any increase in the number of Council members; it effected a change in Council membership, and secured the admission of a State belonging to the same group as Sweden, which would represent the neutral point of view. As for the stubbornness of Brazil, it had been hoped that she might relinquish her demand. It was her attitude alone which had brought about failure of the suggested Swedish solution.

Before the Council adjourned in March 1926, a Committee on the Composition of the Council was named to make a thorough investigation of the whole problem of the Council's reorganization. M. Sjöborg sat for Sweden, the only Scandinavian member of this committee of fifteen. His speeches ably express the Swedish point of view.[53] The "Observations of the Norwegian Government," dated

[50] The Swedish offer was discussed by the Swedish Cabinet, and the Committee on Foreign Affairs (*Utrikesnämnden*) was consulted before the Cabinet agreed to the offer. *The Times*, March 17, 1926.

[51] *The Times*, March 25, 1926 [15B].

[52] *U.N.F.* (1926), pp. 15 ff., and the above citation.

[53] The Report and Minutes of the Committee on the Composition of the Council are contained in *L. of N. Doc.*, C. 299, M. 139, 1926, V, and C. 394, M. 137, 1926, V.

May 12, 1926, and submitted to the Committee, furnish an additional evidence of the Scandinavian attitude.[54] With regard to the increase of the permanent members of the Council, the Norwegian Government remarked: "From the outset the Covenant placed *all* the original members of the League, except the Principal Allied and Associated Powers, on a footing of equality as regards membership of the Council. The right of certain members of the League to permanent seats on the Council is a concession which was made to them because they were beyond question 'Great Powers.' If an exception were now made in favour of *one country* to the principle that only 'Great Powers' are entitled to permanent seats, it would be exceedingly difficult thereafter to refuse the same privilege to other countries which could adduce equally plausible arguments in support of their claims to permanent seats."[55]

Norway and Sweden were also hostile to an increase of the non-permanent seats. To quote again from the "Observations of the Norwegian Government": "It seems superfluous to enlarge upon the undesirable effects this would have upon the work of the Council and the League; for it is an essential condition of the satisfactory working of the League that the Council—the organ of the League which is executive and whose work is continuous—should have only so many members as are strictly necessary for the proper performance of its important duties."

The reasons suggested for opposing an increase in the Council were as follows: First, "the authority and influence of the Assembly would probably wane in proportion to the increase in the membership of the Council."[56] Such a change was contrary to the interests of the League. Second, the effectiveness of the Council as a working body would be diminished. Third, any increase in the number of members of the Council would seriously endanger the maintenance of the rule of unanimity. In the view of M. Sjöborg, the League would run the risk of dismemberment if this rule were not maintained.[57] On this point, the Swedish delegate agreed with the Italian delegate that the

---

[54] Published in Appendix II, at p. 140, of *Doc.,* C. 299, M. 139, 1926, V.

[55] *ibid.,* p. 140.

[56] Published in Appendix II, at p. 140, of *Doc.,* C. 299, M. 139, 1926, V.

[57] Speech of May 10, 1926. *Minutes of the First Session of the Committee on the Composition of the Council,* p. 18.

use of the privilege of "abstention from voting" when a Council member did not agree with the majority (while it might be conceivable in the Assembly) could not be admitted in the Council. Everyone should have the courage of his opinion.[58] A fourth, and perhaps the most important, reason advanced by the Norwegian and Swedish Governments for opposing enlargement of the Council was the fear that a "Council within a Council" might be formed by representatives of the most influential Powers.[59]

Certain objections to the Scandinavian view were answered. The Belgian representative had emphasized that the number of non-permanent members ought to be greater than the number of permanent members. M. Sjöborg replied that "this theory might be a very good one," but that even with Germany in the League as a permanent member, there would be six non-permanent members to five permanent ones. If other Great Powers—i.e. Russia or the United States—became members of the League the question of increasing the non-permanent members could then be faced.[60] To the argument that an increase was necessary so that the Council might reflect the various aspirations and interests of the members of the League, M. Sjöborg pointed out that, in any case, this desire could not be realized by increasing the Council by only a few members. It was not possible to classify members into a number of small groups. True there were such groups as the Little Entente, the Scandinavian States and Latin America. But other countries, which numbered twenty-three, or at least most of them, could not be put into any group. These desires were therefore beyond the realm of practical politics.[61] The Norwegian Government noted the argument that the Council must be large enough to act with authority in a dispute affecting a considerable number of States. In such event, replied the Norwegian memorandum, "only one institution could intervene with any hope of success, and that would not be the Council, whether small or large, but the

[58] Speech of May 14, 1926. *ibid.*, pp. 63-4. Compare Dr Munch's abstention in the Council vote of April 17, 1935, where Germany was condemned for her unilateral denunciation of the military clauses of the Versailles Treaty. *infra*, p. 251.

[59] Speech of May 14, 1926. *Minutes of the First Session of the Committee on the Composition of the Council*, p. 18; *Doc.*, C. 299, M. 139, 1926, V, p. 140.

[60] *ibid.*, p. 63.

[61] *ibid.*

Assembly of the League as the mouthpiece of the public opinion of the world."[62]

The meetings of the Committee were extended for more than two months. The Swedish member refrained from voting on the proposal for an increase in the number of non-permanent States from six to nine.[63] The Committee adhered to the Scandinavian view that Germany alone should be designated as the holder of a new permanent seat. The principles of rotation and continuity which the Scandinavian delegations had requested since the First Assembly were provided for, but rotation was limited by the acceptance of the doctrine of reeligibility for as many as three non-permanent seats.[64]

The report of the committee was laid before the Council and on September 4, 1926, Viscount Ishii's resolution calling for the increase of the non-permanent members to nine, and the appointment of Germany as a permanent member upon her admission to the League was adopted. Brazil and Spain, having lost their pleas for permanent Council membership, did not impede the resolution, but gave notice of withdrawal from the League.[65] For Sweden, M. Undén made the following declaration:[66]

> The Swedish Government considers—and I know that a large number of other members of the League of Nations are of the same opinion—that the proposed increase of the number of non-permanent members of the Council will entail serious disadvantages in more ways than one.
>
> Nevertheless in order to find an issue from the present difficulties, my Government is prepared to make the sacrifices which, from its point of view, are involved by the adoption of this scheme.

[62] *Doc.,* C. 299, M. 139, 1926, V, p. 140.

[63] *ibid.,* p. 96.

[64] *L. of N. Doc.,* C. 512, 1926. The ratification by France and Spain in the early summer of 1926, of the constitutional amendment of 1921 (now Article IV, 2 bis, of the Covenant) effected the entry into force of this amendment on July 29, 1926, thereby giving the Assembly power to fix rules "dealing with the election of the non-permanent members of the Council." Morley, *op. cit.,* p. 364.

[65] They were not represented at the Council on September 4, 1926. *L.N.O.J.,* VII, 41C., p. 1237.

[66] *L.N.O.J.,* VII, 41C., p. 1241.

Four days later in the Seventh Assembly, Dr Nansen expressed regret that constitutional methods had not been employed in dealing with the problem of Germany's admission. Although he rejoiced in the Council's decision to grant Germany a permanent seat, it was regrettable that such a decision had been taken when she was not yet a member of the League.[67] Apparently the Swedish representative raised no objection in the Council to this disregard of the strict provisions of Article IV. But M. Löfgren, the Swedish Foreign Minister, agreed with Dr Nansen that it was regrettable to connect the question of permanent seats with that of the increase of non-permanent seats, as the General Committee of the Assembly had done. The usual procedure of referring proposals to the consideration of the appropriate committee of the Assembly should have been followed.[68] The Danish delegation was silent on this point. All three delegations from the North, however, expressed pleasure in having a permanent seat granted to Germany. None of them favoured the increase of the non-permanent seats from six to nine.[69] Nansen declared his objection to the procedure which was chosen, as follows:

> The increase in the number of non-permanent members . . . is a new proposal which no one ever heard of until a few months ago and of which most of the members of the Assembly have only had formal notification of this morning. It is a proposal which we consider of vital importance for the future of the League. A similar proposal for an increase from four to six was discussed for weeks in the First Committee and its sub-committee before it was adopted by the full Assembly.

[67] *7 A.P.*, 34.

[68] *7 A.P.*, 35.

[69] The Norwegian delegation had been instructed that in the event of one of the non-permanent members of the Council impeding Germany's entry, the delegation should work for the substitution of a new State on the Council in the place of the impeding State. *St. med.* nr. 3 (1927), p. 9.

See Moltke's expression of Danish enthusiasm for Germany's entry into the League. He seemed less disturbed than the Norwegian and Swedish delegates concerning the enlargement of the Council. [*7 A.P.*, 38.] The report of the Danish Foreign Office to the Rigsdag expresses delight in finally obtaining an arrangement for the successive renewal and change of the non-permanent Council membership, but fails to express regret that the membership of the Council has been enlarged or that reeligibility has been introduced in the rules of the Assembly. *Beretning til Rigsdagen angaaende Folkeforbundets 7. Forsamling i Geneve i September 1926, Rigsdagstidenden* (1926-1927), *Tillæg* A. II, p. 4919.

> This new proposal, which is infinitely more serious because
> it increases the size . . . to the unwieldy number of fourteen,
> we are now asked to accept without a similar discussion. . . .
> I wish to emphasize that only fifteen members out of fifty-five
> have had any opportunity of expressing an opinion on this
> particular proposal, whether in the Special Committee, which
> the Council set up, or in the Council itself or by written
> communication. . . .

He pleaded for the safeguarding of the rights of the Assembly,
"which is and must be the supreme organ of the League."[70] Although
Sweden had been able to express her view in the Special Committee
and in the Council, M. Löfgren supported the same argument.[71]

The Semi-Permanent Seats on the Council

The Scandinavian States were unable to prevent an increase in the
number of the non-permanent members of the Council in 1926. In
vain they also objected to the creation of semi-permanent seats on the
Council. The reason for this opposition is self-evident. It was obvious
that States as small as Denmark, Norway, and even Sweden, could
not hope for classification in a middle group of Powers, such as
Poland, Spain, Brazil and the Argentine.[72] They were indeed "small
States" which could hardly delude themselves with the hope of ever
being recognized as Great Powers. Imbued with the spirit of "equality
of States" for all Powers not truly Great Powers, they naturally
opposed the attempt of France and other Powers to create a new and
more marked classification of States. But the prevailing opinion in
the Committee on the Composition of the Council was favourable to
Cecil's proposal that a State elected as a non-permanent member of
the Council might be declared reeligible, if its request were approved
by a two-thirds vote of the Assembly. M. Sjöborg was forced to
abandon the Swedish preference for the rigid principle of rotation,

---

[70] *7A.P.*, 34.

[71] *7A.P.*, 35.

[72] The population of Denmark (3½ millions), Norway (less than 3 millions), and
Sweden (6 millions) should be compared with Poland (30 millions), Spain (22
millions), Brazil (40 millions). See the excellent book of Paul Mohn, *Sverige i
Utrikespolitiskt Perspektiv* (Stockholm, 1937), pp. 19 *ff.* for his comment on the
hierarchy of States. This study was unfortunately received after my manuscript was
completed.

but he announced that he could not favour the making of applications for reeligibility until a member's mandate had expired.[73]

When the scheme for the election of the non-permanent members was laid before the First Committee of the 1926 Assembly, M. Löfgren stated that the Swedish Government would have preferred a more stringent system of rotation. A compromise, however, had been necessary with those who opposed any regulation whatever that would have prevented the Assembly from reelecting indefinitely any members of the League. Reviewing the plan which allowed three of the nine members of the Council to be reelected, M. Löfgren said that the possibility of reelection should "in no way be considered as a privilege to be conferred on this or that State. It is, on the contrary, a faculty which the Assembly in its sovereignty may exercise whenever it deems the continued services of a State on the Council to be needed."[74] As an evidence of his view that no guarantee was intended for any State to sit indefinitely on the Council, the Swedish delegate pointed out that the Committee had not recommended a proposal allowing a State to be declared reeligible at the time of election. This declaration could take place only at the expiration of a mandate.[75] The Norwegian and Danish delegates expressed agreement with the view of the Swedish Government that it "could never have accepted any scheme that tended to put the members of the League into different classes or categories."[76] In the Assembly, the Swedish Foreign Minister explained that in giving up certain points of view which "we had held without any selfish motive, only believing that we were acting in the interests of the League, we did so in the belief that the long-drawn-out struggle being waged within the walls of the League must be brought to an end, lest the League suffer incalculable harm."[77] The provision for reeligibility was, therefore, interpreted by the Scandinavian States as not creating an intermediary class of States.[78]

[73] L. of N. Doc., C. 299, M. 139, 1926, V, p. 48.

[74] 7A.1C., 9.

[75] See, however, Article IV, paragraph 2 (Temporary Provisions), which permitted "immediate" declaration of reeligibility, in 1926, of three members, if the Assembly so authorized it.

[76] Löfgren (7A.1C., 9), Hambro (7A.P., 49), Zahle (7A.1C., 10).

[77] 7A.P., 70 (September 15, 1926). This was also the view of Denmark. See Zahle's speech, 7A.P., 78-9.

[78] The Norwegian delegation to the Seventh Assembly had been instructed to accept the report of the Committee on the Composition of the Council on condition

Before the rules dealing with the election of the nine non-permanent members of the Council were adopted, the Norwegian delegation secured the addition of a provision, which read:[79]

"Notwithstanding the above provisions the Assembly may at any time by a two-thirds majority decide to proceed, in application of Article IV of the Covenant, to a new election of all the non-permanent members of the Council." The Danish and Swedish delegations supported this resolution, which was adopted.[80]

The Norwegian delegation considered this amendment important in that it gave a reserve power to the Assembly, and the delegation cited as evidence of its importance an article from *The Times* (London) of September 15, 1926, as follows: "The Scandinavian members have more than once stood up for the Assembly's rights, but indifference, timidity, or self-interest usually restrains the others from supporting them. Yesterday, however, the Norwegian delegation succeeded in restoring the clause which authorizes the Assembly to reelect the whole of the non-permanent members at any time. This should go far to retain for the Assembly the influence which, as an organization representative of international opinion, it should exercise over the Council."[81]

Reeligibility in Practice

The *Records of the Assembly* do not reveal how delegations vote for the election of Council members or on the request of members for a declaration of reeligibility. The rules of procedure of the Assembly call for a secret ballot on these votes. Generally the official reports given by the Danish, Norwegian and Swedish Foreign Offices are likewise unrevealing in this matter. Some supplementary remarks, however, can be made to the general view of these States on the question of reeligibility. The Norwegian delegation to the Eighth

that six instead of nine be the designated number of non-permanent members, and that no provision for the reeligibility of members be adopted. "The rule mentioned in point 3 of the proposal allowing the Assembly to hold a new election at any time of all the non-permanent members is of great importance. The delegation should work for its adoption." [*St. med.* nr. 3 (1927), 10.] See also *ibid.*, p. 29, for the execution of these instructions in the First Committee, and its sub-committee.

[79] *7A.1C.*, 15.
[80] *7A.1C.*, 16, 17.
[81] *St. med.* nr. 3 (1927), p. 30.

Assembly was instructed to vote against any possible proposal for the declaration of reeligibility of a Council member.[82] Accordingly, it voted against the application of Belgium at the Eighth Assembly, who received twenty-nine favourable votes where the requisite was thirty-two.[83]

In the Ninth Assembly, on the proposal of the General Committee, a resolution was adopted to the effect that the temporary provisions of 1926 should, exceptionally, remain in force for that year, thus authorizing a State Member to make a request for reeligibility immediately after being elected to the Council.[84] The initiative for this proposal had come from Great Britain, France and Germany, who wished to placate Spain and to renew her cooperation with the League of Nations. As a matter of prestige Spain desired to be declared immediately reeligible after her anticipated election to the Council by the Ninth Assembly.[85] Poland had enjoyed such a tribute in 1926. Although this proposal of the General Committee of the Assembly was adopted on September 7, 1928, by the necessary two-thirds vote, four States opposed. These were Sweden, Norway, the Netherlands and Persia. South Africa abstained from voting.[86] The opposition of Norway and Sweden was based on principle, one which they had insisted upon in 1926. Professor Undén remarked that the temporary provisions of the 1926 rules (which allowed immediate declaration of reeligibility) had only been acceptable on the condition that it constitute a final and complete settlement of the whole problem of the Council's reorganization.[87] He and M. Mowinckel[88] thought it dangerous to make such an exception as was now requested; but they were overruled.

That the Scandinavian opposition was based on principle is assured from the reading of the instructions given to the Norwegian delegation to the Ninth Assembly. Although the delegation was informed

---

[82] *St. med.* nr. 3 (1928), p. 10. At the Eighth Assembly Hambro said that the Norwegian Government was still of the opinion that reeligibility was undesirable. *8A.P.*, 58.

[83] *ibid.*, p. 14. *8A.P.*, 115.

[84] *Monthly Summary*, Vol. 8 (1928), p. 258.

[85] *U.N.F.* (1928), p. 59.

[86] *ibid.*, p. 60. Also *St. med.* nr. 3 (1929), p. 16.

[87] *9A.P.*, 49.

[88] *ibid.*

that the Government preferred that none of the Council members elected that year be declared reeligible immediately after the election (unless weighty reasons should exist for doing so), the delegation was instructed to vote for the election of Spain to one of the vacant Council places.[89] Nevertheless, Spain was immediately declared reeligible with ten delegations voting in opposition. Although the official reports of the Foreign Offices in the North do not disclose this vote of the Scandinavian representatives, the Swedish *Blue Book* for 1930 states that Sweden voted against the Chinese request for reeligibility in the Eleventh Assembly "for reasons of principle."[90]

There is sufficient evidence to appreciate the Norwegian and Swedish view on the question of reeligibility. The Danish attitude is somewhat obscure. The Danish delegation did not express objection to the retention in force of the temporary rules of 1926 when the discussion arose at the Ninth Assembly.[91] It is noticeable that the Danish delegations have been less outspoken and critical than the Norwegian and Swedish delegations on the question of the composition of the Council, as on many other League questions.

In the 1931 Assembly Lord Cecil proposed a resolution requesting the Council "to appoint a special committee to study the existing system of elections to the Council and to report to a future session of the Assembly on any reforms which may appear desirable."[92] This resolution was designed primarily to provide an opportunity for States which, like Portugal, were attached to no group, to obtain election to the Council. The motion was opposed by the Swedish delegate, who, however, denied that he wished to prevent an examination of the problem. He recognized that the existing system

[89] *St. med.* nr. 3 (1929), pp. 9, 13.

[90] *U.N.F.* (1930), p. 84. The Norwegian instructions to the Assembly stated that it must be supposed that Spain will obtain again this year reeligibility. In case this is not the outcome, the delegation ought to vote that the free seat go to Portugal. In view of the importance of China, she should be supported for the place vacated by Persia. *St. med.* nr. 3 (1932), p. 8.

The Norwegian instructions for the 1932 Assembly, *St. med.* nr. 3 (1933), pp. 10-11, stated that Norway should follow her earlier policy in regard to Poland, and to vote for that State's election to the Council under the assumption that she obtains reeligibility. Six States voted against declaring Poland reeligible but the Report does not say if Norway was one of them (*ibid.*, p. 16).

[91] See *supra*, note 86.

[92] *12A.1C.*, 15.

favoured certain States or groups of States, but argued that in any case it would be difficult to devise an ideal system of elections.[93] In the Fourth Committee, the Norwegian delegate voted against an appropriation for a Special Committee which was to make the suggested study.[94] But the committee was created, and, in 1933, the number of non-permanent members of the Council was temporarily raised from nine to ten.

In 1936 a permanent solution of the problem of the Council's composition had not been reached. In a special committee of study M. K. I. Westman of Sweden urged a modification of the group system rather than a further increase of the size of the Council. He reported that, with the assent of Finland, the group of the ex-neutrals (composed of Denmark, Norway, Sweden, the Netherlands and Switzerland) agreed to take Finland into the group, and he asked other groups to make adjustments in the same spirit.[95] The other groups, however, did not find it possible to do so, and again the Council was enlarged, although "provisionally."

The Inner Council

Attention has been directed to the Swedish and Norwegian efforts in 1926 to prevent the increase in the size of the Council lest such action encourage the tendency of an "Inner Council." Previously in the Second Assembly M. Branting had criticized the methods which the Council had at times employed. The discussions in the Council, he said, "have sometimes produced the impression that a decision has been prepared and even agreed upon, not at the actual meetings, but elsewhere. Obviously such procedure is scarcely compatible with the letter and spirit of the Covenant."[96] The Scandinavian attitude on this point is founded on the desire to have matters of concern to the League considered by the machinery of the League, and not outside it. There have been many evidences of this attitude since 1920. Especially in the 1927 Assembly the Swedish, Norwegian and Dutch delegations referred to the impression which had been gained in vari-

[93] Undén, *12A.1C.*, 17, 19, 20.
[94] *12A.4C.*, 40.
[95] *Report of the Committee Appointed to Study the Composition of the Council* (adopted by the Committee on April 28, 1936). *L. of N. Doc.*, A. 9., 1936, V, 3.
[96] *2A.P.*, 59.

ous quarters that there existed an "Inner Council" or a "Supreme Council." The Norwegian delegate reminded the Assembly that "one of the soundest principles of the Covenant is that an interested State is present as a member of the Council when a question of interest is being discussed."[97] He felt that "every non-permanent member had been justified in watching with jealousy the 'half-private' deliberations at Geneva."[98]

The same principle was involved in other instances. In the Corfu affair, the Scandinavians objected to workings of the "Inner Council" through the medium of the Conference of Ambassadors.[99] During the Italo-Abyssinian conflict, sharp criticism of "Great Power" policy was made by the President of the Norwegian Storting in a speech at Gothenburg on January 17, 1936.[100] M. Hambro contrasted the spirit of the Hoare-Laval plan of December 1935, with the previous French and English reply to the Italian protest against the League's action against Italy. The latter, but not the former (which disregarded the unanimously decided action of the League), had been taken after consultation with the small States, including the Scandinavian. M. Hambro expressed the hope that France would become clear concerning what was already recognized in England, namely, that the Great Powers can no longer act independently of the smaller States in international politics.

Whatever may have been the correctness of M. Hambro's view in regard to public opinion in England, it can definitely be asserted that the Northern people, or at least many of them, have little faith in the methods of "Great Power" diplomacy.

Proportional Representation

When the report of the Committee on the Composition of the Council was submitted to the 1926 Assembly, the Norwegian delegate, M. Vogt, expressed the desire of his Government that the elections of the non-permanent Council members should be made by a system of proportional representation.[101] Viscount Cecil had already given a

[97] 8A.P., 57.
[98] ibid.
[99] See infra, p. 254.
[100] Göteborgs Handels- och Sjöfarts Tidning, January 18, 1936.
[101] 7A.1C., 10, 33-4; 7A.P., 80-1.

lead in the Committee on the Composition of the Council by indicating the possibility of some such arrangement.[102] The Norwegian proposal was motivated by a desire that the Council should be fully representative "of the whole world, politically, intellectually, geographically." "Only some form of election which gives the right to possible minority groups to be adequately represented on the Council can give proper security to all the interests of the Assembly."[103] Norway was dissatisfied that under present conditions, "private conversations, underhand arrangements and agreements more or less binding interfere in the preparation of the election and are of deciding importance for their results."[104]

Although the Assembly adopted a resolution requesting the Council to instruct the Secretariat to study the question of the single transferable vote and the principle of proportional representation,[105] the opposition of France, Britain and Italy was so great that the Council on December 7, 1926, refused to do so, merely instructing the Secretary-General to communicate to the members of the League the two memoranda received from the Norwegian Government.[106]

Despite this discouragement, the Norwegian delegation to the Eighth Assembly was instructed to work for the alteration of the Assembly's rules along these lines, and M. Hambro renewed his efforts to rid the League of "electoral wirepulling."[107] But the Assembly dismissed the matter by agreeing that the existing scheme should be given a fair trial before any action was taken in this new direction.

[102] *L. of N. Doc.*, C. 299, M. 139, 1926, V, p. 143.

[103] *7A.1C.*, 33-4.

[104] Letter of November 27, 1926, from the Minister of Foreign Affairs of Norway, submitted to the Council, March 7, 1927. *L.N.O.J.*, VIII, 4, 54C. (Annex 940), pp. 448 *ff*. See also Letter of January 18, 1927, and the Second Memorandum from the Norwegian Government (Annex 940a). *ibid.*

[105] *7A.P.*, 121.

[106] *L.N.O.J.*, VIII, 2, 43C., pp. 125-8. Briand expressed sympathy for Count Ishii who, as Rapporteur, "from motives of conscience," had submitted the problem to the Council. If, however, there were some way of losing the question in by-paths, so that the Council would never see the question again, in Briand's view, it would be a good thing.

[107] *St. med.* nr. 3 (1928), p. 10; *8A.6C.*, 10-11.

Personnel of the Council

It is a commonplace that in international work the personality of the individuals concerned is an important factor. I do not think it is immodest to say that, although some nations are far greater than other nations and have larger populations, it does not always follow that the individuals representing them can be measured in the same way. We from the small States, as a rule, come to Geneva, or to any international conference, in the hope that the representatives of the great nations will be found to be proportionately greater than the delegates from our own countries; but that hope is not always fulfilled. In every field of activity in which the League has been attended with success during the last fifteen years, that success has been due to individuals and personalities and not to political prestige.[108]

These words enunciated by *Stortingspresident* Hambro in an address given at Chatham House on December 10, 1935, serve as a fitting renewal for the consideration of the question of the "personal factor" at Geneva, this time with respect to the Council.

In 1921, before any Scandinavian State had been elected to the Council, M. Branting was emphasizing that "the members of the League should be represented on the Council by their most distinguished statesmen."[109] Indeed, he himself, when Prime Minister of Sweden, had come to St. James's Palace in July 1920, to sit on the Council for the special consideration of the Åland Islands question.[110] As soon as Sweden became an elected member of the Council in January 1923, Branting again sat for Sweden at a time when the Great Powers did not deem the Council's meetings of sufficient importance to require the attendance of their heads of Government or Foreign Ministers. Later Norway and Denmark generally followed this policy, which Branting had emphasized, when M.

[108] *International Affairs,* Vol. XV, no. 2 (March-April 1936), p. 168. See also M. Hambro's speech reported in *Göteborgs Handels- och Sjöfarts Tidning,* January 18, 1936.

[109] *2A.P.,* 61.

[110] *L.N.O.J.,* I, 5, p. 246. Branting also sat as the representative for Sweden at the Ninth Session of the Council in Paris, September 1920 [*L.N.O.J.,* I, 7, p. 392] and at the Thirteenth Session in June 1921. *ibid.,* p. 691.

Mowinckel, M. Braadland, Dr Koht and Dr Munch made frequent journeys to Geneva.[111]

At the Eighth Assembly when the Scandinavian and certain other small States were bitter in their criticism of the "Inner Council" tendency of the Great Powers, M. Hambro urged that it would perhaps give greater political weight to the deliberations of the Council if its members were not too closely tied to the diplomatic centres of the Great Powers."[112] In a critical speech before the "Congrès pour la défense de la paix et la Société des Nations" in Brussels, February 15, 1934, this Norwegian statesman stated that the effectiveness of the Council was impaired by the shifting of representatives of a given State on the Council. For example, during a single day one State was represented by three persons on the Council. Such a practice, said Hambro, destroyed the continuity of the Council's work.[113] In the same speech the President of the Storting complained that the representatives of the Great Powers on the Council are too often not properly informed concerning the business to be transacted. The first demand to be made of the Council is that those which compose it are quite clear concerning the important matters which come before it. What actually takes place is that the members usually look blindly to the Secretariat. Such a system is clearly not perfect, even if the information given by the Secretariat is the best.[114]

Presidency of the Council

It is natural to suppose that the non-permanent members of the Council would prefer the definite and open rotation of the presidency to an election system which would mean rotation by tacit agreement, and probably among the representatives of the Great Powers only.[115] Yet M. Hambro in 1934, the year after the presidency of the Council

[111] Norway was a member of the Council from 1930 to 1933 and Denmark from 1933 to 1936.

[112] *8 A.P.*, 57-8.

[113] This speech is printed in Norwegian under the title of "Folkeforbundet Idag" in *Nordisk Tidskrift för Vetenskap, Konst och Industri*, Årg. 10 (1934), Häft 2. For this information, see p. 80.

[114] Hambro, "Folkeforbundet Idag," *op. cit.*, p. 81.

[115] Morley, *op. cit.*, p. 394.

fell upon M. Mowinckel, his own countryman, attacked the practice of rotation of the presidency on the ground that such a transfer does not provide the greatest effectiveness.[116] It is a tribute to the international public spirit of M. Hambro that he should have taken this view. The selection of a Council President "through alphabetical exigencies" does not always enable the Council to command its highest authority. But the suggested change has not been proposed officially by the Norwegian or other Scandinavian Governments.

[116] "Folkeforbundet Idag," *op. cit.*, p. 80.

CHAPTER IX

PERMANENT OFFICIALS OF THE LEAGUE

The Nationality Question

AFTER more than a decade of service as Secretary-General of the League of Nations, Sir Eric Drummond wrote as follows: "The real difficulty of the organization of the Secretariat lies in the clash of two principles: the first that a post should be filled by the best available man or woman, the second that there shall be a reasonable and fair distribution of posts among the nationals of the countries members of the League."[1] In practice, from the very outset the Secretariat was bound to both principles, and the Secretary-General when making appointments found it necessary to treat "each case on its own merits." As Lord Balfour in his often-quoted report concerning the Staff of the Secretariat said: The Secretary-General in making his appointments "had primarily to secure the best available men and women for the particular duties which had to be performed; but in doing so, it was necessary to have regard to the great importance of selecting officials from various nations. Evidently, no one nation or group of nations ought to have a monopoly in providing the material for this international institution. I emphasize the word 'international' because the members of the Secretariat once appointed are no longer the servants of the country of which they are citizens, but become for the time being the servants only of the League of Nations. Their duties are not national but international."[2]

In a recent book on the League, Sir Alfred Zimmern has maintained that the realization of the principle of an international Civil Service is incompatible with the desire of "making the Secretariat as

[1] In "The Secretariat of the League of Nations," *Public Administration,* IX, April 1931, p. 234.

[2] *L.N.O.J.,* I (1920), 4, 5C., pp. 136 *ff.* This report was adopted by the Council on May 19, 1920.

widely representative of the League membership as possible."[3] If this view is correct, it is well to remember that responsibility lies with the Great Powers who were determined from the outset to entrench themselves in the key posts of the Secretariat. The Coordinating Committee on the League of Nations in 1919 indicated to the first Secretary-General that political reasons suggested the creation of a Deputy Secretary-General and three Under-Secretaries-General to be filled by nationals of the Permanent Council members.[4]

This action with regard to the higher posts made it natural and certain that smaller States would press their claims for appropriate representation in the Secretariat. In 1920 the First Assembly heard expressions of regret that certain countries had none of their nationals in the Secretariat.[5] The Assembly readily followed the Council's lead by adopting a resolution "that in filling the various posts, whilst having special regard for efficiency, at the same time consideration should be given to the international character of the League."[6]

Until M. Hambro made his début in Geneva at the Seventh Assembly, the delegations of the Scandinavian States had offered little criticism of the distribution of appointments to the Secretariat. The arrival of the newly elected President of the Norwegian Storting, whose previous years of criticism of the League in his own country equipped him to become "a leading figure on the Opposition front bench of the League,"[7] changed the atmosphere of the Fourth Committee. Few men at Geneva have been M. Hambro's equal in this, his chosen rôle of delight. Unusually sensitive to Great Power domination of the League, he saw an opportunity for a "revolt" of the small States, under his leadership. M. Hambro began with an effort to get representation for nationals of all countries on the Permanent Staff of the League. This would naturally rally to his standard States which had complaints to raise on this score, and they were not few, even as late as 1926.

[3] *The League of Nations and the Rule of Law,* p. 477.
[4] See Drummond, *op. cit.,* pp. 229 ff. Also his speech in the Fourth Committee of the Ninth Assembly (September 13, 1928), *9A.4C.,* 37.
[5] For example, by the delegate of India, *1A.P.,* 659.
[6] *1A.P.,* 664.
[7] Sir Alfred Zimmern's characterization. See *International Affairs,* XV, no. 2 (March-April 1936), p. 179.

In the Fifth Assembly, M. Barboza-Carneiro of Brazil had expressed the desire of the South American States for a larger number of appointments of their nationals to the Secretariat.[8] The following year he pointed out that the salaries of the Latin American officials in the Secretariat and Labour Office represented only 4.6 per cent of the contribution of those countries to the expenses of the League. This might be contrasted with that of Austrian officials who drew 576 per cent of Austria's contribution, and with British and French officials whose corresponding figures were 133 per cent and 122 per cent respectively. The Brazilian delegate thought the aspirations of the countries of Latin America should be considered when new appointments were made.[9]

M. Hambro reopened the question in the Seventh Assembly, but not on the ground that Norway had been discriminated against.[10] According to figures he submitted, Norwegian nationals recovered 60 per cent (and Danish nationals 50 per cent) of their countries' contributions. He did not, however, attach much importance to those figures. But there were seventeen States, members of the League, without a single national in the Secretariat, and in the International Labour Office twenty-three. Surely it was reasonable for every member State to have at least one of its nationals in the employment of the League. Thirteen South American States were without nationals in any of the League's three permanent staffs. This fact, he suggested, may have had its influence upon public opinion, or the lack of public opinion, in some of these countries.[11]

The Secretary-General in reply regretted the necessity of making the same speech he had made the year before. He quoted from the report of the Committee to the Sixth Assembly in which "the Committee noted with satisfaction the assurance given by the Secretary-General that States 'represented' inadequately or not at all should, presupposing equal qualifications in their candidates, have priority when new posts were to be filled." He had adhered to his promise, but the difficulty was that vacancies were not common, since most occu-

---

[8] *5A.4C.*, 34.

[9] *6A.4C.*, 19-20. *Monthly Summary,* VIII, no. 9, pp. 282-3.

[10] "I do not criticize and I do not complain, especially as my country has no reason to complain," he said. *7A.P.*, 141.

[11] *7A.4C.*, 20-1, 21-2, 22.

pants held contracts for periods of seven, fourteen or twenty-one years.[12]

M. Hambro then requested that the members of the Fourth Committee thereafter be given in advance copies of the Staff Regulations and a list of appointments made since the preceding Assembly, indicating the salaries and the precise number of different nationalities. This would perhaps reduce the number of unnecessary speeches in the future.[13]

In the Assembly he emphasized "the need of all small nations and all distant nations for a better representation in the Secretariat and in the International Labour Office."[14] In the Mixed Courts of Justice in Egypt the small States had been privileged "because it was felt that they were likely to be politically impartial." In support of this argument for wider representation he pointed to the importance of each delegate to the Assembly having someone on the Staff who could understand him when he spoke his own language. In regard to the merit of individuals, M. Hambro stated that given equal conditions of competition, "the men of small nations have an opportunity to obtain the posts *which we all want them to have.*"[15]

This last clause suggests a "call to colours." For whom can "we" mean but the secondary Powers? A moment later, M. Hambro was assuming the rôle of spokesman of a "small-State bloc" in the remarkable sentence which follows: "I know the obstacles of pride and prejudice that have to be overcome in dealing with these questions, but I have spoken these words with the feeling that, being the delegate of a nation which is in the happy position of living in friendship with every neighbouring nation, and never having any claim upon the League, it is also our duty to try to express the wishes felt by the delegations of all the small nations, wishes to which not every delegation can feel it politically wise to give expression from this rostrum."[16]

[12] *7A.4C.*, 21.
[13] M. Adelswärd of Sweden in the committee of the First Assembly had requested a list—giving the salary and nationality of members of the Secretariat by classes. *1A.4C. (II)*, 17
[14] *7A.P.*, 141.
[15] *ibid.* The italics are mine.
[16] *ibid.*

The Higher Officials and the Great-Power Monopoly

The practical considerations which Sir Eric Drummond called to the attention of the President of the Storting greatly weakened the force of the latter's plea for greater representation of the small States on the Secretariat. Sir Alfred Zimmern would have objected on grounds of principle to M. Hambro's position. But the distinguished Oxford Professor of International Relations in his treatise *The League of Nations and the Rule of Law* strongly supports a position adopted by the Scandinavian States in regard to the higher officials of the Secretariat.[17]

It was again M. Hambro who was chief spokesman of the objectors to the over-representation of the Great Powers in the higher staff. In the Eighth Assembly he inquired of the Council members whether it had been laid down as a principle that there should be an Under-Secretary-General for every Great Power, and that no such high position should be filled by a person of any other nationality.[18] If the Council did not choose to answer, the same cannot be said of Professor Madariaga. In a concise article published in *The Times* (London) he demonstrated that the principle of nationality entered the Secretariat when the four highest posts of the office were tacitly reserved for the Great Powers. In the edition of September 5, 1928, he writes:

> . . . neither competence, nor necessity, but nationality, was the criterion upon which these high positions were created and allotted.
>
> The Secretary-General was an Englishman; the Deputy Secretary-General a Frenchman; the two Under-Secretaries-General, an Italian and a Japanese. A fifth Under-Secretary-General, an American, was in office until the United States refused to ratify the Covenant. His resignation then, and the acceptance thereof, gave a somewhat official sanction to the view that League members have a kind of proprietary right to Secretariat posts, and that Great Powers can claim this right

[17] See pp. 477-8.

[18] *8A.P.*, 58. The previous year Hambro had said that care should be taken not to give the world at large the impression that only nationals of Great Powers will have the opportunity of filling these positions. *7A.P.*, 141. He had been instructed to obtain clarification of the basis of appointment of higher Secretariat officials. *St. med.*, nr. 3 (1927), p. 11.

to apply to the highest grades. This view was confirmed first when, on Signor Anzilotti's election to a Hague judgeship and the vote of the Committee Four of the Assembly suppressing as unnecessary the post of Under-Secretary-General which he occupied, measures were taken to have the vote reversed in order to ensure a high post for Italy. . . . A similar case occurred on Germany's arrival. A new and wholly unnecessary post of Under-Secretary-General was created in order to acknowledge Germany's right to add to the imposing array of upper League officials one more exalted personage. . . . Through this series of decisions, the approval (or suggestion) of which shows a lamentable spirit in the Council, the Secretariat has lost much of its splendid tradition of internationalism. A national hierarchy has replaced the hierarchy of competence.[19]

On September 13, 1928, M. Hambro again raised the issue of the international character of the Secretariat. His speech in the Fourth Committee led M. Reveillaud, the delegate of France, to say that "M. Hambro had energetically opened a large window, and a breeze had passed through the room."[20] What the Norwegian delegate said was this: It was desirable to have a reconsideration of the Staff Regulations and rules of appointment and to have the Secretariat place before the Fourth Committee at the next Assembly a revised edition of the same. The recent discussion of the Secretariat in the press of many countries (such as by M. Madariaga in *The Times*) had brought the matter to the forefront of attention. A thorough consideration must therefore be undertaken.

M. Hambro agreed with the allegations that a remarkable change had occurred in the character of those who filled the higher posts. There were now more diplomats chosen and an extension of the influence of Foreign Offices in the work of the League. "It was against the constitution of the League that any Government should try to influence appointments made in the League. It was against Article VI. No State had a right to fill any single post on the Secretariat. . . . The fact that representatives of one single nationality had, on three successive occasions been appointed to the

[19] *The Times* (London), September 5, 1928. 13F. "The League Staff : Nationality and Merit."
[20] *9A.4C.*, 36.

same position was against the principles adopted by the Assembly. If those who entered the service of the League had to work under the conviction that higher posts were reserved for the candidates of a Government, it would be more difficult to secure the right people."[21]

The Norwegian delegate referred to the principle stated in the report of the Noblemaire Committee, calling for systematic changes in the higher posts "in order to enable them to be filled by persons of *any country whatsoever* who are of recognized importance and widespread influence among their own people, and whose views and sentiments are representative of their national opinion."[22] Was there any member of the Fourth Committee who would declare that this principle had been adhered to, even during the last year?

M. van Eysinga, the Dutch delegate, warmly supported the Norwegian view, agreeing that the monopoly of the Great Powers in the five highest posts, and the near monopoly in case of the Members of Section should be ended. He introduced resolutions that the Assembly reaffirm its faith in the principles of the Balfour report of 1920.[23]

Sir Eric Drummond in reply washed his hands of responsibility. He declared that before he had assumed responsibility for appointments to the Secretariat, the League of Nations Organizing Committee, which had been set up in Paris, definitely informed him that he was to take as Under-Secretaries nationals from France, Italy and Japan. As for the additional Under-Secretary, it was the Fourth Commission which had created that particular post with full knowledge that it was going to be filled by someone of German nationality. A certain responsibility, therefore, rested with the Fourth Committee.[24]

Although the effect of the Norwegian-Dutch initiative was to rally support for a reexamination of the Staff Regulations from various quarters, including the French,[25] it was not until the following year that a committee was appointed by the Assembly itself to make fundamental inquiry of the organization of the League's civil

[21] *9A.4C.*, 32-3. This debate of September 13, 1928, is printed in full in an appendix to M. Hambro's report on the work of the Fourth Committee. *St. med.* nr. 3 (1929), pp. 56-64.

[22] The italics are mine. This quotation is from p. 7 of the report.

[23] *St. med.* nr. 3 (1929), p. 54, *9A.4C.*, 34-6.

[24] *9A.4C.*, 37, 38, 39.

[25] *9A.4C.*, 36.

service. But before the 1928 Assembly closed, the Secretary-General
was led to say, in effect, that the time had arrived when the various
high posts in the Secretariat should be open to any member of any
nationality.[26]

At the Tenth Assembly, Count Moltke of Denmark referred to the
growing feeling of anxiety in many circles lest the present method of
recruitment to the higher posts should ultimately make the League a
sort of preserve for the Great Powers, thereby excluding the spirit of
democracy and equality on which the founders of the League had so
strongly insisted. The pressure of national influences should be felt
only in the Assembly and its committees, if the true League spirit was
to be maintained inside the Secretariat.[27] The difference between the
tone of this speech and that of M. Hambro, previously indicated, well
characterized the difference between Danish and Norwegian methods
at Geneva. The Danish speech was more moderate, less aggressive,
than that of the Norwegian delegate. It was made a year after the
initiative had been launched by the spirited M. Hambro.

The Committee of Thirteen, as the body set up to investigate the
Secretariat was called, met in 1930, and submitted to the Assembly of
that year two reports dealing with the principal officers. The majority
(which included representatives of Great Britain and France) stated
that "any arrangement of the higher posts which excludes the nationals
of certain States Members of the League would seem very difficult to
defend."[28] If their proposal were accepted, every post in the Secretariat, from that of the Secretary-General downward, would be open
to the nationals of all States Members of the League.

[26] 9A.P., 189.

[27] 10A.4C., 49. It is not clear whether or not Count Moltke's omission of the
Council in this connection was intentional. There was an inclination in the Scandinavian States to object to the expression of the strictly nationalistic point of view in the
Council. For example, M. Hambro has said that "So long as public opinion in the
respective countries demands of its respective representatives in the Council that
first and foremost and exclusively they shall take a nationalistic political point of
view, the Council will not be able to come to a settlement of a wider scope of
problems." "Folkeforbundet Idag," op. cit., p. 79.

[28] 11A.4C., 299-300. Report of the Committee of Enquiry on the Organization of
the Secretariat, the International Labour Office and the Registry of the Permanent
Court of International Justice. L. of N. Doc., A. 16, 1930. The minutes of the committee were not printed.

"Essentially, the minority proposed to maintain unimpaired the privileged position of the permanent representatives on the Council. But, in addition, they proposed that a select committee should be formed consisting of the Under-Secretaries-General, to which any Director would be invited for the discussion of questions concerning his department. The Secretary-General would be bound to consult this select committee. They further suggested that the Directors should be grouped under the various Under-Secretaries-General, instead of being directly responsible to the Secretary-General. The result of this arrangement would, by depressing the position of Directors, be still further to accentuate the difference between classes of States, and so far from removing the grievance felt by some of those States, it would aggravate it."[29] The minority report was signed by Count Bernstorff (Germany) and Signor Gallavresi (Italy).

The declarations of the Danish, Norwegian and Swedish members of the Fourth Committee of the 1930 Assembly indicate their agreement with the principle of the majority report that the monopoly which had thus far existed in respect to the highest posts of the League should be abolished. M. Hambro, the only Scandinavian member of the Committee of Thirteen, expressed pleasure that the delegates of Great Britain and France shared the feeling of the majority of the League's members as to the importance of abolishing this monopoly. He reminded the committee that the fifty lesser Powers not represented among the Under-Secretaries-General were not so small after all. It was not only a majority of fifty to five in the number of States, but a majority in terms of population of about the same standing.[30]

The Scandinavian representatives raised a chorus of protest against the minority view enunciated by M. Scialoja in the Committee of Thirteen. M. Boheman, the Swedish delegate, said: "The idea of setting up within the Secretariat a sort of Council consisting almost exclusively of nationals of Powers permanently represented on the Council of the League seems to me to be due to a misconception of the Secretariat's function. It would almost amount to replacing the Council of the League when not in session by a Council of the League

[29] *11A.4C.*, 299.
[30] *11A.4C.*, 89.

Secretariat to discharge political functions in a technical organization."[31] M. Hambro said that the idea of the minority was just the one that he was there to combat. It is the Assembly and the Council, not the Secretariat, that represent the various Powers. The League had a long way to advance if the idea persisted that a group of five Powers should have "a guiding influence on everything that was done by it."[32]

The Swiss, French and other delegates also spoke against the proposal to constitute an Advisory Committee to the Secretary-General, and the proposal was defeated by thirty votes to five.[33]

The failure of the Italian-German proposal, however, was not followed by the acceptance of the majority proposal which recommended increasing the number of Under-Secretaries to eight. M. Hambro was also a leading force in preventing this solution from being adopted. Previously in the Committee of Thirteen, although he had voted with the majority on all questions of principle, his real preference had been to remove the monopoly of the Great Powers by *abolishing* the posts of Under-Secretary-General. He had not pressed his view, however, because of insufficient support and because he recognized "the political difficulties attached at the present time to their abolition."[34]

A few months later when the Assembly met, M. Hambro changed his position and urged abolition as the proper way to rid the Secretariat of the feeling of national jealousy within it. The Swiss and Chinese delegations also favoured abolition. The Norwegian delegate argued that the Under-Secretaries-General did not correspond to any administrative necessity, and that to increase the number added to this anomaly. The abolition of these posts on the other hand would relieve Count Moltke and many other delegations of the economic misgivings they felt in voting for the majority report, because this proposal was the cheapest one suggested.[35]

---

[31] *11A.4C.*, 59.

[32] *11A.4C.*, 91.

[32] *11A.4C.*, 149-54.

[34] See his statement attached to the Report of the Committee of Thirteen (Appendix III), *11A.4C.*, 318. See also *11A.4C.*, 90, where he said that "Mme Kluyver wanted to support me, but she did not do it wholeheartedly."

[35] *11A.4C.*, 90 (September 23, 1930). The Danish delegate had said in the Assembly that although "Everything cannot be brought down to money . . . it is useful,

As the question of the abolition of the posts of Under-Secretary-General had not been discussed by the Committee of Thirteen, the Danish delegate favoured the submission of the whole question to renewed consideration by the Committee of Thirteen or some other committee. He opposed a hasty provisional vote to guide the committee in its further study.[36]

The Swedish Government recognized that the majority proposal had been largely dictated by an actual situation "very difficult to alter," but was "somewhat doubtful" as to the wisdom of creating a larger number of Under-Secretaries-General. Sweden was prepared to vote for the necessary credits for new posts where the need for them was fully established.[37]

M. Hambro did not oppose the desire expressed by various members of the committee (German, British, Japanese) to refer the matter of the Under-Secretaries-General again to a Special Committee of Examination, and this procedure was followed.[38]

The "New Committee of Thirteen," to which M. Hambro was also elected by the Assembly, met from February 2-5, 1931. Fortunately the minutes of the meeting were printed.[39] M. Hambro defined the problem as one of securing a system of real and absolute equality for all members of the League. The only special privilege provided by the Covenant was that permanent membership on the Council was accorded to some States and not to others.[40] The only solution that he could see was to abolish all posts of Under-Secretary-General. At the other extreme stood M. Gallavresi of Italy who was opposed in principle to equality. In vain Viscount Cecil tried to effect a compromise. M. Hambro would not accept his proposal that the Secretary-General be allowed to nominate two or three new Under-Secretaries-General, and himself choose the most appropriate time for appoint-

before taking a final decision, to know the financial aspects of the question."
11A.4C., 77.

[36] *11A.4C.*, 158.

[37] *11A.4C.*, 59.

[38] *11A.4C.*, 154-8.

[39] See *L. of N. Doc.*, A. 8, 1931, X : "Committee Appointed to Give Further Consideration to Certain Questions Relating to the Organization of the Secretariat, the International Labour Office and the Registry of the Permanent Court of International Justice."

[40] *ibid.*, p. 21.

ments. The Norwegian had no hesitation in saying that the Secretary-General possessed far too much power already—an arbitrary power of promotion and of making special allowances. In any case, how could such appointments be made without increasing expenditures? He referred to the difficulty already existing of getting credits for the League voted by some parliaments.[41]

Lord Cecil's anxiety to be rid of the *status quo* led him to say harsh things of M. Hambro. The Norwegian and the Italian, he said, differed on practically every point and neither was prepared to make the slightest concession. M. Hambro had been very critical of those who would not accept his solution and had almost accused them of intellectual dishonesty. M. Hambro believed that all agreed with him, though they had not the courage to say so.

Lord Cecil further pointed out that in the previous year in the Committee of Enquiry, M. Hambro had himself accepted a proposal to increase the number of Under-Secretaries-General by five, without any qualification as to the avoidance of expenditure. The question was indeed a political one. M. Hambro desired to abolish the posts of Under-Secretaries-General because that would satisfy the countries which had no Under-Secretaries-General. As the question was a political one, the committee's task was to face the facts and conciliate opinion. Could not M. Hambro and M. Gallavresi make some concessions?[42]

In reply the Norwegian member denied that the committee was bound by purely political considerations. While a year ago he had agreed to increasing the number of posts from five to ten, that was quite different to the present proposal of increasing the number to six or seven. For "by increasing the number of Under-Secretaries-General from five to ten they would have created a situation so absurd that it could not have endured. The fallacy would have become apparent. . . . He could not agree to increasing the number by two."[43]

The proposal in the committee for abolition of the posts of Under-Secretary-General was defeated by seven votes to three, with one abstention. In addition to M. Hambro, Count Bernstorff (German) and M. Osusky (Czechoslavakian) voted for abolition. The proposal

[41] *ibid.*, p. 22.
[42] *ibid.*, pp. 23-4.
[43] *L. of N. Doc.*, A. 8, 1931, X, p. 24.

to increase the number of posts (the number being left in abeyance) was defeated by six votes to five. The Italian, Japanese and Dutch members of the committee joined the above-mentioned gentlemen in defeating this proposal.[44]

As the committee could not agree on the major issues, it expressed its opinion that the present posts of the principal officers should be provisionally maintained, but that within a period of three years at the latest, or in the event of the resignation of the present Secretary-General, the Council and the Assembly should resume their examination of the problem. The Twelfth Assembly adopted these conclusions.[45]

In view of the resignation of Sir Eric Drummond, the Fourth Committee of the 1932 Assembly renewed the study of the question of the higher officials. On October 5, M. Hambro moved the following draft resolution :[46]

> The Assembly decides that the posts of Under-Secretaries shall be abolished as and when such posts become vacant, at the same time expressing its wish that the principle should be followed that if the Secretary-General be a national of one of the States Members of the League permanently represented on the Council, the Deputy Secretary-General shall be a national of one of the States Members of the League not represented, and *vice versa.*

This motion made possible a final—may we say "full dress"—debate between the "leader of the Opposition front bench" and the retiring Secretary-General. At great length, M. Hambro stated again his whole case for the abolition of the posts of Under-Secretary-General, and for a greater democratization of the League.[47] He had the support of M. Wohlin of Sweden and of M. Moltesen of Denmark, who emphasized that the economies to be effected were not to be underestimated.[48] He had the approval of M. de Madariaga of

[44] *L. of N. Doc.,* A. 8, 1931, X, p. 28.
[45] *Monthly Summary,* XI (1931), p. 56.
[46] *13A.4C.,* 57.
[47] *13A.4C.,* 65-7 (October 6, 1932).
[48] *13A.4C.,* 69. As early as February 1926, Hr. Lindhagen had described the Secretariat as "the most over-organized institution in the world." He introduced a motion in the Upper House of the Riksdag, that the Government take the initiative

Spain, of the German, Chinese and Finnish delegates.[49] The Dutch spokesman did not necessarily favour abolishing the Under-Secretaries-General but he wished an arrangement which would lessen the inequality in the position of nationals of Small and Great Powers in the Secretariat. In his argument, M. Hambro was able to point out that Viscount Cecil had declared in the "Second Committee of Thirteen" that he was personally prepared to accept M. Hambro's proposal for the suppression of the Under-Secretaries-General.[50] The French representative in the committee, moreover, had said that he would not support any system which created a privileged position for certain States. Count Bernstorff had voted for the abolition of the Under-Secretaries-General. It was a very grave thing that the Secretary-General should be more reactionary than these members of the Committee of Thirteen.[51]

In reply Sir Eric Drummond denied that the Secretariat was responsible for the League's success or failure in its first twelve years. The real question was not whether the League had succeeded, but whether it would have been more successful if M. Hambro's scheme had been in effect during the lifetime of the League. To this question he would answer "emphatically no."[52] In his judgment it was desirable to effect a *liaison* with the Great Powers through the Under-Secretaries-General. Such officials placing the interests of the League first could exercise a very favourable influence on their countries and Governments by explaining League problems to them.[53]

Despite untiring efforts, M. Hambro's motion was shelved by a sub-committee of the Fourth Committee in which Norway, but not Italy, was represented.[54] The Assembly subsequently decided to consider the Legal Adviser, the character of whose functions made it

for an investigation to ascertain how far the League was over-organized, and how far the budget could be cut. The motion, as often with M. Lindhagen's proposals, was defeated without a recorded vote. *Riksdagens Protokoll* (1926). *F.K.* 10: 39 *ff*. *A.K.* 10: 9.

[49] *13A.4C.*, 58-63.

[50] *L. of N. Doc.*, A. 8, 1931, X, *Minutes of the Committee*, p. 15. This was Cecil's private view.

[51] *13A.4C.*, 66.

[52] *13A.4C.*, 68.

[53] *13A.4C.*, 56-7.

[54] For the members of this committee, see *ibid.*, p. 69. No other Scandinavian State was represented.

undesirable to alter his title, as holding the rank of Under-Secretary-General. And in order to give the members of the League not permanently represented on the Council a larger share in the responsibilities devolving on the principal officers of the Secretariat, it was decided that a second post of Deputy-Secretary-General could be created.[55]

Although the Norwegian delegate had lost his fight for the abolition of the posts of Under-Secretary-General, his seven years of struggle against Great Power domination of the Secretariat had not been in vain. Although the nationality principle still remained in the Secretariat, the position of the smaller States had been improved. The Thirteenth Assembly adopted a resolution that "the offices of the Secretary-General and the Deputy Secretaries-General should not include more than one Member of Section who is a national of the same member of the League as the holders of these posts."[56]

It was further agreed by the Assembly that in order to give effect to a more equitable distribution of nationalities, not more than two nationals of any one member of the League should be included among the highest officials of the Secretariat (Secretary-General, Deputy Secretaries-General, Legal Adviser and Under-Secretaries-General, and Directors), and that the principle should be carried into effect at the earliest possible moment, existing contracts remaining unaffected.

Nationality vs. Merit: Conclusions

To make an estimate of Scandinavian activity for the alteration of the organization of the League's Civil Service requires an assumption of value. Most students of international relations would agree with M. de Madariaga that the ideal Secretariat would be "one in which competence, not nationality, would be the governing factor."[57] There are strong reasons for believing that the Scandinavian Governments

[55] See the Report of the Fourth Committee to the Assembly (Annex 27), *13 A.P.*, 185-8.

[56] *13A.P.*, 186. (Article II, 3.) The following quotation is at Article II, 5: "In the Twelfth Assembly, M. Hambro had objected to the continuance of the practice of appointing (within a single office) Members of Section of the same nationality as the Under-Secretaries-General. He thought that no true international spirit could exist in an office in which all the members belonged to the same nationality as their superior." *12A.4C.*, 30.

[57] *The Times*, September 5, 1928 [13F.].

have held this view during the past fifteen years. Unfortunately, however, the "evil of nationality entered the body of the Secretariat at its very birth."[58] By 1926, when the Norwegian representative began his demand for a fairer distribution of nationalities in the Secretariat, it had become evident that the evil of "double loyalty" in some of the higher posts was poisoning the international character of the service. Appointments were in fact reserved for some of the Great Powers.[59] M. Hambro found that the rules of the game were already determined. The true spirit of internationalism could only be hoped for if the national hierarchy were broken. This he set out to do. As Viscount Cecil said, the fight over the higher officials was a political fight.[60] But there is evidence to support M. Hambro's denial that his attitude was determined by purely political considerations. On February 2, 1931, in the new Committee of Thirteen he opposed the Irish proposal that: "In future there shall, as a general rule, be no appointment of more than one national of any State among the higher officers of the Secretariat, from and including the rank of Director of Section upward."[61] His reasons for doing so reveal his faith in the principle of competence, and his judgment of the appropriate relation between it and the principle of nationality. M. Hambro said that under the existing system the Secretary-General was already tied too closely by considerations of nationality. The Irish proposal would restrict him even more. It was essential, if the best qualified man or woman was to be appointed to any post, that the Secretary-General should not be bound by considerations of nationality, although the fact that a candidate belonged to a special nationality or system of civilization might in itself constitute a qualification.

It must be reckoned in favour of the Scandinavian States that their desire to break the monopoly of the Great Powers in the highest posts of the Secretariat did not induce them to advocate at the 1930 Assembly the increase of the number of Under-Secretaries-General. They did not clamour for the appointment of their nationals to the highest posts in the service. Their chief desire for the Secretariat was to see it an efficient, technical body which was international in spirit and in

[58] *ibid.*
[59] Zimmern, *op. cit.*, p. 477.
[60] See *supra*, p. 145.
[61] *L. of N. Doc.*, A. 8, 1931, X, pp. 10-11.

which there were no reserved seats for the nationals of particular States. The position taken in the Second Assembly by the Danish and Swedish delegates was dictated by a desire to create a feeling of security and stability among the officials. Unlike the Dutch delegate and others they did not urge the use of rotation and of short-term appointments in the higher staff. Although M. Zahle agreed that this principle was a desirable one, he thought it would be satisfied if reengagement was prohibited in the case of the Secretary-General, the Deputy Secretary-General, and the Under-Secretaries-General. He insisted on the importance of making possible the reengagement of Directors.[62]

Another contrast with the Dutch view indicates Scandinavian regard for a lengthy period of service for members of the higher staff. In the Ninth Assembly, M. van Eysinga called in question the Secretary-General's failure to abide by the principle of the seven-year rule. Sir Eric Drummond then replied that if the rule had been applied he would have lost practically simultaneously all his department heads.[63] Foreseeing this, he had submitted to the Council in May 1924, a definite memorandum asking for power to reappoint them subject to the approval of the Council. The Council, on which Sweden was represented, approved, with no objection from that State's representative.[64]

In the Committee of Thirteen which met in 1930, M. Hambro aligned himself with the majority, who recommended that officials of the First Division, other than the principal officers (as to whom there was unanimity in excepting from permanency), should in principle be permanently employed.[65]

International Character of the Secretariat

To complete the picture of the attitude which the Scandinavian States adopted toward the Secretariat, a few instances may be cited in regard to their view of the international character of the League's

[62] *2A.4C.*, *(II)*, 38, 39, 40. Baron Ramel's statement of principle, to the effect that these officials may in exceptional cases be reappointed, was adopted by the Fourth Committee.

[63] *9A.4C.*, 37.

[64] *L.N.O.J.*, V (1924), pp. 914, 991.

[65] *11A.4C.*, 296-8, 312-13, compare M. Hambro's statement, p. 318.

Civil Service. Mention has already been made of the danger which
M. Hambro saw in the practice employed by some members of the
League of choosing their nationals who were members of the
Secretariat to be governmental representatives at League meetings. It
was unwise to ask an international official to serve in the capacity of
a national official.[66]

On one occasion objection was brought by M. Hambro, who was
often critical of M. Albert Thomas, Director of the International
Labour Office, that a member of the staff of the Labour Office had,
while on leave, stood as a candidate in the parliamentary elections in
his country and had not previously resigned his post at Geneva. For
an official of the International Labour Office to be engaged in national
politics was obviously an unsound procedure if the impartiality of
the Civil Service was to be maintained.[67]

In the same speech, M. Hambro accused M. Thomas of unwar-
ranted action for one in his position. The Director of the Labour
Office had been reported in the press as having said at a banquet
given to his own political party in France, that he hoped that the
Socialists would come into power in France and in other European
countries.[68] An amusing debate followed. M. Thomas replied that he
made that speech everywhere; that he regarded it his duty to engage
in propaganda on behalf of the League, and the Labour Office, before
the Pope and the Devil alike. Why should he abstain from such
propaganda before his own political party?

M. Hambro then pointed out that M. Thomas would appreciate
the difference between engaging in propaganda for the League and
for a political party. To use M. Thomas' metaphor, he feared that if
M. Thomas when visiting Hell had proposed the toast of the Devil,
wishing him success in every direction, this might perhaps lessen his
influence when he went to Rome to extend the same wishes to
the Pope.[69]

[66] *10A.4C.*, 51. It is only fitting to call attention to the important part which
persons of Scandinavian origin have played in the Secretariat, I.L.O. and Registry
of the Permanent Court. To this considerable number of able and devoted servants
of the League praise is due especially for their genuine loyalty to and achievement
of the spirit of internationalism.

[67] *10A.4C.*, 58.

[68] In *Le Populaire*, July 1, 1929.

[69] *10A.4C.*, 59-60.

Paradoxically, M. Gallavresi of Italy and M. Hambro, who could not agree on principles—Cecil later said, "on a single principle"—concerning the reorganization of the principal officers of the Secretariat, made a joint attack in 1930 on the Secretary-General for alleged partiality. The gentlemen from the North and from the South of Europe united in criticism of Sir Eric Drummond for issuing a circular to members of the Secretariat to the effect that only members of the Secretariat whose duties made it necessary should attend the meetings of the Fourth Committee when the latter was discussing the Report of the Committee of Thirteen.[70]

A more serious criticism, and one more generally levelled against members of the Secretariat, is that they are unduly influenced by the Governments of the countries of which they are nationals. It is fitting to end this section with a quotation from M. Boheman of Sweden, who, in referring to this sort of criticism, said:[71]

> I do not think that it is altogether fair to bring this charge against the officials. It is the Governments above all that should respect the international character of the Secretariat officials, and it is the duty of the Governments to refrain from exercising political influence in the League of Nations through the members of the Secretariat.
>
> Governments should also be asked in the general interest to bear in mind that the Secretariat of the League is not a political, but a technical, organ. If all Governments adopted this view in all sincerity, I think that many problems which at present appear almost insoluble would no longer arise.

M. Hambro agreed with the Swedish delegate that the Secretariat should be technical, not political. But he was compelled to recognize that at present it was necessary for the superior officers of the Secretariat to do many things which otherwise would remain undone, owing to the failure of the Assembly fully to recognize its duties and privileges.[72]

[70] *11A.4C.*, 62, 63, 64.
[71] *11A.4C.*, 58.
[72] *11A.4C.*, 91.

CHAPTER X

THE ASSEMBLY AS AN INSTRUMENT OF CONTROL

WE HAVE considered the attitude of the Scandinavian States towards the organization of the Assembly, the Council and the Secretariat. Let us now turn our attention to certain constitutional questions concerned with the general supervision which the Assembly exercised over the work of the League and, especially, over the other League organs.

The reason which led the Scandinavian States to strive for the assertion of the supremacy of the Assembly should be kept in the foreground. It was generally recognized in the North that the Great Powers, "actuated by mixed motives," "who lead the development of the world for good or for ill," would always exercise the greatest influence in the League.[1] But there was a strong conviction among many of the Northern statesmen that the welfare of mankind would be served by "strengthening the influence of those States who, in the very nature of things, were, *above all*, interested in the supremacy of justice in international relations."[2] It was the mission of the small States, whose very existence depended on the realization of justice, to counteract the temptation of the Great Powers to rely upon Might rather than Right. As the Council, because of its organization and technique, obviously offered less hope for realizing this high mission than the Assembly, it was clear to the small States that the importance of the Assembly should be assured. Such statesmen as Branting and Nansen were quick to seize the opportunity of making the Assembly a rostrum from which to arouse world public opinion. Acting on behalf of international morality, the Assembly should be entitled to demand that the other League organs keep step with the Assembly's conscience and wishes.

[1] Hjalmar Branting, in his address of June 19, 1922, in fulfilment of the Obligation as Nobel Prize Winner. *American-Scandinavian Review,* September 1922, p. 534.
[2] See the speech of M. Branting in the Second Assembly at *2A.P.,* 61.

Control of the Council

In August 1920, at a conference of Danish, Norwegian and Swedish Ministers held at Copenhagen, a resolution was adopted stating that "the General Report of the Council presented the Assembly with an opportunity to exercise its right of control and of criticism in respect to the Council."[3] The determination of the Scandinavian States to guide the Assembly to this work was announced to the First Assembly by M. Hagerup, of Norway, who said:

> If we were to establish an analogy . . . we might say that the Council is our Government and the Assembly our parliament. It is one of the most uncontested rights of parliaments to exercise control over their Governments. It is true that the Council, as such, is not present at the Assembly; therefore it cannot defend its action here in the capacity as a Council. But that does not deprive us of the possibility of exercising our control by means of criticism, recommendations, etc. This right of control is in my opinion . . . an essential right which gives the Assembly an appropriate importance.[4]

The Norwegian delegate proposed, therefore, that in the future the Reports and, if possible, the Minutes of the Council's meetings should be distributed to members of the League in time to be studied before the Assembly met. M. Zahle of Denmark supported this suggestion. He wished to see the Assembly express the *vox populi,* which in the long run, he said, becomes the *vox Dei.*[5] The Swedish delegation proposed an amendment to the Assembly's Provisional Rules of Procedure, which sought to assure that the General Report of the Council would be automatically included in the Agenda of the Assembly.[6]

One other instance of Swedish insistence on the Assembly's right to criticize will be mentioned. During the debate in 1923 on the Assembly's right to consider the Polish-Lithuanian dispute, Baron

[3] *U.N.F.* (1920), p. 2; *IA.P.,* 92.
[4] *ibid.*
[5] *IA.P.,* 153-4.
[6] *IA.1C.,* 59-60. The Provisional Rules [Article IX] provided, however, that the Secretary-General should present to each Assembly a report on the work of the Secretariat and on the measures which have been taken to execute the Assembly's decisions. *IA.1C.,* 52 ff.

Marks von Würtemberg, while associating himself with M. Barthélemy's view that the Assembly was not competent to pronounce as a tribunal of second instance on questions which had already been decided by the Council, said that the French delegate had gone too far in stating that the Assembly had not even the right to criticize the Council's action. This right could not be denied the Assembly.[7]

Few States have sent representatives to Geneva who have been more outspoken in their criticism of the Council. Especially during those years when no Scandinavian State was represented on the Council, that is, from 1920 to 1922 and from 1927 to 1929 there was sharp Scandinavian criticism. In 1921 M. Branting insisted that the small States should feel perfectly free to express their points of view, especially as the permanent representative on the Council had not shown a sufficient respect for, and lively interest in, the work of the League.[8] M. Hambro later complained that the Council did not fulfil its duty by properly discussing problems that came before the League, but chose to remain silent and to ignore questions put to it by members of the Assembly.[9]

The pressure of criticism as a means of control has been supplemented by the demand that the Council should scrupulously execute the recommendations of the Assembly. Delegates of the Northern States have taken the view that this obligation rested upon members of the Council because "the seats on the Council have been given them in trust by the Assembly in order to respect and uphold the wishes and rights of the Assembly."[10]

Extension of the Assembly's Control of Finance

Although certain questions, such as mandates, minorities and the Government of the Saar Territory were explicitly entrusted to the Council by the Covenant or by other treaties, this has not prevented the Assembly from exercising some supervision thereof. Such action was made possible by the authorization given the Assembly, by Article III of the Covenant, to deal with any matter within the sphere of action of the League or affecting the peace of the world. The Minis-

[7] 4A.1C., 23.
[8] 2A.P., 61; U.N.F. (1921), p. 2.
[9] 8A.P., 58.
[10] 7A.P., 49. (See the speech of M. Hambro.)

ters' Meeting of the three Northern countries in Copenhagen foresaw the significance of this provision, and through their initiative the question of mandates (also the reduction of armaments) was included in the Agenda of the First Assembly.[11] Year after year Dr Nansen of Norway moved a resolution in the Assembly that the report of the Permanent Mandates Commission should be referred to the appropriate committee for examination. It was M. Branting, Chairman of the Sixth Committee of the 1920 Assembly, who assured Dr Nansen that in the event of the Council's failure to accept the Assembly's assistance, the committee would nevertheless enter upon a discussion of mandates.[12] Dr Nansen thought that the Assembly was more or less morally responsible for the terms of the mandates, and for the manner in which they were carried out.[13]

To the Scandinavian States should go the credit for first making use of this "simple but ingenious" method of subjecting to the scrutiny and criticism of the Assembly questions which had originally been intended for regulation by the Council. On the administration of the Saar, to give another instance, Dr Nansen from the floor of the Assembly took it upon himself to lay down principles for the guidance of the Council's supervision.[14]

There is nothing of substance to add to the account given by Mr Felix Morley as to how the supremacy of the Assembly has been established over the finances of the League.[15] Indeed it is beyond the scope of this study to retell this significant development towards the democratization of the League, which was largely directed by the skillful leadership of M. Hambro. To read Mr Morley's chapter, "The Assembly as Sovereign Power," gives one a clear impression of the important rôle which the Norwegian statesmen played in ousting "the Council from all semblance of control over the Supervisory Commission." Our treatment will consist in giving greater emphasis to the strictly Scandinavian point of view and will make no attempt to recreate a history of the entire development.

[11] *1A.P.*, 92.
[12] *1A.6C. (II)*, 247.
[13] *1A.6C. (II)*, 306.
[14] See, for example, *4A.P.*, 61, where he is reported to have said that "we are all convinced that the Council in electing the members of the Governing Commission will pay due attention to the interests of the inhabitants of the Saar." See *infra*, p. 269.
[15] *The Society of Nations*, pp. 512-44.

In the first six Assemblies the delegations from Scandinavia did not play an inconspicuous part in determining the Financial Regulations of the League. Like certain other States they were concerned with efforts to reduce their quotas in the League's budget, and they, who were prompt in their payment of dues, expressed frequent concern as to the situation created by the disturbingly large number of members in arrears. They waged no large-scale campaign, however, for the extension of the Assembly's control over the finances of the League. Yet there is no doubt that they supported such efforts as were made in the First Assembly to assure the comprehensive Assembly control recommended by Sir George Foster, the former Finance Minister for Canada. Denmark was represented in the Finance Committee of the First Assembly by M. Moltesen, who pointed out that if the Council were to submit to the Assembly preliminary estimates, the Assembly would often be faced with a *fait accompli*. It was therefore necessary that the budget be submitted to the Assembly very early, even if it had not been examined by the Council. Whenever this was impossible, the Council should be empowered to incur only normal expenditure, such as the payment of salaries, and not extraordinary expenditure, such as that resulting from the appointment of commissions or the execution of political decisions.[16]

The Scandinavian States supported the creation by the Second Assembly of a Commission of Control. This "Supervisory Commission," which was designed to secure an effective control over the finances of the League, was to be appointed by the Council. It is noteworthy that M. Bull of Norway opposed the addition of an expert to the commission, on the ground that to do so would involve the risk of the commission's becoming a mere machine, automatically registering the decisions of the expert. The post of expert, recommended by the Noblemaire Committee, was accordingly suppressed.[17]

In the Fourth Committee in 1920, M. Trygger of Sweden opposed an amendment offered by the Japanese delegate which would have given the Council, rather than the Assembly, actual power to determine the allocation of League expenses. The support from other small States who rallied to M. Trygger's position was sufficient to

---

16 *1A.4C. (II)*, 24.
17 *2A.4C. (II)*, 52, 56.

cause the withdrawal of the Japanese proposal. The Assembly then proceeded to recommend an amendment to Article VI of the Covenant which substituted Assembly control over the allocation of expenses for the original apportionment employed by the Universal Postal Union.[18]

At the First Assembly in which M. Hambro represented Norway, that of 1926, he gave some indication of the direction his future activity would take when he said that his sole purpose in the debate on the control of the budget was to bring out the fact that it was with the Fourth Committee that the duty lay of causing economies to be effected.[19] He further intimated that the improved method of control should come, not through some superior organ, but perhaps through the medium of a sub-committee of the Fourth Committee.[20] M. Hambro's intended reform of the League, dominated by a "tacit alliance between representatives of the permanent members of the Council and the executive officers of the Secretariat," was sufficiently well known to make it desirable in some quarters to remove him from the Finance Committee where decisive debates took place. "In the Eighth (1927) Assembly, at Secretariat instance, M. Hambro was named Chairman of the Fifth (Opium and Social Questions) Committee. Instead of participating in the constitutionally important debates of the Fourth Committee, he consequently spent his time in presiding over discussion on such subjects as the protection of women and children in the Near East." Prior to the Ninth Assembly, "the effort to shelve the Norwegian Progressive took the form of offering him the Assembly presidency, which [he said] 'I refused because I wanted to start something in the Fourth Committee.' "[21]

In the Ninth Assembly, M. Hambro was free to begin operations. These took the form of an amendment to Article I of the Financial Regulations, wherein he proposed that in the future the Supervisory Commission should be appointed by the Assembly rather than by the Council.[22] The Norwegian proposal was opposed mainly by States

[18] 2A.4C. (II), 155, 156.
[19] 7A.4C., 39, 40.
[20] 7A.4C., 60.
[21] Morley, op. cit., p. 528.
[22] 9A.4C., 15, 89.

with permanent representatives on the Council.[23] The British delegate, for example, expressed fears that if the election of the Supervisory Commission were to rest entirely with the Assembly, political
considerations might play an undue part. As a compromise, he suggested that the formal right of appointment be given the Assembly,
but that nominations remain with the Council. M. Hambro replied
that he did not share with his British colleague the same distrust of
the Assembly nor the same confidence in the Council with regard to
political intrigues. His amendment was based on a universally recognized principle that a parliamentary body providing credits should
control their expenditure. The British proposal was incompatible
with that principle. Since the Assembly alone could approve expenditure, the Assembly alone should appoint the controlling body.[24]

The egalitarian forces rallied to the logic and oratory of M.
Hambro to secure the adoption of his amendment by thirteen votes to
six. Then on September 26, 1928, after triumphant M. Hambro had
proclaimed to the Assembly that it must awaken to its latent powers,
the Plenary Session adopted a resolution withdrawing the Council's
authority to appoint the Supervisory Commission.[25] The Norwegian
statesman had done more than preach the gospel of power to his
fellows in the Assembly: he also had urged the delegations of the
Assembly to realize that they had a responsibility for every resolution
passed by the Assembly.

Although the Assembly had gained control over the important committee which scrutinizes the annual budget, M. Hambro was not
satisfied; for the arrangement accepted for the nomination of the
Supervisory Commission was one by which the Great Powers *in fact*
were in a favoured position. The General Committee of the Assembly,
upon whom the duty of nomination had been conferred, was composed of fourteen members, among whom the permanent members
of the Council were traditionally represented. M. Hambro decided,
therefore, to oppose this new system and to demand nomination by
the Fourth Committee. Such an arrangement would assure the control
of the choice of the Supervisory Commission by the small States, as

[23] Morley, *op. cit.*, p. 527.
[24] *9A.4C.*, 89-90. The Polish and South African delegates expressed approval of
the British view.
[25] *9A.P.*, 188-9.

the Great Powers would be hopelessly outnumbered in the Fourth Committee, where each State has one vote.[26]

In the Tenth Assembly M. Hambro served warning by demanding a regular vote at the election of the Supervisory Commission, rather than silently giving consent to the nominees of the General Committee, thereby emphasizing that the Assembly now had within its hands the sole power of determining the personnel of the Supervisory Commission. Then in 1930 the Norwegian delegate proposed this additional alteration.[27] He argued that the General Committee was unsuited to the task of submitting names; for it had never had an opportunity to follow the work of the Supervisory Commission, and the majority had never served in the Fourth Committee and hence knew little about the League's budget.[28]

The immediate support given by a large number of the small States, including Sweden, indicated "a certain amount of preliminary preparation."[29] Italy, whose representative, according to Mr Morley, "greatly desired small-Power support," was the only Great Power openly to declare approval of M. Hambro's proposal. There is no evidence to suggest that Denmark, whose delegation gave no expression of its view, was not also favourably disposed to control by the Fourth Committee. It is probable, however, that the Danish Government attached less importance to the constitutional changes which were effected between 1928 and 1930 than did M. Hambro. In this whole development the Danish, and even the Swedish, activity was much less conspicuous than that of the sister State, some of whose representatives appeared eager to have their country win "a place in the sun." Notice should be taken of the characteristic Danish moderation and caution which is in sharp contrast to the aggressive tactics of the Norwegian representative. Perhaps it is the character of M. Hambro himself which was chiefly responsible for the Norwegian initiative which achieved the "control of the purse" by the Assembly. To compare his activity with the instructions which he was given by his Government suggests that the prominence of Norway in effecting

[26] Compare Morley, *op. cit.*, pp. 537-40.
[27] *10A.P.*, 140.
[28] *11A.4C.*, 81.
[29] Morley, *op. cit.*, p. 539.

this significant change came largely from the determination and ability of the *Stortingspresident.*[30]

It was a fitting tribute to M. Hambro that he, who had manifested such a concern for the finances of the League, should have been elected to membership in the Supervisory Commission by the Twelfth Assembly.[31]

Control of Committees

The question of control of committees, which was raised in the above discussion, merits further treatment. It has already been indicated that in the opening years of the League, the Scandinavian delegations had not pressed the issue of control of committees to any great extent.[32] The origin of the special and determined policy in this regard seems to lie in the *Utenriks- og Konstitutionskomité* of the Norwegian Storting. This committee (which may be designated as the Foreign Affairs Committee) expressed great concern that Norway was not represented on the committee created by the Council in December 1924, to study the possibility of the Progressive Codification of International Law. In the report of the Foreign Affairs Committee dated May 28, 1926, and signed by Carl J. Hambro, its chairman, special complaint was expressed that Norway was not represented in the sub-committee investigating the law of territorial waters, a question of more importance to Norway than to almost any other State.[33] These omissions led the Storting's committee to consider the whole question of Norway's representation in the various organs of the League. A table was introduced into the report showing that

[30] See *St. med.* nr. 3 (1929), pp. 8, 55. The delegation was merely authorized to work for the application of constitutional procedure throughout all the activity of the Assembly and Council, and to strengthen the position of the Assembly. The instructions given to the delegation to the Eleventh Assembly [see *St. med.* nr. 3 (1931), pp. 9-12] contain no instructions to work for the nomination of the Supervisory Commission by the Fourth Committee. The delegation was instructed not to support a proposal for the increase of the number of Vice-Presidents of the Assembly from six to eight. *ibid.,* p. 9.

[31] *12A.4C.,* 46; *12A.P.,* 152. Hambro was nominated by the Fourth Committee, receiving, however, only 19 of the 35 votes cast, one more than necessary. The vacancy was created by the resignation of Count Moltke of Denmark, who had been elected by the Tenth Assembly [*10A.P.,* 140]. Lord Meston, whose term had expired, was reelected. He received 30 votes (in the committee) for renomination.

[32] *supra,* Chapter VII, p. 103.

[33] *Stortings Forhandlinger* (1926), Vol. 6a, pp. 212-18. (*Innst. S.* nr. 100.)

sixteen Swedish nationals were thus represented, and twelve Danish nationals, but only six Norwegian nationals.[34] The Storting's committee interpreted Norway's slight representation as an evidence that the Norwegian delegation to the Assembly had not always acted as a national and collective unit, and that perhaps it had been more actively occupied with international rather than national considerations. The committee, however, did not intend this as a compliment, but indicated its desire to have the Norwegian delegation to the next Assembly instructed to take care of "national" interests.[35]

The subsequent debate in the Storting on July 2, 1926, indicated that although there was disagreement as to the justice of the criticism brought by the committee against the delegation, the general attitude of the House was that of M. Johan Castberg, who said, "we as a small nation desire and demand that the small States should get a greater influence" in the League.[36] M. Mowinckel agreed with M. Hambro that the welfare of the League would have been better served in the past if the small States had been able to act with more independence and force, so as to counterbalance the strength of the victorious Powers.[37]

In view of this debate and the attitude of the Committee on Foreign Affairs, M. Lykke's Conservative Government instructed the delegation to the Seventh Ordinary Assembly to express the desirability "that the Council should see to it that all members of the League as far as possible should be represented in the commissions of the League, especially in the permanent commissions. In this connection the delegation should indicate the possibility of making permanent regulations for the choice of membership in commissions."[38]

Armed with instructions which were largely of his own making, M. Hambro came to Geneva in September 1926 to express the opinion of the Norwegian Government that "it would be natural" to distribute the seats on the League's commissions and committees more

[34] *Fortegnelse over de skandinaviske landes repræsentation i Folkenes Forbunds organisationer og kommissioner* (Appendix to the Innstilling), *ibid.*, pp. 216-18.
[35] *ibid.*, p. 216.
[36] *Stortings Forhandlinger* (1926), Vol. 7b, pp. 2576 ff.
[37] *ibid.*, p. 2576.
[38] *St. med.* nr. 3 (1927), p. 8.

evenly among the members of the League, and, preferably, under a system of rotation.[39]

Again in 1929 the Scandinavians raised the question of committee distribution and appointment. In the Assembly the Socialist Prime Minister of Denmark, M. Stauning, referred to the tendency to concentrate the real work of the League in the Council and in the commissions appointed by the Council, in which States members of the Council exercise a preponderant influence. The consequence, he said, has been that the number of Council seats have been increased to an extent "which many of us hold to be undesirable," and still the struggle to obtain seats continues. M. Stauning wondered if the difficulty could not be overcome by giving the Assembly a more active rôle in the League's work. He raised the question whether it would be better in certain cases to elect commissions consisting both of members appointed by the Council and by the Assembly.[40]

Although nothing came of the Danish suggestion, an expression of the spirit which motivated it appeared in the objection which the Norwegian and Danish delegations offered to the British and Italian proposals that the Council should appoint the committee studying the Secretariat.[41] The Scandinavian view was that this inquiry was one which, to a special degree, reposed in the Assembly's authority; the Assembly, therefore, should make the appointment. The Fourth Commission approved of this position, with eight negative votes. Despite M. Hambro's opposition, it was decided, however, that the General Committee should suggest the personnel of the Committee of Enquiry to the Assembly for election.[42]

Control of the Permanent Staff

It will be recalled that a Danish initiative at the Hotel Crillon on March 20, 1919, had led to an alteration in the Draft Covenant of the League, requiring the Secretary-General to be chosen not by the

[39] *7A.P.*, 49.
[40] *10A.P.*, 41.
[41] *10A.4C.*, 38, 50, 51.
[42] *10A.4C.*, 68; *St. med.* nr. 3 (1930), p. 68, wherein Hambro remarks that "it was shown here as at the preparation for the election of the Supervisory Commission that the General Committee of the Assembly is not suitable as an election committee."

Council but by the Assembly on the motion of the Council.[43] This action was a prelude to a policy later championed by the Scandinavian States to assure the Assembly's control over the Civil Service of the League.

Although the Covenant specified that the "secretaries and staff" should be appointed by the Secretary-General with the approval of the Council—not of the Assembly—the latter body by virtue of its control over expenditures was able to exercise a wide control over the League's permanent employees.[44] As it was feared that the Council might exercise too wide a control over the Secretariat, Scandinavian policy in the early years of the League tended to emphasize the independent character of the Secretariat as a distinct organ of the League responsible for its own action.[45] This was but the first step in asserting the Assembly's right of control through the medium of criticism and budgetary regulation. In 1920, M. Trygger was among those who objected to M. Albert Thomas' proposal that a lump sum be given to the International Labour Office with full discretionary power to the governing body for its expenditure.[46]

When M. Hambro came to Geneva in 1926, he emphasized the positive obligation of the Fourth Committee to regulate effectively the work of the Secretariat. His manner was hardly mild and his speech included the use of "censorious phrases," for which he later apologized and explained as due to his "imperfect command of the English language." "His attitude," he said, "had been influenced by an old parliamentary prejudice that as a member of a committee one should make some pretence of preserving at least a remnant—even though it were a rather superficial remnant—of control. . . . He hoped that if he had left a disagreeable impression in the mind of the Secretary-General," it might serve as a reminder of the principle of the Fourth Committee.[47]

There can be little doubt that the campaign of 1928, 1929 and 1930 led by M. Hambro for budgetary control was "directed as much

[43] *supra*, Chapter IV, p. 61.
[44] *supra*, this Chapter, p. 160.
[45] See, for instance, M. Trygger's speech reported in *3A.1C.*, 33.
[46] *1A.4C. (II)*, 30.
[47] *7A.4C.*, 22.

against the assertion of unwritten authority on the part of the Secretariat as against the existence of authorized supremacy on the part of the Council."[48]

If we turn to the Scandinavian attitude towards the Assembly's supervisory functions with regard to the International Labour Office, the situation is little different. Norway, through the mouth of M. Hambro, was most outspoken in demanding control of the budget. So sharp was this gentleman's criticism on September 15, 1928, that *The Times* (London) correspondent at Geneva wrote as follows: "It is a long time since there was so outspoken a criticism of an international organization as that made this afternoon by the Norwegian delegate (M. Hambro) in the Fourth Committee," which is dealing with the International Labour Office.[49] In addition to his demand for an effective control which would make it possible to achieve economies, M. Hambro said that the distribution of nationals in the Labour Office was "badly balanced," even less satisfactory than that in the Secretariat.[50]

The debate in the Fourth Committee did not stay above the personal level. The "compelling personality" of the Director of the Labour Office, said M. Hambro, made it possible for the Director to obtain the approval of the Governing Body for budgets which the Governments of its members would not accept. Control was necessary because M. Thomas was sometimes, "if not intoxicated, at any rate, carried away by the exuberance of his own verbosity," and able "to carry with him most of those who heard him."[51] On another occasion, M. Hambro implied that the finances of the Labour Office were left to the conscience, or to "the elasticity of conscience" of M. Thomas.[52] Such remarks may perhaps be recognized as an exaggerated application of the parliamentary principle, an application which obviously has more limitations in the international than in the national field.

[48] Morley, *op. cit.*, p. 538.
[49] *The Times,* September 17, 1928 [11A].
[50] 9A.4C., 60-1, 77.
[51] 9A.4C., 60. "Popular humour," writes M. Hambro in his book, *Folkeforbundet og dets Arbeide,* p. 63, refers to M. Thomas as the "Governing Mind," and the other members of the I.L.O. are "exclusively the Body."
[52] 7A.4C., 41.

M. Hambro's violent attacks on the Labour Office ought to be viewed against the attitude of organized Labour in Norway.[53] Until 1935 the official Labour Party (Arbeider Partiet), unlike that in Denmark and in Sweden, consistently voted against the annual appropriation to the International Labour Organization. In a minority report of the Foreign Affairs Committee of the Storting in 1922, M. Magnussen explained this opposition on the ground that under the existing Constitution of the International Labour Organization, the Labour representatives at the conferences would usually be outvoted by the representatives of the employers and Governments, who, he said, usually have common interests.[54] Although the Norwegian delegations to the annual Labour Conferences normally contained employees' representatives in the years from 1919 to 1926, in the following years no representatives of the workers were sent until 1934, when the cooperation of the Norwegian Confederation of Trade Unions was restored.[55]

At two Labour Conferences, the Thirteenth and Fourteenth, the Norwegian Government was unable to send any delegation whatsoever as a result of the quite unexpected refusal of the Storting on April 19, 1929, to grant the funds for Norway's participation.[56] By ninety votes to thirty-one the Storting struck out the budget provision which had been recommended by the Social Committee.[57] The Labour Party as usual voted against participation and many members of the bourgeois parties did likewise. M. Hambro (Conservative), for instance, saw no other way to express dissatisfaction with Norway's representation in the previous Labour Conference. The relation between this delegation and the Norwegian delegation to the Assembly had not been satisfactory. The Government had sent a Civil Service

[53] Frequent references were made by the Norwegian delegation to the position of Norwegian Labour. See, for instance, *12A.4C.*, 25.

[54] *Stortings Forhandlinger* (1922), Vol. 6a, II. *Innst. S. LIV*.

[55] *Records of the Proceedings of the International Labour Conferences.* See also, speech of Mr. Bramsnaes, *ibid., Eighteenth Session,* 1934, p. 5. See also *American-Scandinavian Review,* November 1925, p. 689.

[56] Norway was represented, however, by an observer. *Stortings Forhandlinger* (1931), Vol. 6a. *Innst. S.* nr. 29.

[57] For the debate on the Report of the Social Committee (part of *Budget-innst. S.* nr. 51), see *Stortings Forhandlinger* (1929), Vol. 7a, pp. 1149 *ff.*

delegation and not a political one. This practice resulted in the adoption of numerous Labour Conventions which could not secure ratification. M. Hambro wished also to demonstrate against the methods and the budget of the Labour Office. M. Hundseid of the Agrarian Party (Bonde Partiet) also opposed the appropriation as a disapproval of the Government's choice of delegates to the Labour Conference. M. Norlie, another Conservative, voted "no," for purposes of economy, but not, as the *Stortingspresident,* for a demonstration. The defence of the budget provision for participation in the Labour Conference fell upon Venstre led by M. Mowinckel, who asked how M. Hambro's policy of "critical attention" to the Labour Office could be followed if Norway were not well represented at meetings of the conference.[58]

The following year, 1930, the Norwegian bourgeois parties returned to their customary support, and appropriation was made for participation in the Geneva Labour Conference; but the Labour Party, whose members occupied more than one-third of all the seats in the Storting, was solid in opposition.[59] Not until 1932 did the Norwegian Labour Party desist from voting against participation in the conference.[60] When in June 1934, M. Halvard Olsen, President of the Norwegian Confederation of Trade Unions, took his seat in the Eighteenth Session of the International Labour Conference, it was after a period of seven years in which no representative of employees had been sent from Norway to the annual conferences at Geneva. Under such circumstances it is not surprising that the Norwegian delegations to the Assembly had meanwhile been extremely critical of the growing expenditure of the Labour Office.

The policy of Denmark and Sweden, who also supported general supervision of the Assembly over the budget of the Labour Office, was dispassionately pronounced. These States have been among the

[58] See debate on May 13, 1929, in the Storting. *ibid.,* pp. 1797-812. M. Lykke, leader of the Conservative Party, supported Mowinckel in defence of Norwegian participation.

[59] See the Committee's Report, *Stortings Forhandlinger* (1930), Vol. 6a. *Budgett-innst. S.* nr. 52. On April 3, 1930, the Committee's Report was adopted, but there were 57 negative votes. *Stortings Tidende,* 1930, p. 1026.

[60] (1932) *Budgett-innst. S.* nr. 50; (1932) *Stortings Tidende,* p. 895. See (1933) *Stortings Tidende,* p. 938 (1934), *Budgett-innst. S.* nr. 48.

most active participants in the work of the International Labour Organization. Indeed, it is correct to say that within this organization the Northern countries have worked together in a constructive way, with the result that the social development of their peoples has been notably advanced.[61]

[61] For the part the Northern States have played in this institution, see Erik Brüel, "Norden og den Internationale Arbejdsorganisation," *Nordisk Tidskrift för Vetenskap, Konst och Industri,* Vol. 5 (6) (1929), pp. 417-32.

III. THE ORGANIZATION OF PEACE AND JUSTICE

CHAPTER XI

CONCILIATION, ARBITRATION AND JUDICIAL PROCEDURE

A. The Permanent Court of International Justice

IN EARLIER chapters the pre-League attitude of the Northern States to the organization of international justice through a permanent court was described, and special attention has been directed to the essential characteristics of the court suggested by the Danish, Norwegian and Swedish Commissions in 1918.[1] On the thorny question of the composition of the court it had been provided that the absolute equality of States would be safeguarded. The election of judges, moreover, was to be effected by a body in which one national from each State would cast an equal vote. In short, no exceptional consideration whatsoever was assigned to the Great Powers.

In August 1919 the three Commissions again met in Copenhagen to review their previous scheme in the light of the resolution adopted by the Organizing Committee of the League of Nations at its meeting on June 9, 1919, requesting States to inform the League as soon as possible on questions of general interest. Moreover, having been excluded from participation in the work of creating the League, the Scandinavians were anxious to make their influence felt in the formulation of plans for the Permanent Court referred to in Article XIV of the Covenant.[2]

The meeting of the Scandinavian Commissions at Copenhagen revealed that while the Swedish Commission was satisfied with nearly all the provisions of the joint plan elaborated the year before, the Danish and Norwegian Commissions wished to make certain altera-

---

[1] *supra,* Chapter II, pp. 21-2, and Chapter III, p. 38.
[2] Permanent Court of International Justice, Advisory Committee of Jurists. *Documents presented to the Committee,* pp. 55, 207. Hereinafter cited as *P.C.I.J. (Advisory Committee), Documents.*

tions. It was decided, therefore, that each Commission should draft a scheme of its own.[3]

After this had been done, renewed collaboration took place at The Hague with delegates of the Netherlands and Switzerland at the so-called Conference of the Five Neutral Powers in February 1920.[4] This consultation showed that the opinions of the delegates were already identical upon most points at issue concerning the nature, composition and organization of the future court. Complete agreement was reached on four cardinal principles, namely, "equality of States," "complete and methodical separation of the notions of Justice and Arbitration," "total exclusion of political influences," and "total independence of judges as against their own country."

A few controversial points which arose at the Five-Power Conference merit notice, but should not be considered of great importance, for it is the fundamental similarity of attitude which commands emphasis. The Swedish delegates, after some hesitation, and partly to realize unity, accepted the position that election of judges of the Permanent Court ought to be made by the Assembly rather than by a special body of Hague Court judges. According to Baron E. Marks von Würtemberg, "the Swedish desire to exclude as far as possible political considerations from the election bowed before a desire to fortify the authority of the League as well as that of the court."[5]

Denmark and Norway maintained the propriety of the privilege of challenging judges without indicating reasons; the Netherlands, Sweden and Switzerland opposed such procedure. The Swedish argument was that since the court was to deal with issues of a purely legal character, the personnel of the court should be rendered as independent as possible of the parties to the dispute. To allow such a right of challenge might tend to obscure the principle that no national or

[3] *P.C.I.J.* (*Advisory Committee*), *Documents*, p. 227. For the draft schemes concerning the Organization of a Permanent Court of International Justice, see Annexes 6, 7, 8, *ibid.*, pp. 203-51. The "Reports" and "Considerations" attached to the same explain the variation of views of the three commissions.

[4] *ibid.*, p. 325. The representatives of the Powers at the Five-Power Conference were as follows: Denmark, Otto Krag; The Netherlands, B. C. J. Loder, J. Limburg, C. van Vollenhoven; Norway, Emil Huitfeldt and M. K. Lie; Sweden, Baron Marks von Würtemberg and Baron A. Adelswärd; Switzerland, Gaston Carlin and Max Huber.

[5] P. Munch, *Les origines et L'œuvre de la Société des Nations*, Vol. II, p. 218.

political consideration whatever should be allowed to influence judgments.[6]

On the important question of the competence of the court, the Netherlands, Sweden and Switzerland held that the court should be clothed with compulsory jurisdiction over five classes of legal disputes, including those which subsequently were specified in Article 36 of the Statute of the Court. Although Denmark and Norway also eagerly desired a court of very wide competence, they abstained from any such recommendation on the ground that it would not be possible, in view of the provisions of the Covenant, to convince other members of the League to accept compulsory adjudication.[7]

The draft plan of the five neutral Powers and the separate Danish, Norwegian and Swedish plans were, with certain other schemes, laid before an advisory committee of jurists named by the Council in February 1920, to prepare plans for the establishment of the Permanent Court of International Justice. M. Francis Hagerup, former Norwegian Prime Minister and first delegate of Norway to The Hague Conference of 1907, was appointed to this committee of ten members, which included one other national of a neutral Power, Dr Loder of the Netherlands. The draft statute which the committee elaborated was in many respects influenced by the plan of the five neutral States[8] and included, notably, a provision for compulsory adjudication of the suggested five classes of cases.[9] As a safeguard for the Great Powers, however, the Root-Phillimore plan for election of judges by a majority vote of the Council as well as by the Assembly was adopted. M. Hagerup and M. Fernandes of Brazil regretted that this double vote was given to members of the Council, thereby departing from the principle of absolute equality, and the Norwegian jurist only refrained from proposing an amendment because there was no chance for it to succeed.[10] Professor Manley Hudson has remarked

---

[6] *P.C.I.J.* (*Advisory Committee*), *Documents,* p. 249.

[7] Compare von Würtemberg, *op. cit.,* with "Memorandum of the Work of the Conference," *P.C.I.J.* (*Advisory Committee*), *Documents,* p. 331. The five classes of cases to be referred to compulsory adjudication are given at *ibid.,* p. 309.

[8] The Committee of Jurists found "a very valuable source of information in the plan of the Five Powers." *Procès-Verbaux of the Proceedings of the Committee, June 16-July 24, 1920,* p. 697.

[9] See Article 34 of the draft. The draft statute is given in *ibid.,* pp. 673-85.

[10] *ibid.,* pp. 365-8, 385, 387.

that "many of the committee's proposals with reference to the procedure of the Court were borrowed from provisions in the 'Five-
Power Plan.' "[11] With a few modifications, the most important of
which was to strike out the assignment of compulsory jurisdiction to
the Court, the jurists' scheme was adopted by the Council at Brussels
in October 1920.[12]

Before the Statute of the Court took final form at the First Assembly, the Norwegian and Swedish Governments sent letters to the
League proposing amendments to the draft of the committee of
jurists.[13] Some of these desired changes merit notice as an indication
of the conception of these States in regard to the Court. It was made
clear in the Assembly, however, that these amendments would not be
insisted upon if to do so would imperil the successful adoption of
the Statute.[14]

It was thought preferable that the nomination of judges should be
made directly by the Governments of the Members, rather than by
The Hague Court panels. These panels were deemed unsuitable since
the likely candidates might very generally belong to these panels.

The Committee of Jurists had recommended that the national
groups in the respective countries nominate two persons, but nothing
was said of their nationality. The Scandinavians saw in this arrangement the probability that each country would name its own nationals.
To overcome this objection, they proposed that a fixed proportion of
one's own nationals (for instance, one-third) might not be exceeded
when nominations were being made. This principle was accepted by
the Assembly and inserted into the Statute of the Court.[15]

The Scandinavians were also eager to assure that the judges should
engage in no other public function. Article 16 of the committee's
draft scheme was altered, though not sufficiently to meet their

[11] Hudson, *The Permanent Court of International Justice*, p. 123.

[12] *L.N.O.J.*, I, 8 (10C.), pp. 14-15 (October 27, 1920).

[13] Letter of October 15, 1920, from the Norwegian Ministry of Foreign Affairs.
1A.3C.(I), 500 *ff*. Letter of October 18, 1920, from the Swedish Ministry at
Brussels, *1A.3C.(I)*, 506 *ff*. These letters were laid before the Council at its Tenth
Session (Brussels).

[14] *1A.3C.(I)*, 279.

[15] *1A.3C.(I)*, 303, 554. See Article 5 of the Statute. This suggestion seems to have
originated in the Five-Power Plan, Article 6. Compare Hudson, *op. cit.*, p. 133,
note 78.

desires.[16] In order to safeguard judges as far as possible from national influences it was proposed by the Scandinavians that judges should be required to reside at the seat of the Court. Their wishes on this point were not met, except for the President of the Court.[17]

It was natural that the small States should have favoured a Court sufficiently large to assure the election of an adequate number of judges who were nationals of the small States. The plan of the Swedish Commission had called for fifteen; the Danish and Norwegian plans for twenty-one. These numbers had been unacceptable to the Committee of Jurists, who specified eleven judges and four deputy-judges. But even this number did not satisfy the British, who asked at the Assembly for further reduction to nine. In the sub-committee, M. Hagerup, its chairman, who played a prominent rôle throughout the discussion, explained that the smaller Powers were opposed to so limited a number of judges, and he succeeded in keeping the number at eleven, a figure which in practice meant a fairly even distribution between nationals of the large and small States.[18]

The Council, it was noted, had eliminated the Jurists' recommendation for compulsory adjudication of certain legal disputes. In the Third Committee M. Hagerup did not hesitate to express regret for this action and to disagree with Lord Robert Cecil, who had said that no State was ready to give up the usual reservations of *vital interests* from compulsory jurisdiction of the Court.[19] Even the British and French delegates were compelled to admit that there was a majority in the committee in favor of the Jurists' recommendation.[20] Thus the Great Powers aided by the unanimity rule blocked the wish of the Scandinavians and other small States for the compulsory adjudication by an international tribunal of a limited category of disputes.[21]

[16] Compare Hudson, *op. cit.*, pp. 142-3.

[17] Article 22.

[18] *1A.3C.(I)*, 340.

[19] *1A.3C.(I)*, 289.

[20] See an interesting article in *The New York Times,* November 26, 1920 [1: 5] for the clash between Great and Small Powers.

[21] The sub-committee of the Third Committee reported that "it did not seem possible to arrive at unanimity except on the basis of the principles laid down in the Council's draft." *1A.3C. (I)*, 533.

The Scandinavian States agreed that the "ingenious device,"[22] submitted by the Brazilian jurist, M. Fernandes, and known as the Optional Clause, was all that could be hoped for under the circumstances.[23] Their speedy acceptance of the protocol attached to Article 36 of the Statute of the Court is another clear indication of the loyalty of these States to the principle which had been announced at the Five-Power Conferences. Denmark in December 1920, and Norway and Sweden in 1921, signed the protocol attached to Article 36 of the Statute of the Court. Denmark took first honours, being the first State to deposit ratification.[24] When the Government asked the Rigsdag for ratification of its action, it was unanimously given by both Houses.[25] In the Folketing, however, M. Holstein (Conservative), although acknowledging the interest of small States in the substitution of law for might in international intercourses, preferred delay, especially as Sweden and Norway had not yet given an indication of what action they would take concerning the Optional Clause.[26] M. Moltesen (Venstre) replied that someone must take the lead, and that there was no reason why it should not be Denmark. This step was clearly in line with the arbitration policy developed in Denmark since the treaty with Holland of February 12, 1904. Experience had not shown any objection to it. It must be remembered, he added, that *Rettens Vej er en Livsbetingelse; Magtens er Døden* ["the way of right is essential for life; the way of might is death."].[27]

When the Swedish Riksdag was asked to ratify adherence to the protocol attached to Article 36, this was done in both Chambers on June 4, 1921, without an important debate or without a recorded vote. Herr Trygger, leader of the Conservative Party in the Upper·

[22] See the speech of M. Bourgeois (France), *L.N.O.J.*, II, 2, p. 184.

[23] See M. Hagerup's speech, *1A.P.*, 492. Professor Manley Hudson says that "The Italian Council for Diplomatic Litigation seems to have first suggested a 'separate convention' for the acceptance of the Court's compulsory jurisdiction." *The Permanent Court of International Justice*, p. 118.

[24] Sweden, however, had been the first State to deposit ratification of the Statute of the Court (February 21, 1921), *L.N.O.J.*, XI, p. 1692. Denmark deposited ratification, June 13, 1921. (Date of signature, before January 28, 1921.) Norway deposited ratification, October 3, 1921. (Date of signature, September 6, 1921.) Sweden gave signature August 16, 1921; ratification not required.

[25] *Rigsdagstidenden* (1920-1921). *Folketinget*, II, p. 5949 (April 27, 1921) ; *Landstinget*, p. 2180 (April 29, 1921).

[26] *Folketinget*, II, pp. 5908-15 (April 27, 1921).

[27] *Folketinget* (1920-1921), p. 5908.

House, traditionally opposed to compulsory arbitration, supported ratification.[28] On July 21, 1921, the Norwegian Storting, without debate, accepted the report of the Constitution Committee, which unanimously advised adherence to the Optional Clause and to the Statute of the Court.[29]

The fight of the small States, chiefly the former European neutrals, for compulsory jurisdiction has been a hard and slow one. At the end of 1921 only eight States were bound by the Optional Clause. Most of the Latin American States had not signed the Optional Clause by 1930, and eleven of them had not even ratified the Protocol to the Statute of the Court by that year.[30] As for the Great Powers, they too were hesitant. When the Assembly opened in 1924 only fifteen States had accepted Article 36, and not a single Great Power was included in the number. Dr Nansen and other representatives of the small nations of Europe expressed their keen disappointment.[31] The reticence of the Great Powers (and indeed some of the smaller Powers) to accept in advance judicial settlement for justiciable disputes strengthened the conviction of the Northern States that they were a unique "group," with a chosen mission to perform. For some purposes the "group" was larger than for others, depending on the number of supporters that could be won for the Scandinavian or "Five Neutral Powers" point of view. Too often this special outlook was referred to in the debates in the Danish, Norwegian and Swedish parliaments as the "small State" point of view, probably because of an underlying feeling that all small States had a common interest (whether they acted upon it or not).[32]

When the doctrine of compulsory jurisdiction of the Court was finally accepted by all the permanent members of the Council (except

[28] *Riksdagens Protokoll* (1921). *F.K.*, 43: 65 *ff.*; *A.K.*, 53: 57.
[29] *Stortings Forhandlinger* (1921), Vol. 6a. *Innst. S.L.XVI*; and Vol. 7b (*S. Tidende*), pp. 2930-1.
[30] *L.N.O.J*, XI (1931), pp. 1692 *ff*.
[31] *5A.P.*, 38.
[32] See for instance Dr Munch's speech in the *Folketing*, October 22, 1924. *Rigsdagstidenden* (1924-1925), *Folketing*, I, p. 511; also on November 15, 1928, *Rigsdagstidenden* (1928-1929). *Folketing*, I, pp. 1419-20. Concerning the unity of outlook of the non-Great Powers in the League of Nations, see W. E. Rappard, "Small States in the League of Nations," *Political Science Quarterly*, XLIX (December 1934), pp. 544-75.

Japan),[33] it was only after many Assemblies in which the Scandinavian delegations had well played their rôle as "the conscience of the Great Powers."[34] During this period the Great Powers were told that the other Powers would have gladly taken them as an example, if they had been more deserving of it.[35] Meanwhile in true Ibsenian fashion, some time before the body politic had been converted and had accepted the position of the leaders, the leaders themselves had moved on to a new and better programme. Later in this chapter another Scandinavian initiative will be considered, which sought to circumscribe power-politics in a network of compulsory arbitration agreements of a more far-reaching nature.

One of the arguments which had been advanced in the Committee of Jurists against writing into the Statute of the Court a provision for compulsory jurisdiction was the constitutional argument that to do so would be contrary to Article XIII of the Covenant. This article provided:

> Disputes as to the interpretation of a treaty, as to any question of international law, as to the existence of a fact which if established would constitute a breach of any international obligation, or as to the extent and nature of the reparation to be made for any such breach, are declared to be among those which are generally suitable for judicial settlement.

As it was deemed "desirable to make this obligation to have recourse to arbitration more absolute and more precise," the Danish, Norwegian and Swedish Governments introduced amendments at the First Assembly to remove the word "generally"[36] from this article. This proposal, however, was declared unacceptable by the committee on amendments which met in 1921, on the ground that it was contrary to the spirit of the Covenant, which did not wish to introduce compul-

[33] More than forty States were bound by the Optional Clause in May 1935. *Oppenheim* (fifth ed.), Vol. II, p. 58. Germany deposited ratification as of February 29, 1928; Great Britain, February 5, 1930; France, April 25, 1931; Italy, September 7, 1931. *L.N.O.J.*, XIV (1933), pp. 14 *ff*.

[34] This expression was used by the Norwegian Prime Minister, M. Lykke, in the Storting in 1927. See *Stortings Forhandlinger* (May 21, 1927), Vol. 7b, p. 1518.

[35] See M. Hambro's speech, *8A.P.*, 57.

[36] See the "Comment by the Swedish Government" attached to the draft amendments proposed by that Government. *L.N.O.J.*, I (1920), p. 356. For the Danish, Norwegian and Swedish Amendments, see *ibid.*, pp. 353 *ff*.

sory arbitration.[37] The Scandinavian States were therefore reduced in their efforts for extending the acceptance in advance of judicial settlement, to agitation for wider adherence to the Optional Clause.

The most notable occasion in which Scandinavian efforts have been directed towards implementing the use of the Permanent Court arose during the Corfu affair of 1923. The situation which resulted from Italy's aggressive action against the Greek island, led Council members to recognize the need for referring certain questions of interpretation of the Covenant to trained jurists. When it was proposed to utilize the services of a special committee of jurists, M. Branting objected.[38] He thought that the questions formulated by the committee should be referred to the Permanent Court of International Justice for an advisory opinion. In the Council he stated that no matter how competent a committee of jurists might be, in public opinion it would not hold the same position of authority and impartiality as the Permanent Court of International Justice. Moreover, Article XIV of the Covenant provided for advisory opinions in such cases. The opposition to the Swedish view was unyielding, and on Cecil's appeal, Branting refrained from voting against the motion to refer the question to a committee of jurists.[39] He reserved the right, however, to explain his view to the Assembly, where his renewed defence of the Court was supported by his Danish and Norwegian colleagues.[40]

In practice, Scandinavian States have demonstrated their willingness to abide by Court settlement. On July 12, 1931, Denmark filed application against Norway, requesting the Permanent Court, by virtue of its jurisdiction under the Optional Clause, to declare unlawful the declaration of occupation of East Greenland promulgated two days before by the Norwegian Government.[41] No objection was raised by the Norwegian Government to the jurisdiction of the Court under Article 36, paragraph 2, despite the fact that the question in dispute was one involving the extent of the national domain.[42] Yet

[37] 2A.1C.(I), 151.
[38] L.N.O.J., IV (1923), 26C., pp. 1330, 1331, 1341-2, 1349.
[39] ibid., pp. 1350, 1352.
[40] 4A.P., 60, 140, 141-2.
[41] Publications de la Cour Permanente de Justice Internationale, Series A/B No. 53. Judgment of April 5, 1933, p. 23.
[42] Compare Hudson, op. cit., p. 405.

the feelings aroused as a result of this long-continued dispute ought not to be underestimated. As one writer said in 1931, "what makes the loss of Greenland rankle so much in retrospect[43] is the Norwegians' acute consciousness of their ascendancy in Arctic pursuits, which has rendered most of them blind to the merits of Danish colonization among the Eskimos."[44]

The decision of the Court, which by a vote of twelve to two upheld Danish sovereignty,[45] brought, in addition to natural disappointment in Norway, a feeling of relief at the removal of a factor so disturbing to the friendly relations of the two peoples of such different temperaments.[46] At no time did the Governments, or any of the political parties in either country, recommend the use of non-pacific means for the settlement of this ancient and vexing controversy. If it had become an established tradition that Denmark and Norway should quarrel within certain bounds, the words of Oscar I, King of Sweden and Norway, spoken in 1856, had not been forgotten; he then declared at a great student festival in Stockholm that "henceforth a war between the Scandinavian brethren will be impossible."[47]

In the 1928 Assembly the Norwegian and Swedish delegates again urged the use of the Permanent Court for an interpretation of the Covenant.[48] It was suggested that the League's authority would be increased by the speedy settlement of the question whether the Council is entitled to ask the Permanent Court for an advisory opinion on legal matters by a majority vote, or whether unanimity is required, with or without the votes of the parties to the dispute. This question had frequently arisen during the consideration of previous international disputes, and time and again the Council had failed to ask for an advisory opinion when objected to by one of the disputants. Since the Council was not clear as to its own competence, the Court, it was argued by the Scandinavians, should be invited to decide this point.[49]

[43] He is referring to the time when Norwegian sovereignty over Greenland was unquestioned.

[44] Special Correspondent (Stockholm) of *The Times*. *The Times*, August 4, 1931 ("Three Northern Neighbours").

[45] *Series A/B* No. 53, p. 75.

[46] *American-Scandinavian Review*, June-July 1933, p. 365.

[47] Svanström and Palmstierna, *A History of Sweden*, p. 338.

[48] *9A.P.*, 73.

[49] *St. med.* nr. 3 (1929), p. 27.

At a later meeting of the Assembly the Swiss delegation followed this lead by introducing a resolution which invited the Council to consider the advisability of obtaining the Court's opinion.[50] But the opposition of the delegates of all the States permanently represented on the Council (except Germany) made necessary an amendment, to the effect that the Council might authorize the study of this question "when circumstances permit." This courteous way of rejecting the Scandinavian-Swiss proposal was unsatisfactory to Dr Nansen, who again urged, though unsuccessfully, that the Court should be asked to clear the confusion.[51] M. Frede Castberg, in the committee, took the untenable position that the Court's prestige would not suffer if an advisory opinion were not accepted by all States, since an advisory opinion has no legal binding force.[52] It was really to counteract this view that the Great Powers had opposed the Swiss amendment. For, as M. Fromageot of France pointed out, since in practice an advisory opinion had become of the same importance as a judgment, it would be improper to request the Court for an advisory opinion without the consent of both parties. To do so would be equivalent to enforcing members to submit a dispute to arbitration, which was not required by the Covenant.

In 1936 the Danish, Finnish and Swedish Governments reaffirmed the Norwegian view that an advisory opinion is not to be considered as possessing authority equal to that of a judgment strictly so-called, and they maintained that a simple majority either in the Council or the Assembly was adequate to authorize a request.[53]

The Election of Judges and Registrar of the Permanent Court

A word should be said of the position which nationals of Denmark, Norway and Sweden have held on the Permanent Court of International Justice. The Swedish Foreign Office stated in its official report on the Second Assembly of the League that the election of judges in 1921 ought, from the Swedish standpoint, to be considered as satisfactory even though the Swedish candidate was not elected; for the small neutral States obtained a good representation, in that

[50] See *9A.1C.*, 40, 43, 57.
[51] *9A.P.*, 139.
[52] *9A.1C.*, 46.
[53] *L. of N. Doc.*, C. 543, M. 351, 1936, V, 9.

among the eleven judges chosen were a Dane, a Swiss and a Dutch-man, and, among the four deputy-judges, a Norwegian.[54]

The election was indeed a tribute to the reputation for impartiality which these States enjoyed. On the other hand, nationals of the eight European States (excluding the Great Powers) which participated in the War were awarded only two judgeships.[55]

The election, however, gave M. Johan Castberg a much desired opportunity to attack in the Storting Scandinavian collaboration, or, as he called it, "Scandinavian politics."[56] It appears that the national nominating groups of Denmark, Norway and Sweden had sought to make an agreement concerning the persons named. Each group nominated two judges from its own country and one each from the other two Scandinavian countries.[57] M. D. G. G. Nyholm (Denmark) was nominated by each of the three groups, as was Baron Marks von Würtemberg (Sweden). But the Norwegian official candidate, M. F. V. N. Beichmann, was not supported by the Swedish group, who nominated M. G. Gran (Norway) instead. As M. K. H. L. Hammarskjöld, former Swedish Prime Minister, the other Swedish nominee, had been supported by the Italian and Chinese groups, Baron Marks von Würtemberg withdrew his nomination. The resulting situation made it appear that Judge Nyholm was the special candidate of ·the Northern countries as his name alone appeared on all three lists.[58] At any rate, he was elected to the Court, and M. Beichmann was elected to the post of deputy-judge. M. Castberg condemned such political scheming and pointed to the unsatisfactory outcome as one reason for not resorting to Scandinavian "group" politics. It may be noted, however, that Norway had fared better than Sweden, whose Foreign Office had declared itself "satisfied."

The practical disadvantage of failure to agree on a common ticket was demonstrated at the second regular election of the Court in 1930, when not a single Scandinavian was elected to the Court, despite the fact that the number of judges had been increased by four. Both the Norwegian and Swedish delegations explained the

[54] *U.N.F.* (1921), p. 3.
[55] *St. med.* nr. 5 (1922), p. 6.
[56] *Stortingstidende* (September 27, 1921), at pp. 3448-9.
[57] *L.N.O.J.*, II (1921), pp. 811-18.
[58] For the Norwegian version, see *St. med.* nr. 5 (1922), p. 5.

outcome on the ground of a "lack of accord."[59] By the closest of margins M. Åke Hammarskjöld, the Registrar of the Court (not to be confused with the Swedish nominee in 1921), was defeated for the fifteenth place by M. Urrutia of Colombia, after both Assembly and Council had given M. Hammarskjöld a majority vote on different ballots. It is fitting to say of M. Hammarskjöld, who was Registrar from the origin of the Permanent Court in 1922 until 1936, that the way he has organized the registry of the Court "has brought great credit to the country from which he comes."[60] Finally, on October 8, 1936, M. Åke Hammarskjöld was chosen as a judge of the Court at the special election of that date.

B. The Development and Codification of International Law

The legalistic tone of "Scandinavian internationalism" permeated nearly all of the schemes for a League of Nations which were contributed in the North during the War. We have frequently stressed the Scandinavian desire to institute the rule of law. The rule of the Court rather than the rule of the Concert of Great Powers was the end to be pursued if justice were to reign in the world.

The Scandinavian Governmental Commissions of 1918 had recognized a distinction between justiciable and non-justiciable disputes, and the fact that, under existing condition of international law, many disputes would not be capable of settlement by an international court on strictly legal lines. They had recommended, therefore, that the codification and development of international law must be effected "in order that the legal method might become more and more the general means of action."[61] International conferences on the model of those at The Hague in 1899 and 1907 should meet at fixed intervals to prepare conventions bearing on all questions of general world interest.

This Scandinavian proposal was examined by the Committee of Jurists which prepared the Statute of the Permanent Court of Inter-

---

[59] *U.N.F.* (1930), p. 84. The Norwegian delegations state that no Scandinavian judge was elected "because of a lack of accord and certain other circumstances." *St. med.* nr. 3 (1931), p. 14. Compare, *Beretning til Rigsdagen Angaaende Folkeforbundets Ellevte Forsamling i Genève*, pp. 48-9, where it is said that the Danish vote was given to Åke Hammarskjöld after the first ballot.

[60] Bellquist, *op. cit.*, p. 318.

[61] Article 73 of the "Draft Convention for an International Juridical Organization."

national Justice, who in turn suggested that the work begun for codification by The Hague Conferences should be continued and supplemented.[62] The question, however, was indefinitely postponed by the First Assembly after Lord Robert Cecil had declared that conditions were not then favourable for this undertaking.[63]

No special initiative was made by the League to advance the codification or development of international law along definite lines until the Swedish Minister for Foreign Affairs, Baron Marks von Würtemberg, introduced a proposal at the Fifth Assembly.[64] He referred to the keen interest which public opinion in a number of countries was showing in the development of international treaty law. In view of what had already been done in this field without following a definite plan, he thought that much could be expected if its work were systematically organized. He did not classify himself with certain theorists who thought it possible to codify international law in short order. But the Swedish statesman advocated efforts for the building up of "a system of inter-State engagements, particularly in fields where certain main principles of international law are already accepted," but where a degree of vagueness existed regarding details of application. He also wished efforts to be made in certain fields "where there are no recognized rules," but a growing need for them, or where existing rules no longer meet present requirements.[65]

To give effect to these suggestions the Swedish delegation proposed that the Council should be asked to request the members of the League to submit subjects of international law, which they believed expedient to examine with a view to reaching international agreement. The Danish delegate, M. Andersen, "noted with lively satisfaction" the Swedish initiative, and proposed that States not members of the

[62] See Finch, *American Journal of International Law*, Vol. 19 (1925), p. 538. *Procès-Verbaux of the Proceedings of the Committee of Jurists*, pp. 747-8. Mr Philip Marshall Brown states that the Committee of Jurists "did not specifically urge the *codification* of international law. The conference to be called was to be termed 'a Conference for the *Advancement* of International Law.' Though individual statesmen and jurists were undoubtedly thinking of statutory legislation, which should include not only *accepted* law but also *new* law, the general purpose in mind was the *clarification* of international law." See Mr Brown's article "The Codification of International Law," in *A.J.I.L.*, Vol. 29 (1935), at p. 27.
[63] The League of Nations, *Ten Years of World Cooperation*, p. 165.
[64] *5A.P.*, 82-3.
[65] *ibid.*

League be invited to participate in the preparatory work.[66] On September 22, 1924, the Assembly adopted a resolution which modified only in detail the Swedish proposal, and in December the Council adopted Professor Undén's report to proceed with the preliminary business of codification.[67] A former Swedish Prime Minister, M. K. Hjalmar Hammarskjöld, was made Chairman of the Committee of Experts for the Progressive Codification of International Law.[68] No other Scandinavian was represented. The omission of a Norwegian national was particularly irksome to that Government, and led to a complaint by M. Hambro at the Seventh Assembly. He thought it unfair that Norway, "for whose very existence the questions concerning territorial waters are of the utmost importance," and who had "a longer and more broken coast line than any other European country," was not represented.[69]

In the years of preparation for the conference (1925-1930), the three Northern States gave their unqualified support to the work which was being undertaken. They, more than many, were convinced of its importance.[70] In the Assemblies they opposed all obstructions[71] placed in the way. While for many objects they were proposing economy, for codification they suggested an increase of funds.[72]

In September 1929 prior to the meeting of the First Conference for Codification at The Hague, Baron Marks von Würtemberg was already proposing that the experts should meet soon after the Assembly in 1930 to consider the results achieved by the conference, and to prepare for a second conference to continue the law-making function of the League.

The failure of The Hague Conference of 1930 to effect important agreements on the subjects of nationality, territorial waters, and responsibility of States, subjects on which accord had seemed most likely, naturally aroused genuine disappointment in Scandinavia.[73]

---

[66] 5A.1C., 26.
[67] L.N.O.J., VI, 32C., pp. 120-1.
[68] St. med. nr. 14 (1925), pp. 20-1.
[69] 7A.P., 49. See also St. med. nr. 3 (1927) p. 8, supra, p. 161.
[70] See M. Moltesen's speech, 8A.P., 52.
[71] 8A.P., 57; 9A.1C., 11; 9A.4C., 96.
[72] 8A.4C., 62-3; St. med. nr. 3 (1928), pp. 11-12.
[73] The results of the conference were a draft convention on nationality, a protocol on military obligations, and two protocols on statelessness.

When the Eleventh Assembly met a few months after the adjournment of the Conference, Baron Ramel of Sweden was compelled to
admit that the conference "did not yield the positive results which
we were justified in expecting after such detailed and preparatory
work."[74] He urged that discouragement should not tempt the League
to abandon the work, for "international legislation is, in the very
nature of things, slow." The Norwegian Government, for its part,
"was of the opinion that a new conference cannot be called with
benefit until further preparatory work has so far advanced that
positive results of value can be expected."[75] Both Governments
introduced a resolution asking the Council to institute an inquiry
concerning how best to continue the work towards codification.[76]

The failure of the First Codification Conference led to renewed
reflection on the real object of codification. Was the purpose of the
conventions drawn up at The Hague to be declaratory or enactory?
That is, was the object to convert customary law into written law, or
was it merely to supplement it with new law? At the 1930 Assembly,
resolutions were introduced by the Belgian,[77] and by the British,
French, German, Greek and Italian delegations,[78] stating the principle
that "codification," as applied to the work of developing international law undertaken by the League, should be limited to the laying
down of rules for the future which do not already exist as customary
law. On the other hand, the Norwegian and Swedish delegations
asked that the codification work of the League should include the
effort to formulate international conventions containing definite rules
"either based on customary international law or being entirely new
law."[79]

These conflicting views were amplified in a number of letters submitted to the League following a resolution of the 1930 Assembly

[74] *11A.P.*, 62.

[75] Instructions given the delegation to the Eleventh Assembly. *St. med.* nr. 3
(1931), p. 11.

In the Fourth Committee the Swedish delegate urged an appropriation of 45,000
Swiss francs for the Committee of Experts on the Progressive Codification of International Law, whose work should be continued. *11A.4C.*, 44-5.

[76] *11A.1C.*, 159.

[77] *11A.1C.*, 160.

[78] *11A.1C.*, 158-9.

[79] *11A.1C.*, 159.

which requested the observations of the Governments on the future work of codification.[80]

The letter of the Swedish Government of July 6, 1931, although admitting that the results of the First Codification Conference were of little practical value, deemed it important for the League to continue the work of codification. The Swedish Government therein objected to the view of certain delegations to the 1930 Assembly[81] that the League should make no further attempt at the determination and codification of existing customary law. In its view "consolidatory codification" as well as "legislative codification"—to use terms of the British Foreign Office[82] had a proper place in the League's work. The Swedish Government stated:[83]

> The Swedish Government is not convinced that it is wise to begin by excluding certain important subjects from the preliminary investigations in view of a new codification conference. The customary law of nations is a singularly vague conception, and several of the principles of law which it is made to include are so general that courts of law find it difficult to use them as a basis of decisions, while in other instances they give rise to differences of opinion involving considerable practical inconveniences. It is also conceivable that the principles of customary law of a previous age no longer meet the needs of our time, and consequently require revising by means of international legislation taking the form of a general convention.
>
> The Swedish Government, however, considers that it is not to a codification conference that one should assign the task of defining the scope and effect of existing customary law. This task, in its opinion, belongs rather to the international courts

[80] *12A.1C.*, 98-114. See especially the letters from the British, French, Swiss and Swedish Governments. See also Manley O. Hudson, "The Prospects for Future Codification," *A.J.I.L.*, Vol. 26 (1932), pp. 137-40. A large majority of the Governments replying were in favour of continuing the work for codification. "Only the Indian, Italian, and to some extent, the British, Governments expressed strong doubts as to the wisdom of attempting to proceed with the work of codification." *ibid.*, p. 140.

[81] See the draft resolution of the British, French, German, Greek and Italian delegations, *11A.1C.*, 158-9, and draft resolution submitted by the Belgian delegation. *11A.1C.*, 160.

[82] *12A.1C.*, 101 *ff.* "Letter of the Government of Great Britain and Northern Ireland" (April 28, 1931).

[83] *12A.1C.*, 111. Apparently no reply was made by the Danish and Norwegian Governments.

and to writers on doctrine. A codification conference should adopt such principles as it deems necessary and valuable without deciding whether their adoption constitutes a consecration or a revision of existing customary law. It is to this extent only that the Swedish Government supports the view that a future codification conference should not concern itself with the determination of customary international law.

The Royal Government is, therefore, of the opinion that the committee entrusted with the preliminary work of deciding what questions are suitable for codification should also be left free to examine matters in respect of which rules of customary law are thought already to exist, if it considers that codification of the law relating to them would be advantageous from a practical point of view—whether because the existing rules are not generally recognized, are too vague for the courts of law to use them as the basis of decisions, or stand in the need of revision.

This interesting declaration was, however, of no great practical value for, as Dr Lauterpacht has written, "in the present state of international organization, codification must be left out of account as an effective means of developing international law. The resolution of the Assembly of the League in 1931 leaves little doubt on the matter."[84] So low were hopes for "consolidatory codification" that even before the 1931 Assembly the Norwegian Government informed its delegation that it "found no grounds, under the existing international situation, for seeking an acceleration of the work of codification."[85]

During the years of preparatory study for the Conference on the Codification of International Law, the work proceeded largely on the basis that the task of the conference was one of "consolidation," that is, one of establishing "in precise and accurate legal phraseology" rules of international law already in existence. While the experts were searching for subjects "ripe for consolidation," another process of determining international rules, which the British Foreign Office

[84] Lauterpacht, *The Development of International Law*, p. 4. Professor Hudson wrote that "The general effect of the Assembly's resolution is to bestow a blessing on codification as a hope for the future, to shift the responsibility to Governments. and to leave it wholly problematical whether any second codification conference will ever be held." *A.J.I.L.*, Vol. 26 (1932), p. 143.

[85] *St. med.* nr. 3 (1932), p 8.

had discreetly labelled "codification," was in full swing.[86] A flood of international conventions dealing with social, economic, financial, industrial, technical and cultural inter-State relations appeared on the Geneva front, many of them concluded under the auspices of the League of Nations. It was necessary to recognize, however, that great was the disparity between the number of conventions adopted by technical conferences and bearing an array of signatures, and the number which had actually come into force. At the Tenth Assembly, the Danish delegation introduced a proposal designed to alter this serious situation.[87] M. Andersen urged that a mixed committee of enquiry be named by the Council and the Assembly to ascertain why States signed conventions which they were not prepared to ratify. He indicated two methods which might be tried to eradicate this evil. A special period should be laid down in a proposed convention within which it would have to be ratified, with a stipulation whereby a new meeting of the contracting States might be held if the ratification had not been brought into force. It might also be useful to have delegations report at each Assembly on the progress of ratification in their respective countries.

The Danish delegation attached great importance to this question. M. Stauning, who had but recently returned to power at the head of a Socialist-Radical coalition, admitted that Denmark was not blameless on this score. His Government, however, was prepared to make amends, and had already examined all conventions which had been signed, with a view to submitting a large number for ratification at the opening of the next session of the Rigsdag. To improve the general situation, the Danish Prime Minister urged caution before the conclusion of conventions for which there was no guarantee of a sufficient number of accessions. He alluded to the danger of adopting conventions "so detailed that they lack the elasticity which would render them adaptable to the internal conditions of the various countries."[88] The Norwegian delegate, M. Hambro, stated that if the Government delegates had the moral courage to vote against conventions which they thought irrelevant or of little value, the number

[86] Letter of the Government of Great Britain and Northern Ireland (April 28, 1931). *12A.1C.*, 102.

[87] *10A.1C.*, 34.

[88] *10A.P.*, 41-2 (September 4, 1929).

of conventions that States would be asked to ratify would no doubt decrease.[89]

As a result of the proposal made by the Danish delegation, the Assembly instructed the Secretariat to compile annually double-column tables giving the position with regard to signatures, ratifications and accessions in respect of conventions concluded under the League's auspices.[90] The Council was requested to appoint a committee of investigation, which, under the chairmanship of M. Scavenius of Denmark, reported to the Eleventh Assembly certain recommendations designed to secure the ratification of existing League conventions.[91] The subsequent resolution fixing the preparatory procedure to be followed for general conventions negotiated under the League's auspices must, therefore, be considered as due partially to the Danish initiative made at the 1929 Assembly.[92]

C. Conciliation and Arbitration.

It is sometimes said that "the foreign policy of Sweden (as of Norway) is to have no foreign policy." Whatever service, if any, this half-truth may have rendered as a characterization of the period before the War, it cannot be considered as applicable to the period following Sweden's entry into the League of Nations. One of the clearest proofs of a positive Swedish foreign policy lies in her activity in behalf of the organization of machinery for the pacific settlement of disputes. In addition to judicial procedure before the Permanent Court of International Justice, the technique of conciliation and arbitration has been energetically sponsored by the Swedish, as indeed also by the Danish and Norwegian Governments through their Geneva policies.

The conversion of prominent peace advocates and political leaders in Scandinavia to the merits of conciliation as a method for dealing with political disputes had become widespread by the end of the War. In a previous chapter emphasis was laid on the conciliation proposals made by the official Scandinavian Commissions which in 1918 studied

[89] 10A.1C., 40.
[90] Monthly Summary, Vol. IX, pp. 283-4.
[91] 11A.1C., 141 ff. (Annex 7).
[92] For the text of this procedure, see Monthly Summary, Vol. XI, pp. 266-7.

the question of the neutral States' interests.[93] At Paris the following March representatives of the Northern States had endeavoured, although in vain, to include in the Covenant a definite provision for obligatory reference of all non-legal disputes to permanent conciliation commissions modelled on the lines of the Bryan commissions of 1914.[94]

Unsuccessful at Hotel Crillon, the Scandinavians prepared for a modification of Articles XII and XV at the First Assembly, where amendments were introduced by Norway and Sweden requiring members of the League to set up bilateral conciliation commissions, the recourse to which would be obligatory for non-justiciable disputes.[95] It was another expression of the traditional Northern aversion to "international politics," which it was feared might operate within the Council acting as conciliator. The object was to "depoliticize" conciliation,[96] that is, to assure "an expert, independent, and non-partisan type of conciliation as compared with that conducted by the Council, whose members are in law representatives of their States, and as such are not always free from political bias and from the influence of political considerations not necessarily connected with the merits of the actual dispute."[97] Although Dr Lie said in the 1921 Assembly that the Norwegian proposal "was in no sense conceived in a spirit of distrust of the Council's high and delicate duties as *pacificator mundi*,"[98] his arguments do not seem to have been the essential motivating force for the Norwegian and Swedish initiative. Bilateral conciliation commissions, he said, would not only serve as useful

[93] *supra*, Chapter III, pp. 37, 38.
[94] *supra*, Chapter IV, p. 56. In Dr Max Habicht's view, the Bryan commissions are not entrusted with the task of proposing a scheme for the settlement of the dispute and therefore should be called Commissions of Investigation, rather than Commissions of Conciliation. Habicht, *op. cit.*, pp. 1021-2.
[95] Draft Amendments and Additions to the Covenant of the League Transmitted by the Norwegian Government, *L.N.O.J.*, I, 6, pp. 357 *ff*. Amendments to the Norwegian Draft Amendments to the Covenant, submitted by the Swedish Government. *1A.1C.(I)*, 82-9.
The Norwegian proposal assigned powers of arbitration to the commissions as well; the Swedish proposal limited the commissions' rôle to that of conciliation. *3A.P. (II)*, 140-1.
[96] Zimmern, *op. cit.*, p. 344.
[97] Oppenheim, *International Law*, Vol. II, p. 17 (fifth ed., edited by Lauterpacht).
[98] *2A.P.*, 823-4.

"filters" to relieve the Council of excessive burdens;[99] they would strengthen the participation of individual League members, who under the existing arrangement played too passive a rôle in the work for peace.

The Swedish Foreign Office, in the Introduction to its Report on the work of the League in 1922, more accurately states the reason which prompted this initiative two years before. "The Council had a quite too marked political character to make it appropriate to serve as a conciliation organ in first instance."[100] Indeed the "Explanatory Statement" of the Swedish Government laid before the First Assembly had openly expressed the same view.[101]

The Committee on Amendments, whose report was submitted to the 1921 Assembly, admitted the Norwegian and Swedish claim that "in theory, the commission best qualified to fulfil successfully the rôle of mediator was, beyond doubt, one composed of members chosen by the parties, and therefore of a more intimate character."[102] But it could not recommend the adoption of the proposed amendments because it feared that a world-wide system of conciliation commissions might result in the submission of disputes to bodies of insufficient authority to effect a peaceful settlement. It seemed more advisable not to make this particular procedure obligatory, but to leave the choice of method to the discretion of the Council, which could act in accordance with the requirements of the particular case.[103]

The Second Assembly, however, was willing to refer the question of conciliation to a special committee for renewed study, which took place in 1922, and led to the adoption of a resolution by the Third Assembly recommending that League members conclude conventions between one another providing for the establishment of bilateral conciliation commissions.[104] A model convention was agreed upon similar

[99] *3A.1C.,* 17.

[100] *U.N.F.* (1922), p. 9.

[101] *1A.1C.(I),* 82. It should be noted that the Norwegian amendments assigned the commissions arbitral powers as well, while the Swedish Government insisted that it was unwise to confuse conciliation and arbitration procedures by use of the same commissions for both. *ibid.,* p. 83.

[102] *2A.1C.(I),* 148-9.

[103] The sub-committee of the First Committee's Report, *2A.1C.(I),* 148-51; *2A.P.,* 823-6.

[104] *2A.P.,* 830; *3A.P.(I),* 196-7 (Report of the First Committee).

to that already entered into by Sweden and Chile at Stockholm on March 26, 1920, which was "the first post-War treaty of conciliation."[105] The Council was authorized to make use of such a commission, if this were deemed advisable in executing its obligations under Article XV.

The Swedish Government accepted the Assembly's resolution, but declared that it could not abandon its view that an obligation to set up conciliation commissions should be laid upon States.[106] In the treaty which had been negotiated with Chile, the parties agree not to submit a dispute to the Council of the League before first having laid it before the conciliation board to be instituted.[107] The Norwegian Government considered the Assembly resolution as only a "first step," nevertheless a "not unimportant step in the direction at which the Norwegian proposal was aiming."[108] The Danish Government, which had introduced no proposal of its own and which was unfavourable to the compulsory requirements of the original Norwegian and Swedish amendments, was now able fully to support the resolution of the Assembly.[109] It will be remembered that at the meeting with the committee of the Paris Peace Conference in 1919, the Danish delegation had proposed a central conciliation board, distinct from the Council.[110]

Desirous of carrying into effect the principle laid down by the 1922 Assembly, the representatives of Denmark, Norway, Sweden, and Finland signed similar conventions on June 27, 1924, for the establishment of permanent conciliation commissions.[111] That is to say, each of these States concluded bipartite conventions with the other

[105] *League of Nations Treaty Series*, IV, pp. 273-9. Habicht, *Post-War Treaties for the Pacific Settlement of International Disputes*, p. 1022.

[106] *3A.P.(I)*, 198.

[107] Article I.

[108] *St. med.* nr. 8 (1923), pp. 10-11; *3A.1C.*, 15.

[109] See *2A.1C.(I)*, 33; *3A.1C.*, 17; *Rigsdagstidenden* (1922-1923); *Tillæg* A. II, pp. 5500 ff.

[110] See *supra*, Chapter IV, p. 56.

[111] Convention between Norway and Sweden. *Treaty Series*, XXVII: 310.
Convention between Finland and Sweden. *Treaty Series*, XXIX: 20.
Convention between Finland and Norway. *Treaty Series*, XXIX: 404.
Convention between Denmark and Finland. *Treaty Series*, XXXIII: 132.
Convention between Denmark and Norway. *Treaty Series*, XXXIII: 174.
Convention between Denmark and Sweden. *Treaty Series*, XXXIII: 150.

three for the setting up of bilateral commissions of enquiry and conciliation. It was agreed to endow these commissions with authority to investigate and propose a settlement of "all disputes of any nature whatever which it has not been possible to settle within reasonable time through diplomatic channels, and which should not, under the terms of the Statute of the Permanent Court of International Justice or of any other agreement between the parties, be submitted either to the Permanent Court or to a court of arbitration."[112] This exception to the jurisdiction of the Scandinavian conciliation commissions was a departure from the Bryan treaties which these States had made in 1914, according to which legal disputes might also be submitted for investigation. The inter-Scandinavian treaties also differed in this respect from the Swedish-Swiss treaty of June 2, 1924,[113] and the Danish-Swiss treaty of June 6, 1924,[114] which in Article I, paragraph 3, stated that the parties may agree that a dispute which is capable of judicial settlement under Article 36, paragraph 2, of the Statute of the Court shall be previously submitted to the procedure of conciliation.[115]

The commissions set up by the inter-Scandinavian conventions consist of five members, of whom each Government chooses one of its own nationals and one from a third State, while by common agreement the Governments choose the fifth member, who must be a national of a State not otherwise represented on the commission. If the Governments fail to agree, appointment is made by the President or Vice-President of the Permanent Court of International Justice. Members of the commissions are chosen for three years, although each of the parties may, in certain circumstances, substitute for an ordinary member a person having special knowledge with respect to the dispute in question. Unlike the Bryan commissions, which

112 Article I of these conventions.
113 *Treaty Series,* XXXIII: 200. The expression "inter-Scandinavian" does not include Finland.
114 *Treaty Series,* XXXIV: 176.
115 As Herr Eliel Löfgren points out, there are exceptions even in the inter-Scandinavian conciliation conventions to the principle that legal disputes should be referred directly to the Court. This would occur if the parties expressly agree to submit the dispute to conciliation, if objection is not raised against the jurisdiction of the commission, or if a legal question perchance should fall outside the competence of the Permanent Court of International Justice or special arbitration Tribunals. See citation in note 118.

strictly speaking were commissions of investigation ("fact-finding") rather than conciliation commissions,[116] the Scandinavian commissions are required to propose a settlement, "if a settlement is possible and if at least three members agree to the proposals."[117] The proposals for conciliation which need not rest on legal grounds, but only upon a "free judgment" may or may not be accepted by the parties to the dispute.[118]

The Scandinavian States made other bilateral conciliation treaties in the period between 1924 and 1927, but by 1926 the more common practice, as we shall see, was to combine within one treaty a procedure of conciliation with that of arbitration and court settlement.

When the Stauning Government submitted the Finnish, Norwegian, Swedish and Swiss conventions of conciliation to the Danish Rigsdag for ratification, objection was raised by the Conservative minority in both Houses that matters solely within the domestic jurisdiction of States could, under these conventions, be investigated by the commissions, even without the consent of the parties.[119] In future conventions consideration should be taken of the principle laid down in Article XV, paragraph 8, of the Covenant of the League, which exempts domestic questions from mediation. Nevertheless, all of the members of the Select Committee of the Folketing, except Dr Axel Møller, Professor of International Law at the University of Copenhagen, recommended ratification by the Rigsdag.[120] He, like the Conservative minority in the corresponding committee of the Landsting, dissented.[121] When approval was asked of the Chambers, no

[116] See the classification of Dr Habicht, *op. cit.*, pp. 976-7, 1022.

[117] See Article 14. The convention of conciliation between Chile and Sweden of March 26, 1920, merely said that a settlement should be submitted "if circumstances permit."

[118] On these treaties, see Eliel Löfgren, *De Nordiska Förliknings-och Skiljedomsavtalen i deras Ställning till det Internationella Rättsystemet*, pp. 12-13, 40-4. Axel Møller, *International Law in Peace and War*, Vol. II, pp. 4-7.

[119] See the report of the *Folketing* committee of December 10, 1924. *Rigsdagstidenden* (1924-1925), *Tillæg* B, pp. 79-84; and the report of the *Landsting* committee of November 14, 1924, *ibid.*, pp. 15-20.

[120] Holger Andersen, the other Conservative member of the committee, agreed with Dr Møller on the question of "excessive jurisdiction" of the conciliation commissions.

[121] See the minority report of M. Ellinger and M. Schovelin, both Conservatives.

opposition votes were cast against any of these conventions, but some of the members of the Right abstained from voting.[122]

In the Swedish Riksdag no objection to ratification was voiced,[123] and in Norway the conventions were ratified by Royal Resolution without consultation in advance of the Storting.[124]

Although the Danish Government became a party to the Scandinavian conciliation treaties of 1924, it was not wholly satisfied with the typical bilateral agreements which had been effected, at least not in the generalization of this procedure. At the 1925 Assembly a memorandum was submitted which recommended the establishment of a conciliation commission attached to the Permanent Court of International Justice.[125] There were two reasons which prompted this idea. One was to prevent the restriction of the competence of the Court, the other to secure centralization of conciliation. Attention was directed to the tendency of some States, such as Switzerland, to negotiate conventions stipulating that legal disputes should, if desired, be referred to bilateral conciliation commissions before going to the Court. Since a preliminary resort to conciliation might often be very desirable, and since it was deemed undesirable to restrict still further the competence of the Court, the Danish Government thought it advisable to attach a conciliation commission to the Court.[126] This suggestion met with criticism in the Assembly on the ground that the rôle of judge and that of conciliator ought to be kept distinct, and that this proposal created the danger of establishing too close contact between the Court and the proposed conciliation commission.[127]

The second motive was perhaps the more important. For practical and theoretical reasons centralization had much in its favour. The only existing centralization resulted from that provision of Article

[122] *Folketing* (1924-1925), pp. 5674 *ff.* (March 7, 1925); *Landsting* (1924-1925), pp. 205-6.

[123] *Riksdagens Protokoll* (1924). F.K., 28: 50; A.K., 28: 44. See "Constitution Committee's Report nr. 20 (April 4, 1924)—Saml. 5. *Kungl. Maj:ts prop.* nr. 183.

[124] *Stortings Forhandlinger* (1925). *Innst. S.* nr. 113. In this report the *Utenriks- og konstitusjonskomitee* states that the Conciliation treaties were ratified by the Royal Resolution of July 18, 1924.

[125] *6A.1C.*, 51-3.

[126] See also "Statement of Reasons" presented by the Danish delegation to the First Committee. *6A.1C.*, 53-4.

[127] By M. Adatci (Japan) and M. Motta (Switzerland) and others. *6A.1C.*, 11. See also *6A.P.*, 103.

XV of the Covenant, which, however, dealt only with disputes which might lead to rupture. In the Danish view it was desirable to centralize the conciliation treatment of all other conflicts. For one reason it was difficult to find a sufficient number of competent persons to serve on the commissions set up by the ever-growing number of bilateral treaties.[128]

The Danish proposal, however, met with little favour, and the Assembly adopted a resolution calling for the adjournment of the question until a subsequent session.[129] The Danish view should be thought of as an exception to the unity of outlook among the Scandinavian States on the question of conciliation procedure.[130]

In the autumn of 1924, after the Scandinavians had negotiated the Stockholm conciliation conventions with one another and with Finland, the Fifth Assembly drew up the "Geneva Protocol," which sought to fill in the "gaps" of the Covenant by finding a peaceful settlement of every dispute without exception which might arise between States. The Protocol was little influenced by the previous conciliation activity of the Northern States. Its sources were different. Arbitration, not conciliation, was the keystone of this system.

For the moment let us consider the Geneva Protocol, not as an "indivisible whole," but in the light of the Scandinavian attitude towards its provisions for peaceful settlement of disputes. Therein it was specified that all disputes covered by Article 36 of the Statute of the Permanent Court of International Justice should, as the Scandinavian delegations had urged since the foundation of the League, be referred to the Court. M. Lange declared in the Assembly that he was "overjoyed at the prospect of seeing all the Powers, great and small, adhere to Article 36 of the Statute of the Court."[131] The Protocol, moreover, went further. In the last analysis all political disputes (except those aiming at the revision of treaties or which

[128] See also Zahle's speech. 6A.1C., 10.

[129] 6A.P., 103.

[130] In the First Committee, the Norwegian and Swedish delegations were silent in the discussion on this proposal, which was not in accord with their hitherto-expressed policy. For that reason it is difficult to explain the instructions given the Norwegian delegation to support in principle the Danish proposal. St. med. nr. 3 (1926), p. 10.

[131] 5A.P., 210.

sought to jeopardize the existing territorial integrity of States) would find obligatory settlement.[132]

What was the attitude of the Scandinavian States in 1924 towards the compulsory arbitration of all disputes without exception? Although the Northern countries had not previously worked through the League for the acceptance of a general obligation for the pacific settlement of all disputes without exception, it was largely because to do so seemed visionary when, despite their repeated efforts, the Great Powers and many other States had been unwilling to accept compulsory adjudication even to the limited extent of the Optional Clause. In the Fifth Assembly, however, when the British and French Governments gave indications of a determination to join the company of those States which had an advanced arbitration policy, the Scandinavians heartily approved of the effort to realize compulsory arbitration "in so complete a form." M. Zahle pointed out that Denmark had already for a long time advocated this principle, and had applied this system in all arbitration treaties which Denmark had concluded, even on vital questions, "whenever we have obtained the consent of the other party thereto."[133]

On the other hand, Norway and Sweden, like most States, had not yet entered into any treaty providing for compulsory arbitration of political disputes, without making certain reservations as to the *honour, independence* or *vital interests* of States. In a previous chapter, however, it was seen that prior to the War, Norway and Sweden had developed an arbitration policy more far-reaching than the principal Great Powers.[134] When the Fifth Assembly opened, apparently no declaration had been made by the Norwegian and Swedish Governments specifically indicating their willingness to accept compulsory arbitration without exception for all disputes. The report of the Swedish Commission in December 1918, which dealt with an "international juridical organization" stated that it would be "vain et peut-être aussi peu sage" to wish for the achievement of a general accord concerning the judicial or arbitral settlement of all

---

[132] The literature on the Geneva Protocol is voluminous. For purposes of reference D. H. Miller, *The Geneva Protocol,* is convenient. See especially *Records of the Fifth Assembly,* and *Records of the First and Third Committees.*

[133] *5A.P.,* 213. See also, Munch at *5A.3C.,* 56-7.

[134] *supra,* Chapter II, p. 21.

categories of international disputes; but it asked if, for States in the position of the Scandinavian countries, a convention exempting from all reservation the settlement of disputes by arbitration would not on the whole, if it were possible to conclude one, be advantageous.[135] The latest expression of Sweden's arbitration policy, prior to the Fifth Assembly, is found in a letter of the Swedish Government, dated August 24, 1924, to the Secretary-General of the League. It affirmed the adhesion of Sweden to the principle of the extension of arbitration, but expressed doubt whether the majority of States were prepared to accept the submission of all disputes to the decision of a court or other international authority. This letter does not state that the Swedish Government is prepared to do so.[136] When, therefore, M. Branting said in the Assembly on October 2, 1924, that "nothing could give greater satisfaction to the lesser States than to see the principle of compulsory arbitration realized in so complete a form," he seemed to have implied approval of the principle of compulsory arbitration for political disputes.[137] The Norwegian delegation at the Fifth Assembly appears not to have expressed its view on this particular point. In view of the Greenland dispute considerable opinion in Norway was somewhat doubtful of the advisability of extending arbitration to cover "interest" disputes, although in point of fact that dispute was covered by the Optional Clause which had already been accepted almost unanimously.[138]

If the acceptance of compulsory adjudication of justiciable disputes was a victory of the policy faithfully championed by Denmark, Norway and Sweden, the rather complicated system provided in the Protocol for the settlement of political disputes owed much less to Scandinavian activity. However, their wishes were met by providing that a special "committee of arbitration," rather than the Council, should, on the demand of one party, be set up to decide such dis-

---

[135] See *Rapport du Comité d'experts chargé par le Gouvernement Suédois de l'examen du Protocole dit de Genève, relatif au Règlement Pacifique des Différends Internationaux*, pp. 47-8, 107-8.

[136] *L. of N. Doc.* A. 35, 1924, IX (signed by E. Marks de Würtemberg).

[137] *5A.P.*, 220.

[138] In the Sixth Assembly, however, M. Mowinckel, the Norwegian Prime Minister, said that his Government considered it of "primary importance that as many States as possible shall undertake, so far as is feasible, to submit all disputes . . . to pacific settlement by judicial or other means." *6A.P.*, 45.

putes.[189] The preference of the Scandinavians for a "board of Solomons" of their own choice rather than for the Council, whose decision might be coloured by the interests of its members, is understandable in the light of what has already been said with reference to conciliation.[140]

Although the Geneva Protocol was never ratified, it had an influence on the development of the arbitration policy of the Scandinavian States at Geneva. By a decision of the Swedish Government of October 24, 1924, a committee of experts was named to examine the probable consequence of Sweden's adherence to the Protocol.[141] Before the experts finished their assignment, however, the British Government on March 12, 1925, announced at the Council that it found the Protocol unacceptable.[142] The committee interpreted this declaration as a death-blow to the Protocol, but obtained permission from the Swedish Government to present their conclusions on the chief problems raised by the Protocol. The committee's pronouncement on the question of obligatory arbitration of political disputes constitutes an advance from the previous Swedish view. It was declared that if the States were really ready to accept the principle of "arbitration"—that is, pacific settlement whether by judicial decision, arbitral award, or unanimous report of the Council—for political as well as juridical disputes, "Sweden assuredly would have every reason for seeking to assist an advance of such exceptional importance for international organization along juridical lines," and "could only greet with joy the decision of the community of nations to engage in a general convention for the obligatory submission for settlement by pacific means of juridical and political disputes by the methods indicated in the Protocol."[143]

This declaration made by a non-partisan committee appointed by the third Branting Government was supported by members of the committee who had formerly been Prime Ministers in Conservative

[189] See Article 4 of the Protocol.

[140] *supra*, pp. 191 ff.

[141] (*Statens offentliga utredningar 1925:17*) *Utrikesdepartementet, Betänkande rörande det S.K. Genèveprotokollet angående avgörande på fredlig väg av internationella tvister avgivet av tillkallade sakkunnige,* p. 5. The work cited in note (135) *supra* is the French translation, published by the Swedish Foreign Office.

[142] *ibid.*, pp. 6-7.

[143] *Rapport du Comité d'Experts,* p. 108. (Swedish text, *op. cit.*, p. 109.)

and Liberal Governments.[144] The Social Democrat Government, therefore, in which Branting had named Professor Undén as Foreign Minister, decided to press the question of arbitration at the 1925 Assembly. Recognizing that the hope of securing arbitration through the Geneva Protocol was dead, Professor Undén, "like a true pilot setting the new course for the World Ship,"[145] proposed that the Council be asked to resume the study of the principles of compulsory arbitration. In view of the British opposition he questioned the desirability of continuing efforts for a general treaty, suggesting that concentration on bilateral treaties might be a better means of arriving at the same goal.[146] The outcome of this initiative was an Assembly resolution recommending that States conclude special arbitration treaties with a view to facilitating the conclusion of a general treaty in the near future.

If there had been any doubt about Sweden's attachment to "inclusive" arbitration treaties in the previous Assembly, M. Löfgren's speech on September 25, 1925, dissolved those doubts for the future. In contrast with Lord Robert Cecil, who declared that Britain intended to apply the principle of arbitration "from case to case," he stressed the need of the small States for assurance "in advance" that "all disputes, even those concerning the vital interests of the rulers of the world," would be submitted to peaceful settlement.[147]

When Professor Undén directed the League's attention to the advisability of making special rather than general arbitration treaties, he was realistically doing for "arbitration" what Lord Balfour's memorandum of March 12, 1925, did for "security"; that is, while Balfour was preparing the way for Locarno, a regional guarantee-treaty, Undén was christening the beginning of regional "all-in" arbitration-treaties in the North, as a means of increasing the security of that part of Europe.[148] On October 23, 1925, the Norwe-

---

[144] The members of the committee were: N. Edén, former Prime Minister (Liberal), O. von Sydow, former Prime Minister (Conservative), T. Höjer, Swedish Minister at Oslo, and S. Wallengren, Professor at the University of Lund. Also Eliel Löfgren, legal expert in the Ministry of Foreign Affairs, who did not, however, sign the report.

[145] Madariaga, *Disarmament*, p. 137.

[146] *6A.P.*, 39-40.

[147] *6A.P.*, 129.

[148] Compare Eliel Löfgren, *op. cit.*, p. 47.

gian Government, supported by previous unofficial enquiries, took the initiative for the negotiation of an unlimited arbitration treaty with Sweden, which was signed at Oslo, November 25, 1925. A few days later the Danish Government approached the Norwegian Government for the purpose of making a similar treaty between those States, which was signed at Copenhagen on January 15, 1926. By February 3 each of the Scandinavian States had entered into a "Convention for the Pacific Settlement of Disputes" with each of the others, and with Finland.[149]

These conventions are substantially alike. Any legal dispute as defined in Article 36, paragraph 2, of the Statute of the Court, which it has not been found possible to settle by diplomacy, is to be submitted to the Permanent Court of International Justice. Disputes labelled by previous treaties for judicial or arbitral procedure are to be dealt with as therein provided.[150] All other disputes are to be submitted to a specially created Arbitral Tribunal, if it has not been found possible to settle them by the procedure of enquiry and conciliation provided for in the conventions of June 27, 1924, previously described.[151] This Arbitral Tribunal is to be set up in accordance with Title IV, Chapter II, of The Hague Convention of October 18, 1907, and it shall give its award "in accordance with the principles of law and equity."[152] No reservations are made for questions involving the *honour, independence or vital interests* of the Parties; domestic questions are not excluded, nor are disputes belonging to the past. No exception of jurisdiction is made other than that permitting questions, which under

[149] The following Conventions with dates of signatures were negotiated:
Norway and Sweden (November 25, 1925), *Treaty Series,* LX: 295.
Denmark and Sweden (January 14, 1926), *Treaty Series,* LI: 251.
Denmark and Norway (January 15, 1926), *Treaty Series,* LX: 311.
Finland and Sweden (January 29, 1926), *Treaty Series,* XLIX: 367.
Denmark and Finland (January 30, 1926), *Treaty Series,* LI: 367.
Finland and Norway (February 3, 1926), *Treaty Series,* LX: 353.
[150] Article I. This leaves untouched, for example, the Karlstad Arbitration Convention of October 26, 1905. See Löfgren, *op. cit.,* p. 54.
[151] Article II.
[152] M. Eliel Löfgren, the legal expert of the Swedish Foreign Office, who became Minister of Foreign Affairs shortly after the treaties in question were negotiated, writes that the expression "in accordance with the principles of law and equity" is considered to constitute a translation of the maxim *ex aequo et bono.* Löfgren, *op. cit.,* p. 55. But see Hudson, *op. cit.,* pp. 530-2 and notes.

the laws of the country against which an application is made, are within the competence of the courts, including the administrative courts, to be *first* submitted to national courts.[153]

This scheme for the settlement of political disputes was arrived at by prefacing the principle of the Deuntzer "all-in" treaties by the Scandinavian conciliation conventions of 1924. The procedure of conciliation, advocated previously especially in Norway and Sweden as a substitute for the seemingly unacceptable procedure of arbitration for disputes involving important interests, was now made to serve as an important preparatory work for arbitration.[154] Unlike the system of the Geneva Protocol the Scandinavian treaties of 1925-1926 retain the preliminary conciliation procedure for political disputes, and avoid entirely recourse to the Council of the League. Only if a dispute is such as to threaten the peace of the world would the Council, according to the Scandinavian view, be entitled to intervene, and in that event not to settle the merits of the case but to see that peace was not endangered.[155]

M. Eliel Löfgren, former Swedish Minister of Foreign Affairs, has pointed out that, even if the Geneva Protocol's fate showed that the time was not yet ripe for the general realization of compulsory arbitration, that effort was calculated to effect the coming of separate and "inclusive" arbitration treaties in a considerable degree.[156] To this development the Locarno treaties naturally contributed something by the central position ascribed to obligatory arbitration in their procedure for peaceful settlement. But the Scandinavian arbitration treaties went beyond these agreements. They had a much more important example in the conciliation and arbitration convention which Switzerland had made with Italy on September 20, 1924, which seems to be the first European treaty to combine an "inclusive" conciliation procedure with an "inclusive" provision for arbitration of all disputes without reservation not settled by conciliation.[157] Unlike this treaty

[153] Article 7.
[154] Löfgren, *op. cit.,* pp. 40-1.
[155] *ibid.,* p. 45.
[156] *ibid.,* p. 49.
[157] *Treaty Series,* XXXIII: 92. Compare Habicht, *op. cit.,* p. 984. Dr Habicht's statement "that this was the first post-War treaty to introduce the compulsory adjudication of non-legal as well as legal disputes" should be read in the light

the Scandinavian arbitration treaties of 1925-1926 did not provide that "all disputes," including "legal" disputes, should be first submitted to a preliminary obligatory procedure of conciliation.

The Swedish Government was the first to ratify the arbitration conventions which had been made by the four Northern States in 1925-1926.[158] No opposition was recorded in the report of the Riksdag's constitution committee.[159] In the lower chamber of the Riksdag on February 24, 1926, Admiral Lindman, leader of the Conservative Party, expressed agreement with the committee that no dispute between two Northern States could be visualized of which submission to arbitration would occasion any hesitations. For that reason he would support the proposition introduced by the Social Democrat Government. But the future Prime Minister felt obliged to declare his conviction of principle that a State "cannot and ought not to permit the question of its territorial domain and integrity to be submitted to any court of arbitration," except in case the State itself "in every particular instance" so authorize it.[160] Although he would offer no amendment, his view remained that arbitration treaties ought not to go further than the Swedish-Norwegian treaty of 1905 and the Swedish-Danish treaty of 1908, wherein no obligation in advance was accepted for disputes affecting a State's integrity. Spokesmen of the Liberal and Socialist Parties expressed pleasure over the three treaties, and Herr Engberg of the latter cynically remarked that he did not wonder that Admiral Lindman would be willing to venture on these treaties when such a man as Mussolini had been able to accept a similar undertaking. Both chambers, without a recorded vote, gave assent to ratification on the same day.[161]

In the Danish Rigsdag, the four principal political parties declared their support of the Northern Arbitration Treaties.[162] Herr Holger

of his classification made on p. 977. See the Austria-Hungary treaty of arbitration of April 10, 1923. *Treaty Series* XVIII: 94-100.

[158] *Riksdagens Protokoll* (1926), *Bihang*, Saml. 1, *Kungl. Maj:ts. prop.* nr. 62.

[159] Report of February 19, 1926. *Bihang till Riksdagens Protokoll,* Saml. 5, nr. 8, pp. 20-1.

[160] *Andra Kammaren* (1926), 12 : 54.

[161] *ibid.* Also, *Första Kammaren* (1926), 12 :3. There was no discussion in the Upper House.

[162] See *Forslag til Rigsdagsbeslutning angaaende Afslutning af en Voldgiftskonvention mellem Danmark og Sverige, Rigsdagstidenden* (1925-1926), *Tillæg* A. II, pp. 4983-5000. The corresponding conventions with Norway and Finland follow.

Andersen recalled the Conservative opposition to certain features of the 1924 conciliation conventions, but declared his party's willingness to support all of these more-inclusive treaties now under consideration, despite the opposition of much of the Norwegian press to the Danish-Norwegian treaty.[163] Of the Conservatives in the Folketing, only Professor Axel Møller stated that he had not been won over to the official view of his party and could not vote for the treaty. He objected to the stipulations in Articles 2, 7, and 8 which required the submission of disputes involving strictly domestic questions to the Arbitral Tribunal.[164] The conventions were unanimously approved on March 2, 1926, by the Folketing,[165] and on March 6, 1926, by the Landsting.[166]

In Norway, however, where several important papers of the Conservative and Agrarian Parties, such as *Tidens Tegn, Nationen,* and *Drammens Tidende,* opposed ratification, mainly because of the feeling aroused over the Greenland dispute,[167] there was a year of delay before any of the new conventions were ratified. When the Mowinckel Government introduced a proposition for ratification to the Storting,[168] its Committee on Foreign Affairs was nearly evenly divided pro and con.[169] The majority (seven members), who favoured ratification, consisted of three Radicals (Venstre), the Government Party, three members of the Labour Parties, and one Conservative. The minority (five members) were Conservatives, including M. Hambro, and Agrarians. On July 16, 1926, the Storting adopted the minority, not the majority, report and referred the Government's proposition back to the Committee with instructions for further consideration. When the Foreign Affairs Committee reported the second time on January 26, 1927, the situation had not substantially altered, except that the minority now recommended the definite

---

[163] *Folketinget* (1925-1926), Vol. II, pp. 5374-7 (February 24, 1926).

[164] *ibid.,* p. 5383.

[165] *ibid.,* p. 5421.

[166] *Landstinget* (1925-1926), p. 1210.

[167] *American-Scandinavian Review,* March 1926, p. 174.

[168] *St. prp.* nr. 27 (1926) dok nr. 7 (1927).

[169] *Innstilling fra den utvidede utenriks-og konstitusjonkomité om samtykke til ratifikasjon av avtalene med Sverige, Danmark og Finland om fredelig avgjørelse av tvister. Innst. S.* (1926) nr. 190, dated July 10, 1926.

rejection of the conventions.[170] The minority saw no need to go beyond the conciliation treaties of June 27, 1924, and objected to the reference of "interest" disputes to settlement on the basis of equity.

A protracted debate followed in the Storting, and on February 23, 1927, the Committee's report advising ratification was adopted by 92 votes to 53.[171] The majority consisted of 22 Conservatives under M. Lykke's leadership, all of the Radicals except one, and the Labour members. The minority, led by M. Hambro, included 30 Conservatives, and the Agrarians.[172] The growing desire for solidarity in the North had overridden all objections, and the "island of peace" in the North had been fortified against.internal dissension.[173]

Meanwhile, Denmark and Sweden had been giving expression to the spirit of the resolution of the Sixth Assembly that had advised States to conclude bilateral arbitration conventions, by going outside the family circle and concluding treaties with other States. In 1926 Denmark made treaties with Poland, Germany, France and Czechoslavakia; Sweden made a very far-reaching treaty with Belgium. Negotiations were in progress with other States. Some of these treaties combined conciliation and arbitration procedures; some were entirely without reservation. It is appropriate, however, to think of the inter-Scandinavian "peaceful settlement" treaties of 1925-1926 as the best expression of the attitude of these countries on the most suitable kind of treaty for their own particular needs.

When the Assembly met in September 1926, it fell upon the Third Committee to congratulate the Locarno Powers on their notable success attained the previous October in effecting important regional agreements for peaceful settlement of disputes and security. A Yugoslav delegate introduced a resolution declaring that the general ideas of the Locarno treaties "are susceptible of acceptance as fundamental rules which shall govern the foreign policy of every civilized nation."[174] To this declaration of principle the Scandinavian delegations objected. Dr Peter Munch explained that the principles of Locarno could not be applied in an identical manner to all regions, for

[170] *Innst. S.* (1927) nr. 11, pp. 191 *ff.*
[171] *Stortings Tidende* (1927), p. 605.
[172] Compare *Le Temps*, February 25, 1927.
[173] *American-Scandinavian Review*, May 1927, p. 305.
[174] M. Markovitch, see *7A.3C.*, 36-7.

there were some States which had no need to sign treaties of mutual guarantee between each other.[175] There were States, moreover, which were not entirely satisfied with the principles contained in the "arbitration treaties" of Locarno, in that they preferred a more strictly judicial system. He asked for an amendment which would make it clear that the Assembly did not wish to exclude arbitration treaties of a "superior character," by which he meant the Scandinavian treaties just described. Dr Munch's request was granted.

What, in the Scandinavian view, was the essence of the superiority of their system over that of Locarno? Ignoring the question of guarantees which will be discussed in the following chapter, the essential point was that disputes not deemed suitable for judicial settlement under "Locarno" would, in the event of failure of conciliation, be laid before the Council for consideration (not necessarily for settlement), rather than before an Arbitral Tribunal chosen with respect to the qualification of members as arbitrators.[176]

Certain other distinctions should be drawn between the Scandinavian and Locarno schemes for the pacific settlement of political disputes. The procedure of conciliation in the Scandinavian treaties was regarded more as a "fact-finding" device which would serve as a preliminary to later arbitration, while that of Locarno, which provides no assurance of ultimate settlement of the dispute (for unanimity may possibly not be achieved by the Council acting under Article XV), lays greater stress on the obligation of the permanent conciliation commission to effect an agreement between the parties.[177] The significant contribution of the inter-Scandinavian treaties of 1925-1926 is that they created a region in the North wherein arrangements were made for the peaceful settlement of every dispute, without exception, which might arise. Locarno was less successful. Even for the Rhineland Powers a "gap in justice," if not a "gap in peace" remained. Although the parties undertook never "to attack or invade each other or resort to war against each other," no obligation was

[175] ibid., pp. 36, 37, 38. See also Baron Marks von Würtemberg's speech, 7A.P., 119-20.

[176] M. Löfgren has pointed out that the Scandinavian system is built on the assumption that the parties may not want intervention by the Council, and may prefer a genuine ("verklig") Arbitral Tribunal. Löfgren, op. cit., pp. 64-5.

[177] See also Bellquist, op. cit., p. 332.

accepted to provide for a settlement of political disputes if the Council failed to reach unanimity, the parties to the dispute being excluded. Locarno guaranteed the *status quo,* but provided no equitable remedy for certain kinds of grievances which might prove to be the most dangerous for the peace of Europe. On the other hand, because of the intimate bonds of friendship which unite the North, the Scandinavian scheme took the final step of providing "boards of equity," in the last analysis, clothed with legislative power. Where rules of law are non-existent or inapplicable the sister States of the North would abide by a solution of wise, impartial men given on the basis of *ex aequo et bono.*[178]

Developments at Geneva, 1927-1928

From the North we now turn to Geneva to see what influence the development of the Scandinavian conception of peaceful settlement had upon the course of the League's activity in the same sphere. On September 14, 1927, Dr Nansen introduced a well timed proposal which led to the conclusion a year later of the "General Act for the Peaceful Settlement of International Disputes."[179] The "Draft Optional Convention for Compulsory Arbitration of Disputes" was designed to do for political disputes what the Optional Clause of the Statute of the Permanent Court had done for legal disputes. In short, it was designed to extend the "Scandinavian system" to all States that were willing. In the form in which the Norwegian delegate introduced his proposal, the effect would be to spare members who wished to assume general obligations for arbitration the trouble of making treaty after treaty with individual States. It was not so much an initiative for bilateral treaties *per se* as one to eliminate the confusion caused by the large number of such treaties already made and

[178] See *supra,* note 152. The inter-Scandinavian conventions do not use the expression *ex aequo et bono,* but *"les principes du droit et de l'équité"* (Swedish: *"grundsatserna för rätt och billighet"*). See Dr Max Habicht's argument that this expression should be interpreted, in the treaties concerned, as comparable to *ex aequo et bono, op. cit.,* p. 1052. See, however, Lauterpacht, *The Function of Law in the International Community,* pp. 328, 372-82.
[179] *8A.3C.,* 27-8.

to prevent the danger of treaties conflicting with the Covenant or League system and the creation of a rival system.[180]

The Nansen proposal, like the Geneva Protocol, aimed at securing the peaceful settlement of all disputes without exception. Legal disputes were to be submitted to the Permanent Court of International Justice, a provision equivalent to acceptance of the Article 36 of the Statute. All other disputes in which settlement could not be reached by the Council acting under Article XV were to be decided finally by a committee of arbitration, appointed by the disputants or, in case of their failure, by the Council acting by majority vote. The Norwegian proposal, therefore, was not an unspotted offspring of the Scandinavian conception elaborated in the 1926 inter-Scandinavian treaties. Locarno had exercised an influence, as is evidenced by the provision permitting Council action on political disputes. Because of this digression from orthodoxy, M. Löfgren, who had become Swedish Minister of Foreign Affairs, raised objection.[181] He could not support a proposal which, in reverting to Article IV of the Geneva Protocol (and to Locarno) ignored the trend of later bilateral arbitration treaties, which had taken the procedure out of the hands of the Council and placed it in independent bodies. A different sort of criticism was offered by the delegate of the Netherlands who, more consistent than Dr Nansen with previous Scandinavian policy, expressed regret that the procedure of conciliation by an independent commission had been omitted.[182]

A significant event transpired in December 1927 (after the Assembly had decided to give effect to Dr Nansen's motion by asking the Council to establish a "Committee of Arbitration and Security" to promote, generalize, and coordinate special or collective agreements on arbitration), when M. Löfgren himself addressed a letter to this committee in some respects inconsistent with his stand taken at the

[180] Nansen's proposal, as contrasted with the "General Act," was for a single "whole" treaty which would be open for those States prepared to accept it in its entirety. See *8A.P.*, 174-5 for Nansen's speech *after* discussion in the First and Third Committees.

[181] *8A.IC.*, 22-3.

[182] *ibid.*, p. 23. It was the representative of the Netherlands that suggested that the "committee of arbitration and security" draft a "model treaty."

Assembly three months before.[183] He definitely advocated "building on the principles of Locarno," and the draft convention which he submitted provided that political disputes, after failure of a conciliation commission, should be laid before the Council. No arrangement was suggested for final settlement by arbitration or even by Council decision, unless as in Locarno, unanimity (excluding the parties to the dispute) could be reached.

This letter and a similar one from the Norwegian Government, signed by M. Lykke, the Conservative Prime Minister,[184] evidently indicated a desire to have the prospective treaty fall within the bounds of practical politics. It cannot be supposed that the Scandinavian States had abandoned their view as to the "superior character" of their 1926 treaties. Since they themselves were largely safeguarded from Council interference by the treaties which they had negotiated from 1925 to 1927, they did not insist that recourse to the Council ought, so far as the Covenant allowed, to be excluded from the new "general" convention. The Norwegian letter, however, stated that an optional clause should be included, allowing the parties to use arbitration rather than Council consideration if desired. This was a definite foreshadowing of Chapter III of the "General Act." Perhaps the most important reason why the Norwegian and Swedish Governments did not suggest compulsory arbitration of all disputes without exception as the basis for the collective convention was the over-ambitious nature of such a proposal. It would indeed be asking a great deal of those Powers which had hitherto refused to accept the obligations of Article 36 of the Statute of the Court. The letter of the Norwegian Government indicated that it had altered its position somewhat in order to meet the criticism raised against Dr Nansen's proposal at the 1927 Assembly.[185] In other words, in order to obtain wider acceptance of the new convention, the most advanced Scandinavian position would be made as only an optional clause of a general treaty.

Instead of presenting one collective treaty of arbitration, the committee of arbitration and security evaded the responsibility of

[183] Letter of December 30, 1927. Proposals by the Swedish Government. (*C.A.S.* 10.) *L. of N. Doc.* IX, Dis A, 1928, IX, 3, pp. 44 *ff*.

[184] Letter of December 30, 1927. (*C.A.S.* 10.) *L. of N. Doc.* IX. Dis A, 1928. IX, 3, pp. 47 *ff*.

[185] *ibid.,* p. 47.

choice and submitted to the Ninth Assembly three collective treaties for the peaceful settlement of disputes and three corresponding bilateral ones.[186] These different types of treaties may be thought of as representing pictures of different stages of Scandinavian attitude toward peaceful settlement. "Convention C," which obligated the parties to submit all disputes to a procedure of conciliation, embodies the idea which Sweden was striving, in 1920, to embody in the Covenant. "Convention B" was a collective treaty which combined judicial settlement of legal disputes with a procedure of bilateral conciliation, followed by reference to the Council, if necessary, of political disputes. Clearly this draft was a generalization of the Stockholm conciliation conventions of 1924, added to the obligations of Article XV of the Covenant. In other words, it was essentially the Locarno system stripped of guarantee provisions. As we turn to the third type of peaceful settlement treaties suggested, it will be convenient to speak first of the bilateral draft, "Convention (a)," which was almost a duplicate of the bilateral conventions negotiated in Scandinavia in 1925-1926. Herein the conciliation procedure of "Convention B" was followed by the submission and award of an Arbitral Tribunal, if necessary. "Convention A," the collective draft of the same type as "Convention (a)," the most far-reaching of all in that it was a general treaty open to all comers, represents, as we shall see, Danish policy from 1929 (in reality, since 1904, for in the Danish-Netherlands convention of that year, it was declared that compulsory arbitration without restriction would gladly be accepted for every dispute with any State). The principle of "Convention A," which in its bilateral form owed much to Norway and Sweden, was accepted by Norway in May 1930, when Part III of the General Act was finally accepted; but for Sweden, it has not yet been accepted, a distinction being drawn by the Swedish Government between unlimited arbitration between particular States and the general obligation of the same nature. While Sweden is prepared to accept the obligations of "Convention B" *vis-à-vis* any State, "Convention (a)" is reserved for her more intimate or otherwise acceptable associates in the Family of Nations.[187]

[186] *L.N.O.J.*, IX (1928), pp. 1146 ff.
[187] See *infra*, p. 216.

From this comparison let us turn to the 1928 Assembly where, following a proposal of Professor Undén, Conventions "A," "B" and "C" were knitted together to form "The General Act."[188] By this device it became possible to include in a single comprehensive treaty three optional clauses to the existing peace machinery constituted by the Covenant of the League of Nations. Professor Sir Alfred Zimmern has aptly said that the General Act was "an embodiment of the Scandinavian view of the League as against that of the framers of the Covenant."[189] It may be added that the three alternatives of the General Act represent the various stages of development in the Scandinavian policy for peaceful settlement, and that other States were given the option of declaring which level on the rise to unrestricted arbitration their political position allowed. In every case, the resort to Council mediation was reserved in the background.

An important distinction should be drawn between the most far-reaching option of the General Act—i.e. accepting it in its entirety— and the inter-Scandinavian Arbitration Treaties of 1925-1926. It is not clear upon what basis the Arbitral Tribunal in Chapter III of the General Act gives its award.[190] Article 28 states that when none of the rules specified in Article 38 of the Statute of the Permanent Court of International Justice can be applied to a dispute, the Tribunal shall decide *ex aequo et bono*. But the draft Assembly resolution noted that "respect for rights established by treaty or resulting from international law is obligatory upon international tribunals."[191] The Norwegian delegation unsuccessfully endeavoured to remove this confusion by striking out the obligation placed on the Tribunal to uphold, in their entirety, the formal rights of a State.[192] The retention of this provision placed an obstacle in the way of the Tribunal, whose task, in M. Frede Castberg's view, ought to be to settle in a really satisfac-

---

[188] *9A.1C.*, 27-8. For the General Act, see *9A.P.*, 492-7.

[189] *The League of Nations and the Rule of Law*, p. 381, note 1.

[190] Compare the view of Professor Miroslas Gonsiorowski [*A.J.I.L.*, Vol. 27 (1933), pp. 482 *ff*.], with those of Dr Lauterpacht referred to in note 178 *supra*, and of Professor Brierly in an article entitled, "The General Act of Geneva," *B.Y.I.L.* (1930).

[191] *9A.P.*, 488.

[192] *9A.1C.*, 28, 77.

tory way, on the basis of equity, non-legal disputes. The insistence of the Norwegian and Swedish delegations that the General Act was in no way to affect the interpretation of arbitration treaties, concluded before the General Act, would seem to indicate that the inter-Scandinavian Treaties of 1925-1926 were interpreted as containing no such limitation.[193] Indeed this view is substantiated by M. Löfgren, who states that the expression "in accordance with the principles of law and equity" ("efter grundsatserna för rätt och billighet"), declared the basis of decision for political disputes, is considered as constituting a translation of the rule *"ex aequo et bono."*[194] It would seem, therefore, that some of the Scandinavian treaties may be considered as more far-reaching than the General Act, even when accepted in its entirety and without reservation.

The reception given the General Act by the parliaments of the Northern countries merits a word of attention. In Denmark, the Madsen-Mygdal Government, which had not taken a very active part in the preparation of the General Act, was succeeded in April 1929 by the Socialist-Radical coalition government in which Stauning was Prime Minister and Peter Munch, Foreign Minister. On February 13, 1930, after the four principal parties in the Rigsdag had given their preliminary support to the Government's request for ratification, a select committee of the Folketing submitted a unanimous report in favour of accepting the entire General Act, including Chapter III, which provided for compulsory arbitration of political

[193] *9A.1C.*, 77, *9A.3C.*, 103-4, *9A.P.*, 38.

[194] Löfgren, *op. cit.*, p. 55. When the Swedish-Belgian Treaty of April 30, 1926, was drafted, it was provided (Article 17) that the tribunal shall decide the matter *"ex aequo et bono." Treaty Series* LXVII:93. The Finnish-Norwegian Treaty of February 3, 1926 (Article 2), did not follow the language of the inter-Scandinavian, Swedish-Finnish, and Danish-Finnish conventions of 1925-1926. Power was not given to the Arbitral Tribunal to settle political disputes "in accordance with the principles of law and equity," but it was restricted to an application of the rules contained in Article 38 of the Statute of the Permanent Court of International Justice. *Treaty Series* LX : 368.

The view of M. Löfgren, however, is opposed by Professor S. R. Björksten of the University of Helsingfors; see Eric Cyril Bellquist, "Finland's Treaties for the Peaceful Settlement of International Disputes," in *A.J.I.L.*, Vol. 26 (1932), p. 76 and note.

disputes.[195] The General Act was considered as a desirable supplement to Article 2 of the Kellogg Pact.[196] Shortly afterwards both chambers adopted unanimously the proposition for adherence.[197]

Previously, on May 11, 1929, the Norwegian Storting had accepted without opposition the report of its committee of foreign affairs for adherence to the General Act.[198] But contrary to the proposition introduced by the Mowinckel Government, the report did not include acceptance of Chapter III of the Act. The Prime Minister, whose party occupied but one-fifth of the seats in the Storting, expressed surprise that such action had been taken, indicating that it was to be attributed to a desire of the committee to see what action other States would take. He looked forward to the time when the compulsory arbitration of political dispute as provided in Chapter III might also be accepted.[199] Twelve months later this took place after the committee of foreign affairs had reversed its position because of the favourable action already announced or being undertaken by other States.[200] Only one vote was cast against the report of the committee when the matter was finally settled on May 15, 1930.[201]

In Sweden, immediately after the drafting of the General Act of September 26, 1928, Admiral Lindman came into power at the head of a Conservative Government. Without delay a proposition was submitted to the Riksdag for the ratification of the General Act, exclusive of Chapter III.[202] In the *exposé des motifs*, M. Trygger, the Minister of Foreign Affairs, in stating the reasons for this omission, said that in view of the nature of an arbitral court's function in a political dispute, it was advisable to continue the past policy of inquir-

---

[195] For the support of the four parties, see Dr Munch's speech in the Folketing, October 12, 1929, on the first reading of the proposition. *Folketinget* (1929-1930) I, p. 3306.

For the report of the committee which contains an excellent review of the history of Danish arbitration treaties, see *Rigsdagstidenden* (1929-1930), *Tillæg* B, pp. 695-724.

[196] *ibid.*, p. 714.

[197] *Folketinget* (1929-1930), II, p. 5273 (February 18, 1930). *Landstinget* (1929-1930), p. 998 (March 7, 1930).

[198] *Innst. S.* (1929) nr. 99 (May 2, 1929), pp. 195-8. *Stortings Forhandlinger* (1929), Vol. 7b, p. 1777.

[199] *ibid.*, p. 1776.

[200] *Innst. S.* (1930) nr. 88.

[201] *Stortingstidende* (1930), p. 1587.

[202] *Kungl. Maj: ts. prop.*, nr. 108, *Bihang til Riksdagens Protokoll*, Saml. 1.

ing, in the case of each particular State, if the suppositions existed which would assure that an unlimited arbitration treaty would be safe and necessary. The task before an arbitral court in such an instance was to balance opposing interests and to strike a settlement which would seem most suitable and reasonable, or which from the general political situation was best calculated to settle the dispute. It was appropriate, therefore, to make the most advanced engagements only where the appropriate situation existed between States.[203]

An interesting debate took place in the upper chamber of the Riksdag on April 10, 1929, in which several opposition speakers, members of the Social Democrat Party, urged that the Government should have gone further and asked for approval of adherence to Chapter III as well.[204] M. Vennerström thought it was clearly in Sweden's own interest that political as well as legal disputes be submitted to arbitration. Sweden could not possibly look to war as a means of settling disputes, for her military resources would not allow it. The acceptance of Chapter III offered the advantage of laying disputes involving vital interests before an independent arbitral tribunal rather than before the Council, as in the Åland affair. It was regrettable to turn a cold shoulder to Chapter III which was really the handiwork of a Scandinavian initiative. If the Danish and Norwegian Governments were prepared to accept the General Act in its entirety, why should not the Swedish Government also?[205] M. Lindhagen, another Socialist, said that he had always fancied that if any country should be ready to submit all disputes to arbitration, it would be just such a country as Sweden. The policy of the Government seemed inconsistent with that which had brought into being a similar treaty with Finland in 1926, for it seemed more likely that Sweden should have some serious dispute involving "interests" with Finland than with other countries.[206]

It is hardly surprising that the Conservative Government under the leadership of elderly politicians such as Lindman and Trygger should have failed to free itself from the traditional view on arbitration when men like Hjalmar Hammarskjöld, an Independent member of the

[203] *ibid.,* p. 9. For the constitution committee's report, see *ibid.,* Saml. 5. nr. 8.
[204] *F.K.* (1929), 19 : 102-13.
[205] *ibid.,* pp. 106 ff.
[206] *ibid.,* pp. 108-9.

Utrikesnämnd (committee on foreign affairs),[207] continued to argue
that reservations ought to exist even on legal disputes.[208] But it might
have been expected that when the Social Democrats came to power in
September 1932, an effort would have been made to secure adherence
to Chapter III of the Act.[209] This apparently was not done, and at the
end of 1935, Sweden had not adhered to this additional obligation,
although by that time a number of members of the League were so
bound, including Denmark, Norway, Belgium, Finland, Great
Britain, France and Italy. But the adherence of most of these States
(other than Denmark and Norway) was made conditional on important reservations which substantially altered the effect of the
obligations assumed.[210]

[207] For the function of this committee see Rickard Lindström, *På Helgeandshol-
men: Den Svenska Riksdagen och dess Arbete*, p. 113; Axel Brusewitz, "Parliamentary Control of Foreign Affairs in Sweden," *Foreign Affairs* (London), Vol. 3
(1922), at pp. 103-4. See also Dr Mikael H. Lie and Professor Halvdan Koht, "Parliamentary Control of Foreign Policy," in *Recueil de Rapports sur les différents
points du Programme—Minimum*, Vol. II, pp. 241-51.

[208] *ibid.*, pp. 110-12.

[209] When motions were introduced by Socialist members in the Riksdag early in
1932 requesting the Government to adhere to the General Act in its entirety, the
constitution committee declared that the question of adherence to Chapter III should
be taken into consideration by the Government *before* it came for examination by
the Riksdag. The sorely tried Ekman Government, however, did not propose adherence. *Bihang till Riksdagens Protokoll* (1932), Saml. 5, nr. 16; also Motion 105
in *Första Kammaren*, and Motion 149 in *Andra Kammaren*.

[210] *L.N.O.J., Special Supplement* No. 136.

CHAPTER XII

DISARMAMENT AND SECURITY

SINCE the foundation of the League of Nations the much-used expression *Securité* has generally been associated with the policy of States interested in sanctions, guarantees and pacts of mutual assistance. It will be recognized, however, that some States, notably the Scandinavian, have considered that their security would be served better by the diminution than by the extension of the sanctions provided for in the Covenant.

The scepticism with which the Northern neutrals faced the obligations laid upon members of the League by Article XVI is as understandable as the eagerness of States like France and Czechoslovakia to strengthen the obligations of the Covenant. The latter States deemed it probable that in the event of a future European war they would be involved, and hence they wished to become what has been called "consumers of security."[1] The policy of the three Scandinavian States, however, was founded on the assumption that, in view of their geographical and political positions, the advantages offered by a system of automatic military or economic sanctions were outweighed by the risks involved for them as "producers of security."

This was an obvious conclusion for the Scandinavian Governments to draw in 1920. By that time everybody in Scandinavia had come to regard peace between Denmark, Norway, and Sweden as absolutely assured for the future. The centenary of peace between these peoples had already been celebrated in 1914,[2] and since then the War had strengthened the bonds of friendship and positive cooperation. Moreover, no neighbouring States, great or small, were then felt to

---

[1] Zimmern, *The League of Nations and the Rule of Law*, p. 366.

[2] A. T. Grønborg, "Fredsmonumentet paa den skandinaviske Graense," *Fredsbladet*, 23 Aarg, September 15, 1914, pp. 65-6. Inscribed on the monument dedicated on August 16, 1914, before some 12,000 people were these words, "Hädanefter är Krig mellan skandinaviske bröder omöjligt." Compare words of Oscar I, *supra*, p. 180.

constitute a threat to the security of the Northern Kingdoms.[3] Tsarist Russia had been supplanted by a new Russia no longer threatening the Scandinavian peninsula, and now separated from it by buffer States. Germany lay prostrate at the feet of the victorious Allies, whose territorial ambitions were confined to other quarters of the globe. The only serious contemplated danger was that of a possible future war between the European Great Powers which might again endanger the peace of the North.[4] Should this calamity occur, the Scandinavian States unquestionably would wish to escape being involved. For that reason when adhering to the Covenant their Governments had indicated that they did not admit any obligation to employ military sanctions under Article XVI.[5] But they recognized that this Article required all members of the League to impose an automatic and complete economic blockade against a State which should go to war in disregard of its engagements under Articles XII, XIII and XV. To the Scandinavian States who might, therefore, find themselves obliged to impose penalties against powerful neighbouring States, this obligation was somewhat disturbing. Accordingly, it was decided by the respective Governments to propose an alteration in Article XVI which would recognize that for certain States of secondary importance, especially exposed to powerful neighbours, a complete rupture of economic relations with such neighbours would present grave dangers. As the Swedish Government declared:[6]

> It can, indeed, be imagined that in such a case the Great Power in question might be tempted to occupy the territory of the smaller Power, so as to protect the very important economic interests which, as a result of the blockade, would be at stake.

In view of this consideration, the Danish, Norwegian and Swedish Governments, following the recommendation of the Scandinavian Commissions on League of Nations questions, presented separately a draft amendment to Article XVI empowering the Council to make

[3] P. Munch, *Le Projet Danois de Désarmement et La Société des Nations,* p. 6.
[4] *ibid.*
[5] *Rapport du Comité d'Experts chargé par le Gouvernement Suédois de l'Examen du Protocole dit de Genève, relatif au Reglement Pacifique des Différends Internationaux,* p. 75. See also Chapters IV and V of this treatise.
[6] Comment by the Swedish Government on the draft Swedish amendments to the Covenant. *L.N.O.J.* (1920), I, 6, p. 357.

a relaxation in the obligation of certain members to impose a complete blockade against a State which had resorted to war in violation of its obligations. The amendment provided that: "At the request of a member for whom the application of the above provisions might entail serious danger, the Council may authorize the member to maintain intercourse, in such measure as the Council shall decide, with the Covenant-breaking State."[7]

After discussion of the method of application of Article XVI by the First Assembly, an International Blockade Commission including Admiral Sparre of Norway, was set up by the Council to consider the question further.[8] Subsequently, the 1921 Assembly expressed approval of a series of amendments, including one which gave effect to the Scandinavian desire "to prevent the measures taken from inflicting more harm on the blockading State than on the State blockaded."[9] The draft amendment to paragraph 4 of Article XVI was as follows:[10]

> Nevertheless, the Council may, in the case of particular members, postpone the coming into force of any of these measures for a specified period where it is satisfied that such a postponement will facilitate the attainment of the object of the measures referred to in the preceding paragraph, *or that it is necessary in order to minimize the loss and inconvenience which will be caused to such members.*

In the Assembly, M. Zahle noted that the conclusions adopted by that body were "inspired" by the ideas which the Scandinavian delegations had brought forward at the Hotel Crillon meeting in March 1919.[11]

Although the amendments to Article XVI have never come into force because of the failure of certain States to ratify them, by an Assembly resolution in 1921 it was declared that, nevertheless, they should be considered as constituting rules for the guidance of the League in connection with the application of Article XVI. In 1922,

---

[7] The wording of the drafts submitted by the Government is not identical. *L.N.O.J.* (1920), I, 6, pp. 353-6.

[8] *St. med.* nr. 5 (1922), p. 21.

[9] See Oldenburg's speech, *2A.3C.,* 294.

[10] *Monthly Summary* (1921), I, p. 136. Italics are mine.

[11] *2A.P.,* 439-40.

this and other amendments to the Covenant adopted by the Second Assembly were ratified by Denmark, Norway and Sweden.[12]

If the anti-sanctionist attitude of the Scandinavian Governments was designed to safeguard the security of the neutral North, their disarmament programme at Geneva was to some extent also a function of the quest for security. In view of the small population and military weakness of the Scandinavian countries, little faith was attached to the value of armaments as a means of genuine security. Even many of the Conservative politicians admitted that a *general* reduction of armaments would contribute to Danish, Norwegian, or Swedish security, for it would increase the feeling of mutual confidence between the Powers and would reduce the likelihood of general war which, as has been said, was the only apparent threat to their own safety.[13]

But the Scandinavian statesmen responsible for the vigorous disarmament activity at Geneva based their policy primarily on their estimate of the general international need. World peace, as they saw it, depended on the abolition of the old "war system" of mailed-fist diplomacy, which had led to the catastrophe of 1914. Armaments in themselves, and armaments-races, constituted one of the chief threats to peace. It would be extremely difficult to lay a firm basis for world peace so long as nations maintained numerous professional officers, who, as Dr Peter Munch said, are "les foyers naturels" of the spirit of militarism.[14] It was an ever-present danger to have immense stocks of war materials which created strong vested interests capable of fomenting the spirit of militarism and of exercising influence over public opinion.

When the First Assembly opened in November 1920, the Scandinavian delegations were already prepared to launch the work for

[12] *L. of N. Doc.,* A.6(a), 1935, V (Annex).

[13] The question of a general international reduction of armaments must not be confused with the controversy between Conservatives and Socialists in these countries as regards unilateral reduction of armaments. The Conservative Party, especially in Sweden, in view of the weakness of the League, continually advised the policy of "keeping the powder dry." One writer said in 1927 that "if you were brought up in a fine old Swedish family with traditions handed down from the age of Gustavus Adolphus, then you would want to see your country strongly armed even if there is nobody to arm against. If you weren't, you don't." Special correspondent to *The Manchester Guardian,* November 14, 1927.

[14] *La Politique du Danemark dans la Société des Nations,* p. 23.

disarmament. Their policy, which had been considered at a conference of their Prime Ministers and Foreign Ministers at Copenhagen during the previous August,[15] sought to make a reality of Article VIII of the Covenant. The enthusiasm with which M. Branting and M. Lange pressed the Sixth Committee for immediate preparation, testified to their belief that the primary object of the League was to prevent war, and that disarmament was obviously the most practical way to succeed. Scandinavian leadership was demonstrated when M. Branting, who had been elected chairman of the committee, called on his Norwegian colleague to read a report on disarmament.[16] This was done by M. Lange, who for years had been concerned with the problem of armaments, when, on November 20, he outlined the steps which the League should take to initiate the work indicated in Article VIII.[17] He stressed the view of the celebrated Austrian lawyer Lammasch that "the desire to humanize war is perhaps more utopian than the desire to abolish it."[18]

One of the most important proposals which M. Lange introduced was that for the creation of a commission "consisting of members possessing the necessary political, historical, economical, and social competence," which should be authorized to prepare a plan of general disarmament. This new machinery seemed necessary to the Scandinavian delegates because the Council had "chosen to stultify the effect of Article IX" by creating a commission exclusively composed of military men, the so-called Permanent Advisory Commission on Military, Naval and Air Questions.[19] The Scandinavians were quite convinced of a truth expressed by M. Madariaga that "it was as foolish to expect a disarmament convention from such a commission as a declaration of atheism from a commission of clergy."[20] With the support of Lord Robert Cecil, M. Fock and others, a resolution was adopted which led to the creation by the Council on February 25, 1921, of the Temporary Mixed Commission, the most

[15] *1A.6C.(II)*, 328.
[16] *St. med.* nr. 9 (1921), pp. 45-6. *1A.6C.(II)*, 315.
[17] See Annex 2 and 2A to the *Records of the Sixth Committee* (1920) for the conclusions and statement of Dr Lange.
[18] *1A.6C.(II)*, 322.
[19] Madariaga, *Disarmament*, p. 80.
[20] *ibid.*, pp. 78-9. See *1A.6C.(II)*, 258.

important organ in the elaboration of plans for disarmament before 1925.[21]

M. Lange, supported by his colleagues from Denmark and Sweden, also proposed the creation of a special section of the Secretariat to deal with the collection and exchange of information in regard to armaments.[22] The Assembly was favourable, and the Disarmament Section was set up. This section had performed such service by 1923 that M. Lange felt entitled to express his pleasure for the initiative which he had taken in 1920.[23]

Opposing the Scandinavian plans for hurrying the work for the reduction of armaments stood the French and British delegates, who emphasized that the League must wait until the world was in a more peaceful atmosphere before actual disarmament should be undertaken. Restraining the eagerness of the Northern delegates, they finally secured the adoption of a report that "a comprehensive scheme of disarmament, based on a thorough feeling of trust and security as between nation and nation, could not be looked for at once." The work must "proceed by successive stages."[24]

In the Second Assembly the contention between the Great Powers and some of the small States was more prolonged than in the First Assembly. The Scandinavian delegates spoke vigorously in favour of pushing the plans for disarmament; while the former Allied Powers insisted on delay until after the Washington Naval Conference. During this Assembly M. Lange offered some "sincere and frank" criticisms of the Great Powers on the ground that they were blocking disarmament against the wishes of the majority of the League members.[25] He objected to the "tepid" manner in which the Council gave effect to Assembly resolutions. The 1920 resolution in regard to the limitation on military budgets (a modification of a proposal made by M. Lange) had merely been transmitted by the Council to the Governments without any indication of approval on the part of the Council. The Norwegian representative complained

---

[21] *Ten Years of World Cooperation*, p. 55; *L.N.O.J.*, (1921), II, 7, pp. 744-5.
[22] *1A.6C.(II)*, 315, *1A.4C.(II)*, 7.
[23] *4A.3C.*, 48.
[24] *New York Times*, November 28, 1920; *Ten Years of World Cooperation*, p. 54 (which quotes the Assembly Resolution).
[25] *2A.P.*, 265 *ff*. See also *St. med. nr. 5* (1922), pp. 30-3.

that the Council had departed from the wishes of the Assembly by including in the composition of the Temporary Mixed Commission six military experts from the Permanent Advisory Committee. There was a great need for full publicity of information concerning national armaments; but the interchange of information was entrusted to the Permanent Advisory Commission, a body of officers appointed in fact by the war departments and admiralties and responsible to their own Governments. It was from this ill-chosen commission that the Council took advice on questions of disarmament. The Scandinavian view, in contrast with that of the Great Powers, was neatly expressed in M. Lange's closing remarks:

> M. Balfour says that to disarm is difficult except in a world where troubles have ceased. I tell you that States which still possess great armaments produce distrust by their neighbours and cause international crises. . . .
> The fate of the League is in the hands of the Council.[26]

In the committee dealing with the reduction of armaments, M. Branting was again made chairman and used his influence, as did M. Lange, to force through a proposal of Lord Robert Cecil (representing South Africa) instructing the Temporary Mixed Commission to prepare a general scheme of disarmament as soon as possible.[27]

A resolution was also obtained asking the Council to request the respective Governments to furnish information concerning their military and naval budgets, and concerning the forces they deemed necessary to assure their national security.[28]

The result of these enquiries led the Temporary Mixed Commission to the conclusion that no general plan for reducing armaments could be effected until guarantees of security were made to certain "nervous States." A general treaty of mutual guarantee should be undertaken, based on the principles introduced by Lord Robert Cecil and adopted in the following form:[29]

> No scheme for the reduction of armaments can be successful unless it is general. In the present state of the world, the majority of Governments could not carry out a reduction of

[26] *2A.3C.*, 26. See also *The Times* (London), September 16, 1921.
[27] *2A.3C.*, 329-33.
[28] *St. med.* nr. 5 (1922), p. 32.
[29] *Ten Years of World Cooperation*, p. 57.

armaments unless they received satisfactory guarantees for the safety of their respective countries; such guarantees should be of a general character. And finally, there can be no question of providing such guarantees except in consideration of a definite undertaking to reduce armaments.

Prime Minister Branting and M. Backlund, the other Swedish member of the Temporary Mixed Commission, had made certain reservations with respect to the guarantee proposal during the proceedings of the commission; but these were not included in the report which was laid before the Third Assembly.[30] At that time, the point of view of the Scandinavian States was expressed with remarkable unanimity by the three delegations.[31] The common starting point of their policy was their objection to the acceptance, at least for themselves, of obligations in the nature of a guarantee in addition to what had already been promised in the Covenant of the League. While a connection between disarmament and a "sense of security" was recognized, doubts were entertained as to the desirability of making a general reduction of armaments depend upon the possibility of establishing a general treaty of mutual guarantee.[32] M. Lange did not agree with the commission that "the majority of the Governments" could not carry out a reduction of armaments unless they received additional guarantees.[33] Some Governments, including the Scandinavian, were prepared to make far-reaching agreements for reduction without such promises; indeed, the Northern States asked no further guarantees for themselves.[34] In their view a general reduction of armaments would itself constitute an important guarantee for the security of States.

The Danish, Norwegian and Swedish opposition to the acceptance of commitments to assist a State which might be a victim of aggres-

[30] St. med. nr. 8 (1923), p. 47.

[31] The report of Dr Lange on the work of the Third Committee is of special value. The reports of the Norwegian delegations to the Assembly is annually submitted to the Storting by the Utenriksdepartement, and is often more informative than the Danish or Swedish reports of a similar nature. See also Records of the Third Committee of the Third Assembly.

[32] 3A.P., 274, 279, 284.

[33] The expression "majority of Governments" was altered to read "many Governments" at the insistence of M. Lange.

[34] 3A.3C., 13, 15.

sion led Lord Robert Cecil to reproach the Scandinavians for their egoistic attitude. He asked if they did not recognize an obligation on the part of every State to make some contribution to the maintenance of general peace. M. Undén replied that the Scandinavian States were as much animated by a sense of international duty as any of the other States,[35] and M. Lange added that important pledges had already been undertaken by acceptance of the Covenant.[36] States could hardly be expected to make contributions to the security of other States, if to do so would unduly imperil their own safety. Although the Scandinavian States were doubtful of the utility of resorting to the old method of guarantees as a means of attaining security, the Norwegian delegate said that he would not oppose consideration of the guarantee system, as no doubt it had an importance for some States. He would insist, however, that the agreements concluded should not have an *exclusive* character, for this would inevitably lead to a renewal of the policy of military alliances which had led to the Great War.[37] The Northern neutral States generally took the view that while they themselves were not interested in a treaty of mutual guarantee, if one were made it should be open to all States without being obligatory.[38]

At the same time, M. Branting asked the Assembly not to overlook other important measures which might lead to a reduction of armaments, such as an extension of the Washington naval treaty, Lord Esher's proposals, and possible regional agreements.[39] In this connection it should be noted that the Scandinavian delegations were not quite in agreement with the first principle adopted by the Temporary Mixed Commission, mentioned above, namely, that "No scheme for the reduction of armaments can be successful unless it is general." Although a general reduction of armaments was obviously to be desired, the Norwegian and Swedish Governments were concerned lest regional agreements for reduction of armaments should be excluded from consideration by the League. Already in the 1921

[35] *3A.3C.*, 18.
[36] *ibid.* See also Moltesen's speech in the Rigsdag, *Folketinget* (1922-1923) I, pp. 534-5. (October 24, 1922.)
[37] *3A.3C.*, 17-18.
[38] *3A.3C.*, 53.
[39] *3A.P.*, 274.

Assembly M. Branting had pointed to the advantages that such arrangements would have for certain States forming natural geographical groups, such as the Scandinavian States.[40] At the following Assembly M. Lange introduced and secured the adoption of a proposal asserting the importance of regional agreements, "which might, if necessary, even go beyond the measures decided upon with respect to a general reduction."[41] This initiative seems to have been prompted partly as a safeguard against any attempt which might be made to require States to maintain larger armaments than they desired.[42]

The Third Assembly did not reach a solution of the security-disarmament problem, but contented itself with the adoption of the celebrated Resolution XIV as a guide for the Temporary Mixed Commission, which was instructed to submit a plan to the next Assembly designed to make possible a general reduction of armaments. Meanwhile the Governments were requested by the Council to express their observations on Resolution XIV, a somewhat amended version of Lord Robert Cecil's original proposals. The replies sent by the Danish, Norwegian and Swedish Governments in the summer of 1923 were an amplification of their common attitude expressed at the Third Assembly, and merit careful examination.[43]

The three letters expressed objection to the subordination of the question of a reduction of armaments to that of guarantees. At the most, a treaty of mutual guarantee should be considered, to quote M. Michelet, "as only one of the several means of securing a reduction of armaments."[44] The Danish objection to the conception that a new guarantee not already provided for in the Covenant must be

[40] *Ten Years of World Cooperation*, p. 58.

[41] *3A.3C.*, 38-39.

[42] The Danish and Norwegian Governments in official publications have always held that the Covenant contains no general contractual obligation for members which could make an obstacle to disarmament. Frede Castberg, "Le Droit International et La Défense" in *Acta Scandinavica Juris gentium*, Vol. I (1930), No. 2, pp. 16-17.

[43] See the letter of the Danish Government, signed by Oldenburg and dated June 9, 1923; letter of the Norwegian Government, signed by Michelet, and dated July 17, 1923; and the letter of the Swedish Government, signed by Hederstierna and dated June 1, 1923. The English translation of these replies are published in *L. of N. Doc.* A, 35, 1923, IX, Part I (Report of the Temporary Mixed Commission for the Reduction of Armaments, August 30, 1923).

[44] *L. of N. Doc.* 35, 1923, IX (Part I), p. 40.

offered States in exchange for a reduction of armaments was based on a constitutional argument. Article VIII of the Covenant imposed upon members a clear and unconditional obligation to reduce armaments. This obligation, which was not dependent upon the making of supplementary guarantees, could not be absolved by the difficulties involved. In the Danish view it would be dangerous to accept the basic principle of Resolution XIV, for to do so would constitute the recognition *ipso facto* that present-day armaments are justified so long as no additional guarantees exist.

The weakness of the League strengthened the deeply rooted feeling of the Scandinavian peoples that a system of military guarantees was an inadequate basis for world peace. As the Swedish Foreign Minister pointed out, a proper system of guarantees presupposes world-wide membership; but the existing League lacked authority because of the absence of great military Powers including Germany, Russia and the United States of America. The contemplated defensive military alliances, therefore, might contain the germs of fresh conflicts of interest.

The Danish letter, which included a report signed by members of the four principal parties in the Rigsdag,[45] excluded military assistance on the ground that impartial neutrality was necessary for the very existence and independence of Denmark. "If her entry into the League and acceptance of the obligations of the Covenant were not entirely in accord with the traditionally accepted meaning of neutrality, it was because she originally supposed that the League of Nations would very shortly include all the countries in the world, or at any rate all the countries of any considerable political or military importance."[46] Denmark, however, neither had, nor would accept, any obligation to employ military sanctions.

The Swedish Government, on the other hand, which in 1919 had not excluded the possibility that Sweden might agree to employ military sanctions in particular instances, reaffirmed the view adopted by that country at the time of adherence to the Covenant that individual Governments retain the right of determining whether or not military sanctions would be employed in the cases contemplated in Article XVI.

[45] See also *Redegørelse for Danmarks folkeretlige Stilling efter Folkeforbundspagten og Kellogg-Pagten*, pp. 71-7, for the report dated May 29, 1923.
[46] *L. of N. Doc.* A. 35, 1923, IX (Part I), p. 29.

The following realistic argument was given to explain Sweden's opposition to the system of mutual guarantees visualized in Resolution XIV:

> . . . in the case of Sweden, whose geographical position affords her a fair degree of protection, and whose relations with other States are normal, the obligation arising out of a joint guarantee would increase the danger of her being drawn into war to an extent entirely out of proportion to the increased risk incurred, from the same cause, by certain other countries. There is, no doubt, hope that the day will come when all States will agree to regard any disturber of the peace as a common enemy, against whom they will be prepared to take up arms immediately. But . . . we have not yet reached that stage, and there is no reason to suppose that we shall reach it in the near future. In the present disturbed conditions of the world, no Swedish Government could ask the representatives of the nation to undertake international obligations possibly involving Sweden in warlike operations, which might appear to the nation to be in no way connected with the vital interests and independence of the country.[47]

The Conservative Swedish Government took this occasion to insinuate its disapproval of injustices in the Treaty of Versailles, and stated that an obligation to defend the *status quo* against external aggression exposed members to grave perils, since the existing juridical situation contained many elements of future conflict.

The distinctive feature of the Norwegian reply was the suggestion to restrict the benefit of guarantees to those States which should offer certain assurances of "wise policy." To obtain guarantees of assistance a State must have fulfilled its international engagements in regard to the reduction of armaments, furnished complete information concerning its armaments in accordance with Article VIII of the Covenant, registered all international conventions, and accepted the "Optional Clause" for compulsory adjudication of disputes as defined in Article 36 of the Statute of the Permanent Court of International Justice.[48]

[47] *L. of N. Doc.* A. 35, 1923, IX (Part I), p. 47.
[48] *ibid.*, p. 41.

When the 1923 Assembly considered the draft treaty of mutual guarantee submitted to it by the Temporary Mixed Commission, M. Lange offered an amendment to the proposed Article II along the lines of the suggestion contained in the Norwegian letter of July 13, 1923.[49] Although he and his Scandinavian colleagues took a negative attitude so far as their own acceptance of the draft treaty was concerned,[50] M. Lange tried to alter the draft in conformity with the Scandinavian theory of world peace. In reply to the French demand that a reduction of armaments must depend on greater security, M. Lange demanded that offers of security should only be made to States which had accepted compulsory arbitration. M. Lange had discovered the cornerstone for the Geneva Protocol; but in 1923 the British and French Governments declared it unacceptable.[51] By the small vote of eight to seven, the Third Committee of nearly fifty members rejected the Norwegian amendments for instituting the principle of "wise policy." In addition to the support of Denmark and Sweden, the Netherlands, Switzerland, Greece, and Lithuania voted for the motion in its entirety.[52] Some delegations which favoured the proposal voted against it for fear that the guarantee treaty as a whole would be endangered. M. Lange declared it regrettable that Great Britain and France would not accept compulsory arbitration, for, if they would do so, those small States which had not already adhered to the Optional Clause would no doubt follow their example.[53]

In the plenary session the Norwegian delegate branded the "Treaty of Mutual Assistance" (a title which he greatly preferred to that of "Treaty of Mutual Guarantee")[54] as out of keeping with the spirit of the Covenant which was, "above all, designed to further the development of legal and moral principles."[55] Because he thought that the development of material and economic means of action must be accompanied *pari passu* by the evolution of such principles, M. Lange had striven to obtain approval of the principle of compulsory arbitra-

[49] *4A.3C.*, 23.
[50] *4A.3C.*, 16, 60: *4A.P.*, 150.
[51] Compare Zimmern, *op. cit.*, pp. 344-5.
[52] *St. med.* nr. 8 (1924), p. 40.
[53] *4A.3C.*, 24, 25.
[54] *4A.3C.*, 83.
[55] *4A.P.*, 150.

tion, which the Scandinavians had urged since the foundation of the League. He invited those who look to "material means of force" for security, to contemplate the character of modern warfare, especially of chemical and bacteriological warfare. In view of the opinion of experts it seemed necessary to conclude that "modern armaments are a means of attack and a means of intimidations," and have ceased to be in reality a means of defence and of security.[56]

In order to overcome the objection of the Northern neutrals and other States to commitments of assistance, provision was made in Article 14 of the draft treaty for "partial adherence," which would allow certain States to lessen their obligations under the treaty, provided always that unconditional adherence to the provisions concerning the reduction of armaments should be made. As the meaning of the text of the original draft submitted to the Third Committee was not clear, M. Branting and M. Lange favoured substituting a draft introduced by Lord Robert Cecil, which provided that States might adhere to the treaty on the sole condition that they undertook to reduce their armaments.[57] But the insistence of M. Lebrun of France, led the committee to decide by eighteen votes to four, that "effective assistance"—military or economic—must be given by signatory States; "partial assistance" could not be reduced to mere "moral assistance."[58]

These objections to the Treaty of Mutual Assistance induced the Scandinavian, Swiss and Lithuanian delegations to abstain from voting in the committee on the question of the submission of the treaty to the Governments for consideration. Certain States, including the Netherlands, Italy and Japan, opposed its submission; but following the usual polite manners which were being evolved in the Assembly, that body, in plenary session, unanimously recommended that the treaty be sent to the Governments, although there was little hope for its acceptance.[59] There can certainly be little surprise that the Danish, Norwegian and Swedish Governments found this expression of the "French theory of the League" inadmissible for a traditionally

[56] *4A.P.*, 150.
[57] *4A.3C.*, 60; *St. med.* nr. 8 (1924), pp. 43-4.
[58] *4A.3C.*, 88-9.
[59] *St. med.* nr. 8 (1924), p. 45.

neutral and independent North.[60] The invasion of the Ruhr about the same time strengthened the conviction in Scandinavia of the futility of expecting peace and good understanding if force was to be the method of nations. The occupation of the Ruhr served as a warning against the advisability of making military commitments to defend treaty law, for in practice justice as well as peace might be defeated thereby.[61]

When the Fifth Assembly opened in September 1924, and a fresh start was made towards a comprehensive plan for giving effect to the obligations of the Covenant, Mr Ramsay MacDonald and M. Herriot, the British and French Prime Ministers, came to the agreement that the rejected Norwegian proposal for compulsory arbitration might now be accepted as the cornerstone of the Geneva Protocol.[62] The chief work of this Assembly was to unite the hitherto disconnected principles of security, disarmament and arbitration. The attitude of the Scandinavian States to each of these principles has already been emphasized; it remains now to examine their reaction to the effort to interlock them. In this Assembly they chose the rôle of praising the virtues of disarmament and arbitration, while objecting to the extension of sanctions. Disarmament was the key to the whole solution in the opinion of Dr Peter Munch, the future Danish Minister of Foreign Affairs.[63] Not only was disarmament urged as a means of putting an end to general insecurity; in addition he asked how compulsory arbitration could work as long as States remained armed to the teeth. Sanctions were superfluous, even dangerous, while States

[60] See the letter of the Norwegian Government (August 18, 1924), letter of the Swedish Government (August 25, 1924) in L. of N. Doc. A. 35, 1924, IX. The draft reply of the Danish Government, drawn up by the Ministry of Foreign Affairs and dated September 12, 1924, was never sent as by that time the answer seemed superfluous. It is available in Redegørelse for Danmarks folkeretlige Stilling efter Folkeforbundspagten og Kellogg-Pagten, pp. 77-80.

[61] The critics of the League in Scandinavia were exceptionally outspoken at the time of the Ruhr invasion. The majority report of the Stortings Committee on Foreign Affairs, for example, declared that the League's activity had not entirely answered to the expectations which were attached to it. The League had not dealt with the task which ought to be considered its central sphere of activity. Stortings Forhandlinger (1923), Vol. 6a, II. Innst. S. LIV, p. 5.

[62] Ten Years of World Cooperation, p. 67.

[63] For this and the following information in this paragraph see Dr Munch's lengthy speech on September 12, 1924. 5A.3C., 26-7.

possessed abundant means of aggression; for, if a delinquent State was strong, the only possible means of enforcing the League's decision would be a World War. A complete transformation of armies and navies into police forces was declared necessary if there were ever to be a guarantee by the League of respect for treaties. What the Radical Danish Minister was asking was the international application of the Socialist-Radical disarmament bill introduced in the Rigsdag in 1924.[64] He suggested that if armies and navies of the various nations were cut to about one-fifth of their existing strength, it would be possible for the League to assure an adequate control of military forces and a sufficient degree of security to make possible the acceptance by Denmark of obligations for an enlargement of penalties.

What concessions were the Scandinavians prepared to give on the question of sanctions? MM. Branting, Lange and Munch recognized the necessity of developing the system of sanctions but, in fact, they were prepared to surrender very little ground. In the Third Committee, the Danish delegate emphatically stated that if Article 12 of the Protocol, which dealt with sanctions, was intended to alter the system of Article XVI of the Covenant, he would find it impossible to vote for the Protocol. In his view the draft article meant that the distinction between economic and military sanctions would be maintained;[65] while the Council would be entitled to make recommendations to the various States in regard to military sanctions, the States concerned would be invited to send representatives to the Council. As in the past, the rule of unanimity would remain in force; the States would continue to be free to decide for themselves whether they could take

[64] For the conception on which the proposed Danish Defence Law of 1924 rests, see Dr Munch's splendid monograph, *Le Projet danois de Désarmament et La Société des Nations,* pp. 3-6.

[65] The Scandinavian States have consistently maintained from the beginning of the League that Article XVI of the Covenant placed no obligation upon them to employ military sanctions without their own consent. *ibid.,* pp. 11-15. The Scandinavians often referred to the assurance they were given by Lord Robert Cecil, who as spokesman of the sub-committee at Hotel Crillon, told them that the League would not have the right to require a State not desiring to participate in military sanctions to do so. Dr Munch has said that Denmark joined the League on this clear understanding. Norway and Sweden also have stated that they have accepted no obligation to participate in military sanctions. See J. M. Spaight, *Pseudo-Security,* pp. 64-6. But see Axel Møller, *International Law in Peace and War,* Part II, p. 104.

part in military sanctions. The innovation in Article 12 of the Protocol, in Dr Munch's interpretation, was that there would be no room
for discussion whether or not a situation had arisen involving the
obligation to apply the sanctions provided for in Article XVI of the
Covenant. This view had the support of the Norwegian and Swedish,
as well as the Dutch and British delegations.[66] The Scandinavian
delegates, however, added that they fully intended to "cooperate
loyally" with the other nations in applying economic and financial
pressure.

Did the Scandinavian viewpoint concerning sanctions find its way
into the final draft of the Geneva Protocol? The answer seems to be
in the negative. An important alteration, however, was made in the
text of Article 11 of the Protocol which recognized their special
position. The stipulation that each of the signatory States was "to
cooperate loyally and effectively in support of the Covenant of the
League of Nations, and in resistance to any act of aggression" was,
on Dr Munch's insistence, referred to a sub-committee, of MM. Benes
and Munch, which added to the above provision the expression, "in
the degree which its geographical position and its particular situation
as regards armaments allow."[67] The wording of this amendment had
been first considered by the Scandinavian and Dutch delegates at a
meeting with M. Paul Boncour, and, after acceptance by the sub-
committee, found its way into the Protocol. When later the Swedish
Royal Commission of Investigation gave its opinion on the meaning
of Article 11 of the Protocol, it held that the obligation to impose
military sanctions would still remain on signatories of the Protocol.
This seems to be the correct interpretation and the fear that it might
be was one of the principal reasons for the hesitating, if not unfavourable, attitude taken by the Norwegian and Swedish Governments to
the Protocol.[68]

[66] See Branting's speeches (*5A.3C.*, 28 and *5A.3C.*, 59). In the latter, made on
September 24, 1924, he is reported as saying that he interpreted Article 12 as meaning that acceptance of the draft protocol by Sweden would not impose on her the
obligation of taking part in military sanctions. This he said was also the view of
M. Loudon, Mr Henderson and M. Munch. See also M. Lange's speech (*5A.3C.*,
61) to the same effect.

[67] *Redegørelse for Danmarks folkeretlige Stilling efter Folkeforbundspagten og
Kellogg-Pagten,* p. 94. See also *St. med.* nr. 14 (1925), pp. 73-5.

[68] *Rapport du Comité d'Experts, op. cit.* (*supra,* note 5), pp. 75-6.

On the fundamental and difficult question of defining the aggressor, the Geneva Protocol made use of the idea that "the aggressor would be the one who refused arbitration." It should be remembered that two years previously, in the Third Assembly, M. Lange had already advanced this principle, which was now accepted by the British and French delegations.[69]

It is well to conclude our consideration of the Fifth Assembly's work by returning to the question of reduction of armaments, the topic which the Scandinavian delegations felt obliged to keep in the forefront, and which was, indeed, the admitted "main object for which the Protocol was framed."[71] In order to direct public attention in all countries to the coming "disarmament" Conference, the tireless M. Lange introduced a resolution requesting the Council to instruct the competent organs of the League to examine, in preparation for the conference to be held on June 25, 1925, all proposed schemes submitted to the League concerning the following points :[72]

1. General plan for a reduction of armaments in accordance with Article VIII of the Covenant, in particular:
   (a) Basis and methods of reduction. . . .
   (b) Preparation of a typical budget for expenditure on armaments.
2. Special position of certain States in relation to the reduction of armaments.
   (a) Temporary reservations by countries exposed to special risks;
   (b) Recommendations of regional agreements for the reduction (or limitation) of armaments.
3. Recommendations of the establishment of demilitarized zones.
4. Control and investigation of armaments in the contracting States.

[69] The report made by Dr Lange and Dr Lie concerning "Genfprotokollen" to the Norwegian Foreign Office and published in *St. med.* nr. 14 (1925), adheres to the view that the Protocol provides a common obligation to apply *military* sanctions, subject of course, to the qualification made by amendment just noted. *ibid.*, p. 74. This obligation is recognized by David Hunter Miller in *The Geneva Protocol,* pp. 78-9. *3A.3C.*, 38.

[71] *Ten Years of World Cooperation*, p. 73.

[72] *5A.3C.*, 91. *St. med.* nr. 14 (1925), p. 79.

In the final series of speeches before the exuberant Fifth Assembly, the Scandinavian delegations definitely announced that their vote of approval was not to be understood as in any way committing their Governments to acceptance of the Protocol. M. Branting, who, though leader of the opposition in the Riksdag, had been the chief Swedish spokesman throughout the discussion of the Protocol, indicated that this attempt "to give more definite expression to the principle of international solidarity" might alarm certain sections of Swedish public opinion, "as happened at the time of our entry into the League."[73] But the Swedish statesman, who personally seemed to have approved of the Protocol,[74] added that he felt sure the Swedish people would appreciate that "it is possible to strengthen the bonds of international solidarity without compromising national sovereignty."[75]

It is a matter of conjecture whether the Danish, Norwegian, and Swedish Governments would have adhered to the Protocol if the British Government had not rejected it. From the evidence submitted in the previous chapter it would seem that the Scandinavian States, unlike the new Baldwin Government, were prepared to accept the provisions for universal and compulsory arbitration as provided in the Protocol.[76] It is doubtful that the parliaments of the North would have granted ratification of the sanctions provisions of the Protocol, unless it were definitely understood that no obligation rested on them to employ military assistance without their own consent. The decision as to acceptance or rejection of the Protocol was not, however, made necessary, because of the statement read by Sir Austen Chamberlain in the Council on March 12, 1925.[77] The conclusions reached by the Swedish Royal Commission after this announcement were, however,

[73] 5A.P., 220. See also speech of M. Lange, ibid., pp. 210-11, and of M. Zahle, ibid., p. 214.

[74] On the occasion of M. Branting's death an unsigned article appeared in The Times (February 26, 1925), which stated:
"Branting was entirely in favour of the Geneva Protocol, which he had some share in preparing and which he styled 'The Magna Charta of Europe.' . . ."

[75] 5A.P., 220.

[76] supra, Chapter XI, p. 200.

[77] L.N.O.J., VI, 33C, pp. 446 ff. After the statement of the British representative, M. Undén said in the Council that the Swedish Government in making its decision, would be obliged to take into account the attitude of other Powers, particularly those whose adherence is necessary to make it effective. The Swedish Government reserved the right to submit amendments to the Protocol.

highly critical of the Protocol and of the risks that acceptance would involve for Sweden.[78] No similar commissions of enquiry were named in Denmark and Norway, and the Stauning and Mowinckel Governments played a waiting rôle, a thing easier for them since they, unlike the Swedish Government, were not represented on the Council.[79] The Foreign Affairs Committee of the Storting, nevertheless, criticized the Government for not authorizing a thorough study of the whole question of Norway's attitude to the principles contained in the Protocol. In its report to the Storting signed by M. Hambro and dated July 16, 1925, the view was expressed that the delegation to the next Assembly should be instructed to take a "waiting position," and in no respect to obligate Norway further than was done in the 1924 Assembly.[80]

The Norwegian Prime Minister at the opening of the 1925 Assembly, when the Protocol was obviously dead, called attention to the anxiety which this scheme had caused both to the Government and to public opinion in Norway, "particularly in regard to the provisions which might obligate members to participate in military sanctions."[81] A few weeks later at a political meeting in Oslo, M. Mowinckel said that he did not regret the failure of the Protocol as it was over-ambitious. He thought the position of the present British Government a stronger one and better calculated to serve the peace of the world.[82]

Although the Danish attitude on the sanctions provisions of the Protocol was virtually the same, M. Zahle, in his speech at the Sixth Assembly, seemed more disposed to recognize the "great progress" achieved by the Protocol.[83] He especially noted that it had embraced the principle that all wars of aggression are declared illegal, a principle for which M. Oldenburg of Denmark had asked recognition in the 1922 Assembly. This advance in the field of compulsory arbitration

[78] *Rapport du Comité d'Experts, op. cit.,* pp. 120-5.

[79] See the speech of Prime Minister Mowinckel in the Storting on July 17, 1925. *Stortings Forhandlinger,* Vol. 7b, pp. 2906-8.

[80] *Stortings Forhandlinger* (1925), Vol. 6a, *Innst. S.* nr. 176.

[81] *6A.P.,* 45.

[82] *American-Scandinavian Review,* January 1926, p. 51.

[83] *6A.P.,* 34. On February 12, 1932, in the plenary session of the Conference for the Reduction and Limitation of Armaments, Dr Munch, the Danish Foreign Minister, said: "We [Denmark] regretted the failure of that Protocol." (He was referring to the "Geneva Protocol" of October 2, 1924.)

was in keeping with the policy accepted in Denmark even before the War.

The general point of view of the Scandinavian delegations at the Sixth Assembly was that the peace activity of the League should be undiminished, although new methods might be necessary for progress. In the previous chapter it was seen that M. Undén at this time directed the attention of the Assembly to the consideration of arbitration as a question in itself.[84] For their part, the Locarno Powers were preparing a regional security pact in conjunction with arbitration agreements. In short, the different "schools of internationalism" fell back upon their own particular creeds and inclinations.

It should occasion no surprise, therefore, that the Northern neutrals should have continued their agitation in behalf of a general reduction of armaments. Denmark, who had entered the League "primarily to effect a reduction in armaments,"[85] announced that, despite the view of some States that reduction depended on "guarantees for security," she believed that, in the meantime, preparation should be undertaken by an exhaustive study of all the concomitant problems.[86] While M. Lange was attributing the failure of the Protocol partly to the fact that reduction of armaments had been left in the background, all the Scandinavian delegations supported the Dutch proposal that a special preparatory body should be constituted at once to undertake the technical labours for a future international conference.[87] The decision of the Sixth Assembly to proceed in this manner without awaiting an improvement in the condition of world security was heralded by M. Engberg, the Swedish delegate, as an important advance in the work for peace.[88] But this decision did not mean that the expected "consumers of security" had agreed to the calling of a world disarmament conference prior to the realization of a "satisfactory" feeling of security. Not until 1932 did they permit the meeting of the much delayed conference which the Scandinavian States had been urging since the First Assembly, twelve years before.

[84] *supra*, Chapter XI.
[85] *4A.3C.*, 15.
[86] *6A.3C.*, 15.
[87] *6A.3C.*, 13, 15.
[88] *6A.3C.*, 23.

Meanwhile a number of ways were suggested, discussed and employed by the League, its organs and its members to advance the sense of security for "nervous States." One of these methods, inspired by the example of Locarno, was the drawing up of treaties of non-aggression and mutual assistance by the Committee on Arbitration and Security in 1928. In such treaties the Scandinavian States had "no individual interest," because they did not anticipate any need of their own to conclude treaties of this kind.[89] In the general interest of permanent peace, however, they reaffirmed their conviction, expressed in 1923, that under no condition should States which felt the need for such treaties include provisions which might lead to the formation of rival groups of Powers.[90]

Another attempted method of increasing security was that seeking to give financial assistance to States victims of aggression or the threat of aggression. The discussion concerning the proposal of M. Holsti of Finland, introduced at the 1926 Assembly and, finally, embodied in the form of a draft convention on financial assistance, reveals the necessity of distinguishing between the "sanctionist" policy of the Scandinavian States and that of Finland.[91] That is not to say that the Scandinavian States did not recognize the principle of providing financial aid to a State which was a victim of aggression. On the contrary, the principle was declared admissible.[92] But the approach of the Scandinavian delegations to the Finnish proposals shows that for them there existed a "standing rule" to receive with an attitude of reserve any suggestion, no matter how mild, for the extension of sanctions. The criticisms in this particular instance were numerous.[93] Dr Munch was sceptical of attempting to formulate detailed rules to cover unpredictable future events in the manner prescribed in the convention. Especially did the Scandinavians object to offering financial assistance in case of a mere "threat of war"; for there was the difficulty of determining which State threatened the other, and the Council would obviously lose the possibility of acting as mediator once it named the aggressor. Dr Munch proposed an

[89] *9A.3C.*, 82. *St. med.* nr. 3 (1927), p. 55.
[90] *ibid.*; also *9A.3C.*, 105.
[91] *St. med.* nr. 3 (1929), p. 47.
[92] *10A.3C.*, 23. *St. med.* nr. 3 (1929), p. 57.
[93] See especially the discussion in the Third Committee of the Tenth Assembly.

amendment to the draft convention that financial assistance might not be granted until the Council had attempted mediation without success.[94]

A compromise was effected upon this question. The Danish request that mediation should precede the giving of financial assistance in such cases was accepted, but, on the other hand, it was provided that aid might be given in case of a "threat of war," "provided the Council considers that peace cannot be safeguarded otherwise."[95]

A number of conditions were specified by the Scandinavian delegations in 1929 which they thought ought to be met by a State asking financial assistance. "Correct attitude," in M. Sandler's view, should be evidenced by acceptance of the provisional measures which the Council might make for the purpose of avoiding any aggravation of the dispute and by a willingness to submit the dispute to arbitration or any other procedure likely to bring a pacific settlement.[96] In the 1930 Assembly Baron Ramel of Sweden was particularly anxious to clarify the stipulation that the applicant for assistance must follow the Council's choice of the pacific procedure to be followed in a given instance.[97] These determinants of "correct attitude" found their way into the convention as finally drafted by that Assembly.

The Scandinavian States successfully maintained their policy asserted throughout the decade of the 1920's that no extension of the obligation to employ sanctions should be made until effect had been given to Article VIII of the Covenant. M. Lange was less insistent than his Danish colleague as to the necessity of being exacting on this point.[98] He contemplated a situation in which it would be vitally important to grant financial assistance to a State, even though it had not complied with certain preliminary conditions. Because of the difficulty of application, he considered it preferable not to try to provide specifically for all the contingencies for granting assistance.

It will be seen, therefore, that the Northern States exercised an appreciable influence on the provisions of the Draft Convention on

[94] *10A.3C.*, 23-4.
[95] *Monthly Summary,* X (1930), pp. 168, 212.
[96] *10A.3C.*, 27-8.
[97] *11A.3C.*, 17-18.
[98] *11A.3C.*, 47 (Munch). Compare Munch's and Lange's position *10A.3C.*, 63-4. See also Sandler's speech, *10A.3C.*, 27-8.

Financial Assistance. Although this convention was signed by Denmark, Norway, Sweden and other States, the only ratifications deposited by August 28, 1935, were those of Denmark, Finland and Iran.[99] In view of the failure of the Disarmament Conference, which was opened at Geneva in February 1932, there is no reason to suppose that the Convention on Financial Assistance will come into force in the near future.

The Kellogg Pact and the Covenant of the League

Although Denmark, Norway and Sweden adhered to the Kellogg Pact without reservations, little enthusiasm for this declaration was exhibited in the respective parliaments of the North when ratification was given in 1929.[100] This tepid feeling may be attributed in part to the restricted nature of the anti-war pact, which unlike the Scandinavian peace system, included no positive obligation or procedure for the pacific settlement of disputes.[101] To be sure, the Scandinavian countries favoured the renunciation of war as an instrument of national policy: already they had obviously taken this step for themselves. But, as the Constitution Committee of the Swedish Riksdag noted, the moral value of the Kellogg Pact was considerably reduced by the reservations made by some of the signatories.[102] Members of the Right parties were no doubt influenced in their negative attitude by reason of the opportunity which Socialists were taking to advocate complete disarmament on the ground that war had become a thing of the past.[103]

[99] L.N.O.J., Special Supplement, No. 136 (1935), p. 80.
[100] Rigsdagstidenden (1928-1929), Folketinget II, p. 4743, Landstinget, p. 304. Stortings Forhandlinger (1929), Vol. 7a, pp. 368-9. Riksdagens Protokoll (1929), F.K., 16: 10, A.K., 19: 6 ff. American-Scandinavian Review, March 1929, p. 175; April 1929, p. 239.
[101] See Stortings Forhandlinger (1929), Vol. 6a, Innst. S. nr. 25.
[102] Riksdagens Protokoll (1929). Saml. 5, nr. 7, pp. 8-9.
[103] In 1930 M. Lindhagen introduced a motion into the Swedish Riksdag requesting the Government for an initiative—with regard to the impending revision of the Covenant in connection with the Kellogg Pact—for a provision declaring complete disarmament as the goal of the League. But see the Constitution Committee's report rejecting this motion. Riksdagens Protokoll (1930), Saml. 5, nr. 6. At the time of adherence to the Kellogg Pact, the same committee had rejected a motion by M. Lindhagen that there be attached to the declaration of acceptance, a statement that adherence to the Pact implied approval of general, immediate and complete disarmament. Riksdagens Protokoll (1929), Saml. 5, nr. 7.

Our chief interest in the Kellogg Pact, however, arises from the attempt which was made at the subsequent Assemblies to bring the Covenant into harmony with its provisions. The declaration of principle embodied in the Pact was more far-reaching in its denunciation of war than was the Covenant, and led the British delegation at the Tenth Assembly to propose certain changes in Articles XII, XIII, and XV of the Covenant. Although the British resolution, subscribed to by the Danish and other delegations, offered no amendment to Article XVI, the extension of sanctions would have indirectly resulted from the inclusion of additional classes of prohibited war covered by the Pact.[104] Dr Georg Cohn, legal expert in the Danish Foreign Office, said that Denmark would accept the extension of sanctions which would result indirectly from this proposal, in so far as economic and political sanctions were concerned. The Danish policy rested on the view that *all* cases of war should be combatted in as effective a way as possible. But Denmark considered the extension of military sanctions, even indirect, as undesirable, for in them she saw a vestige of the former law of war and a violation of the fundamental idea of the Covenant with regard to disarmament and the preservation of peace.[105]

Dr Raestad, the Norwegian delegate, admitted the desirability of eliminating from the Covenant such parts as were contradictory to the Kellogg Pact. Although agreeing in principle with Dr Cohn with regard to sanctions, he opposed any extension of sanctions, on the ground that that question should be considered independently of the question of harmonizing the Covenant and Pact.[106]

For Sweden, Baron Marks von Würtemberg held a third view, based on his conviction that the League was not strong enough in relation to States in general to apply even economic sanctions in every war that might occur. He was especially doubtful of the feasibility of applying sanctions when the Council, acting under Article XV, paragraph 7, were not in agreement.[107]

At the 1930 Assemblies the Swedish position was ably explained by M. Undén, who, as a member of the Committee of Eleven set up

[104] *IoA.IC.*, 24, 28-30.
[105] *ibid.*, p. 29. See M. Engell's explanation *IIA.IC.*, 63.
[106] *IoA.IC.*, 30-31.
[107] *IoA.IC.*, 32-3.

to study the question of bringing the Covenant into harmony with the Pact,[108] had objected to the extension of the application of sanctions. After admitting that "penalties and disarmament were part of the same system of security and closely connected," he declared it undesirable to amplify penalties because "no definite forward step" had been taken towards disarmament. And he advanced another reason, as follows :[109]

> My Government is not one of the main adversaries of penalties themselves. On the contrary, it holds that the members of the League are bound to take joint action against any State which threatens the peace. Swedish public opinion regards the joint obligations under Article XVI of the Covenant as one of the cornerstones of the League. But the system of penalties as conceived by the Covenant has certain serious drawbacks, one of which is that there is no guarantee that the members of the League will, at a critical moment, agree as to who is the aggressor. If a serious divergence of views occurred among the members of the League, and if they were thereby divided into two hostile camps of about equal strength, and war broke out, I confidently affirm that it would be cynical in the extreme to call such a war "the joint enforcement of penalties by the League of Nations." Such a war would assume the character of a "private war." The Swedish Government is of opinion that the best method of rendering the system of security more effective at present—apart from the possibility of international disarmament—is to perfect the preventive means which the League can employ in times of crisis.

Professor Undén elaborated further the Swedish view. It was desirable to include in the Covenant a prohibition of all wars covered by the Pact of Paris, and to specify sanctions only for classes of war in which it was likely that sanctions could be imposed. The effectiveness of sanctions would be "subject to conditions or contingencies which it would be particularly difficult to fulfil if the Council were deeply divided."[110] A more reasonable extension of sanctions, one which Professor Undén had proposed in the Committee of Eleven,

[108] *L.N.O.J.*, XI, 58C., p. 101.
[109] The quotations are found in M. Undén's speech published in full in *11A.1C.*, 39-41.
[110] *11A.1C.*, 61.

would be to cover instances where States resorted to war in violation
of a unanimous recommendation of the Council regarding the provisional steps for the maintenance of peace. To the argument used by
M. Rolin of Belgium that the sanctions of Article XVI should be
extended to cover all wars, and thereby lessen the likelihood that a
State would risk aggression,[111] the Swedish statesman replied that
it was not this specification of sanctions in itself which guarantees
the workability of the system. The mere threat of sanctions would
not be sufficient to prevent war "unless both Governments and peoples
were convinced that sanctions would really be applied *with the
necessary efficacy.*"[112] The Italo-Abyssinian conflict of 1935-1936
would seem to bear out this argument.

Although the Norwegian Government, in its letter to the League
dated February 22, 1930,[113] "strongly advised against any simul-
taneous enlargement" of obligations, in the following year it altered
this advice in recognition of the practical difficulties of reaching
agreement on the method of harmonizing the two instruments.[114] In
the Twelfth Assembly Dr Raestad stressed that his Government
could not accept the theory that there may occur within the League
itself only one kind of war, and that penalties are provided for every
form of war. He accepted M. Undén's view that sanctions might be
employed for cases in which there was a unanimous decision of the
Council confirming the measures to restore peace or subdue the
aggressor.[115]

If, however, the Scandinavian States were prepared to make these
extensions in the application of sanctions, the emphasis of their
policy was to develop Article XI of the Covenant rather than
Article XVI. It was because they looked on the League as an instrument for the prevention of war rather than as a criminal court for
inflicting punishment on law-breaking States that their efforts took
this direction.[116] Especially Professor Undén was influential in the

---

[111] *11A.1C.*, 47.

[112] *11A.1C.*, 60-1. Italics are mine.

[113] *11A.1C.*, 130 (Appendix IV of the Report of the Committee on Amendments
to the Covenant).

[114] *12A.1C.* 84-85 (Letter of June 18, 1931).

[115] *12A.1C.*, 34-5, should be compared with *11A.1C.*, 55-7.

[116] *11A.1C.*, 41. See also the declaration of the Norwegian delegation, *St. med.*
nr. 3 (1931), p. 44.

efforts for regularizing and developing the procedure used so successfully in the Greco-Bulgarian dispute.[117] At the 1928 Assembly he
congratulated the German Government for taking the initiative which
led to the drafting of a model treaty for strengthening the means to
prevent war.[118] Later he took an active part in the drafting of a
general convention of a similar character.[119]

The Conference for the Reduction and Limitation of Armaments

At its meeting in May 1931, the Council of the League of Nations
called the long delayed Conference for the Reduction and Limitation
of Armaments to convene in Geneva on February 2, 1932. Shortly
thereafter the Scandinavian Governments began their preparation for
participation.[120] This undertaking was not made a party affair, but
was recognized to be of such general interest that the cooperation of
the various political groups was made possible. In Sweden, M. Ekman,
the Prime Minister, arranged for the appointment of a committee of
eight members from the First and Second Chambers of the Riksdag,
including the Conservative leader, Admiral Lindman, and the
Socialist leader, M. Hansson, to prepare the Swedish policy for the
conference. The work of the committee was directed by the Government with the special collaboration of the Ministers of Foreign
Affairs, Defense, and Finance.[121]

In Norway, where the Labour Party's relations to the bourgeois
parties were less congenial, cooperation was more limited. Although

---

[117] On the question of the development of preventive measures in accordance with
Article XI see especially T. P. Conwell-Evans, *The League Council in Action*,
Part II.

[118] *9A.3C.*, 57.

[119] Records of the Eleventh and Twelfth Assemblies, Third Committee.

The General Convention to Improve the Means of Preventing War, dated Septem-
ber 26, 1931, was signed by Denmark, Norway and Sweden. At the opening of the
Seventeenth Assembly, Norway alone of these States had deposited ratification.
The Convention has not come into force.

[120] The Norwegian *Utenriksdepartement* has published a report entitled "Nedrust-
ningskonferansen, Geneve 1932-33" in *St. med.* nr. 3 (1934), pp. 67-75, which in-
cludes a brief sketch of the preparatory measures taken, a report of M. Lange on
the work of the conference, and the instructions given the Norwegian delegation
in the Royal Resolution of January 15, 1932.

A corresponding Swedish treatment is available in *Utrikesdepartementets blåböcker, U.N.F.* (1932, 1933, 1934). See especially, *U.N.F.* (1932), pp. 66-9.

[121] See *Le Temps*, June 30, 1931.

the members of the Labour Party in the Foreign Affairs Committee of the Storting asked for representation of their party in the delegation and supported the financial appropriation for participation,[122] Professor Edvard Bull, the Labour appointee, refused to join the delegation when the instructions were so drawn by the Government that he would not have been permitted to express an independent view on behalf of complete military disarmament.[123] The Central Executive of the Labour Party then abandoned the idea of being represented at the Conference. When in February 1932 a further appropriation was necessary for the Norwegian delegation, M. Nygaardsvold and his colleagues declared that they had little faith in the prospects of the conference, but that they would again vote for the granting of funds, lest the charge be brought that the Labour Party opposed the work for a general and effective reduction of armaments.[124] If, however, the bourgeois parties in Norway opposed the Labour party's desire to urge complete military disarmament at the coming conference, the Government did go so far as to instruct the delegation to seek the "greatest possible positive results as a first step on the way to the eventual securing of world peace by international disarmament."[125]

In Sweden, however, despite the efforts of pacifists, such as M. Lindhagen, for complete disarmament,[126] the strong Social Democrat Party, and indeed the Government, contented itself with facing the problem of the present, and instructed the delegation to work for "the greatest possible reduction of armaments."[127] The Danish Social Democrat Government, on the other hand, was prepared to accept complete military disarmament, even by unilateral action.[128]

[122] *Innstilling fra Utenriks-og konstitusjonskomiteen* (May 20, 1931), *Stortingets Forhandlinger* (1931), Vol. 6a, *Budg. innst. S.* nr. 11B.

[123] *St. med.* nr. 3 (1934), p. 68. *Manchester Guardian,* January 19, 1932.

[124] *Stortingets Forhandlinger* (1932), Vol. 6a, *Budg. innst. S.* nr. 12. (Report of February 29, 1932.)

[125] *St. med.* nr. 3 (1934), p. 75.

[126] See his frequent motions in *Första Kammaren* of the Riksdag, such as Motion nr. 103 in the session of 1926.

[127] *U.N.F.* (1932), p. 67 (which quotes at length the report of the Swedish Minister for Foreign Affairs in the *statsråds-protokollet* for January 15, 1932, concerning the general policy which the Swedish delegation should take).

[128] See *Forslag til Lov om Omdannelse af Hær og Flaade til et Vagtkorps og en Statsmarine, bestemt til Varetagelse af Danmarks Neutralitets-og Folkeforbundsopgaver. Rigsdagstidenden* (1930-1931) *Tillæg* A. I, pp. 2519-50.

The bill for the disarmament of Denmark which was introduced into the Folketing

Before the Disarmament Conference opened the Assembly met in its twelfth ordinary session and received on September 11, 1931, a draft resolution of the Danish, Norwegian, Dutch, Swedish and Swiss delegations requesting the Council to urge the Governments to abstain, pending the results of the Conference, from any measure leading to the increase in the existing level of their armaments.[129] M. Grandi of Italy also asked the Assembly to recommend an armaments truce, which was subsequently declared for the year beginning November 1, 1931.[130] The Five-Power resolution aimed at securing for the Disarmament Conference the benefit of an active public opinion, enlightened as to the urgent need for mutual concessions; it sought to produce an atmosphere of tranquillity for the better success of the Conference.[131]

It is not within the scope of this study to trace in detail the participation of the Scandinavian States in the ill-fated and long-continued Disarmament Conference. Our interest will be confined primarily to an analysis of their policy as a continuation and development of their past activity in the Assembly.

on October 3, 1929 by Defense Minister L. Rasmussen was adopted by the Folketing on March 11, 1931, by 77 votes to 64. But the bill could not gain a majority in the Landsting. (See *Folketinget*, 1930-1931, III, pp. 5475-6.) When this attempt to disarm Denmark unilaterally was again put to vote in the session of 1932-1933 by the Socialist Government, it was carried in the Folketing by 74 votes to 61 on October 20, 1932, but rejected by the Landsting on March 29, 1933, by 39 votes to 31. (*Landstinget*, 1932-1933, p. 1268.)

On the question of the Socialist Disarmament programme see John H. Wuorinen, "Denmark's Disarmament Program," *Current History*, Vol. 31, pp. 182-3 (October 1929); *New York Times*, September 8, 1929; Peter Munch, "Will Denmark Disarm?" in *Headway*, Vol. II, pp. 128-9 (July 1929); Eric Cyril Bellquist, "Possible Effects of Danish Disarmament," *American-Scandinavian Review*, May 1931, pp. 299-300.

The change in the international situation in 1933-1934 led to a postponement in the efforts of the Social Democrat party to push the plan for disarmament. The present position is that the programme of 1923 will await a more favourable time for being carried out. (*American-Scandinavian Review*, September 1934, p. 269.) See also "Socialdemokratiets Manifest," issued June 24, 1935, at the party Congress at Aalborg, *Aarbog for Rigsdagssamlingen 1934-35 samt Overordentlig Rigsdagssamling 1935*, pp. 523 ff.

[129] *12A.3C.*, 30 ff.

[130] *St. med.* nr. 3 (1933), p. 65. (The Report of the Secretary General to the Thirteenth Assembly.)

[131] See especially *12A.3C.*, 33 (M. Colban's speech).

The instructions given to the Norwegian and Swedish delegations,[132] and the speeches made at the Conference and in its Commissions show that the fundamentals of Scandinavian outlook had not been substantially altered. It was recognized, even by the Danish Government which was then seeking to disarm that country by unilateral action, that emphasis should be placed on the idea of progressive steps for general reduction, as this "First Conference" could obviously not go the entire distance contemplated by Article VIII.[133] The Scandinavian delegations still held the view that "moral disarmament, based on a large reduction of armaments . . . is the best possible guarantee of security,"[134] for as the Danish Foreign Minister said in the plenary session of February 12, 1932, "guarantees of security founded on force will always be imperfect, since it is impossible to foresee the issue of a war even with considerable knowledge of the forces of the belligerents."[135] The delegations, however, accepted the contention that, "in the present state of world politics, it would be necessary, simultaneously with the reduction of armaments, to define and strengthen the international organization which was to guarantee the security of peoples."[136] In this connection Denmark perhaps was prepared to go a little further than Norway and Sweden. Baron Ramel of Sweden, however, stated that the Swedish delegation would give "unbiased and careful consideration to any proposal intended to reinforce security—for instance, by the organization of an international armed force. . . ."[137] The Swedish Government was "fully aware of the necessity of endowing an international juridical organization, which may be set up, with certain means of coercion," and Sweden "would make no attempt to shirk its obligations in that respect." Norway was prepared to accept the idea of constituting an international air force with police power.[138] Its

[132] The Danish instructions were unavailable.

[133] *Records of the Conference for the Reduction and Limitation of Armaments, Series A. Verbatim Records of the Plenary Meetings,* Vol. I, 1932, p. 94 (speech of M. Munch).

[134] See the speeches of M. Munch, *ibid.,* p. 95; Baron Ramel, *ibid.,* p. 88; and M. Colban, *ibid.,* pp. 114-15.

[135] *ibid.,* p. 95.

[136] *Records of the Disarmament Conference, Conf. D/C.G.,* 16 (April 13, 1932), p. 73. (Speech of Dr Munch.)

[137] *Conf. D/P.,* Series A, Vol. I (1932), p. 88. (Speech of February 11, 1932.)

[138] *St. med.* nr. 3 (1934), p. 74.

delegation introduced a proposal to make more precise the rules for the application of economic and financial sanctions. But all the Scandinavians were convinced that a permanent international military, naval or air organization would only be feasible if there were a big reduction of armaments.

The speech of Baron Ramel was hailed by *Le Temps* and others of the French press as equivalent to a support in principle of the French point of view.[139] A debate followed in the Swedish Riksdag on February 26, 1932, on the meaning to be attached to the Foreign Minister's speech, especially with regard to the sympathy he had expressed for a "force internationale." The Conservative leader, M. Lindman, correctly said that no approval was given of the French proposals, but that the Swedish delegate had declared that the French proposals should be investigated and studied, since such consideration must be taken of all proposals put forward at the Conference, if progress were to be made.[140] The overwhelming majority of the Riksdag were of the opinion that the phraseology used by Baron Ramel on February 11, 1932, must not be interpreted to imply acceptance by Sweden of military sanctions. There was, however, disagreement as to the advisability of setting up an international police force prior to actual and sweeping disarmament. M. Hansson, leader of the Social Democrat Party and soon to become Prime Minister, expressed pleasure that the Swedish delegation had taken the stand it did on the question of an international police; he recalled that his party was the only Swedish party which, in its programme, had advocated the conception of an international police, but he stated that the first prerequisite of a successful international police is a reduction of armaments.[141]

Among the provisions which the Danish, Norwegian and Swedish delegations urged at the Conference were the following:[142] total abolition of arms of a special aggressive character, including those dangerous to civilian populations; total prohibition of military avia-

[139] See the speech of M. Engberg on February 26, 1932, in *Andra Kammaren, Riksdagens Protokoll* (1932) *A.K.*, 18: 20 *ff.*
[140] *Riksdagens Protokoll* (1932) *A.K.*, 18: 14 *ff.*
[141] *ibid.*, pp. 17-19.
[142] See especially *St. med.* nr. 3 (1934), p. 74, and in *Conference Documents*, Vol. I, 1932, IX, 63, the following: *Conf. D.,* 83, *Conf. D.,* 89 and *Conf. D.,* 90.

tion and the manufacture, and training in connection therewith; internationalization or strict international control of civil aviation; far-reaching provisions for preventing an armaments race, especially by the limitation of military budgets; a highly developed system of control and supervision of national armaments, and of the provisions of the armaments convention.

The "Straight Eight," as the Belgian, Czechoslovakian, Danish, Spanish, Dutch, Norwegian, Swedish and Swiss delegations were sometimes referred to, submitted a draft prohibiting the use of chemical, bacteriological and incendiary warfare. M. Lange, however, said that it would be a grave error of conception and method to propose in the Conference to render war humane. No distinction could be made between barbarous methods of war and less barbarous methods. If it were desired to make such a distinction, it might be necessary to conclude that chemical warfare was the least barbarous. He thought it necessary to concentrate on abolishing those methods of war which favoured sudden attack, and suggested concentration on air bombardment and chemical warfare.[143]

The Scandinavian States played an active and interested rôle in much of the work of the Conference, but they were well aware that success depended on the Powers which were most heavily armed. In his opening speech on February 11, 1932, Baron Ramel had pointed to the necessity of a political rapprochement between these Powers.[144] As hopes for a positive achievement of any consequence declined, the earlier feeling that the "neutral" countries might play an important rôle in composing international differences began to wane.[145] As the aspirations and hopes of the world were carried to a "suspense account," to use M. Sandler's choice of a budgetary expression, the Scandinavians took the opportunity to assert that responsibility for the disappointing results did not lie with themselves.[146] In the 1933 Assembly Prime Minister Mowinckel remarked that everyone knew that if the Great Powers had been able to reach agreement, "no

---

[143] *Conf. D/C.G.*, Series B, Part I, p. 180. Also pp. 179-80.
[144] *Conf. Dis A.*, Series A, Part I (Plenary), p. 88.
[145] *The Times*, June 4, 1934 (view of the Stockholm correspondent), p. 14.
[146] *Conf. D/C.G.*, Series B, Part I (1932), p. 174.

proposal relating to disarmament would have failed for lack of support from other countries."[147]

The persistency of the Scandinavians in the work for reduction of armaments has testified to the sincerity of their belief as to its importance. The Swedish Foreign Minister in a speech made in the Assembly on September 29, 1933, said that the reference of the problem of armaments to a separate conference "cannot and must not be interpreted as meaning that the League is washing its hands of the question."[148] The obligations of Article VIII of the Covenant remained entirely in force for all members of the League. Although admitting the principle of equality in the application of the common obligations of the Covenant, he pled for a "controlled equality," and warned against a return to the old equality which had meant the "right of everybody to do whatever he liked." To prevent the pre-War equality which produced the "fratricidal fraternity" of the War period and the "impoverished liberty" of the following years, M. Sandler urged the adoption of a convention, "even if it means giving up radical solutions in order to reach sooner a positive and reasonable result."[149]

On April 14, 1934, the Danish, Norwegian, Spanish, Swedish and Swiss delegations to the Disarmament Conference laid a memorandum before the general commission of the Conference with the hope that a final and supreme effort might overcome the *impasse* and achieve at least a limited convention of reduction.[150] The delegations of the European neutral States declared it essential to obtain, to a moderate degree, a practical realization of equality of rights. Even a modest convention, it was avowed, could not be realized without a reinforcement of security beyond the proposals of the British memorandum of January 29, 1934—particularly as regards definite guarantees of execution. But the will to agree was lacking, and once again a compromise proposal came to naught.

[147] *14A.P.*, 29.
[148] *14A.P.*, 43.
[149] *ibid.*
[150] *Conf. D/C.G.*, 158 (*Conf. D./Bureau 57*), pp. 867 *ff.* See also Foreign Minister Rickard Sandler's speech made at Malmö, June 10, 1934, entitled "Nedrustningens Läge," in *Ett Utrikespolitiskt Program*, pp. 87 *ff.*

With the change in the international situation brought about by the departure of Germany from the League, the failure of the disarmament conference and the German denunciation of the military clauses of the Treaty of Versailles, the hopes for any immediate reduction of armaments vanished, and the Scandinavian States were left facing the failure of fifteen years of effort which they, above all, had been active in sponsoring. Meanwhile Denmark, as a member of the Council in April 1935, was confronted with the draft resolution submitted by the French, British and Italian Governments, which condemned the German denunciation of the military clauses of the Versailles *Diktat*. After a meeting of the Danish, Norwegian and Swedish Foreign Ministers in Copenhagen shortly before the Council's meeting,[151] Dr Munch refrained from voting on this resolution in the Council because, as he said, by playing the rôle of a court of justice and condemning Germany's action, the Council was placing difficulties in the way of the successful negotiation necessary to emerge from the existing *impasse* in international politics, and of achieving universality of the League.[152] The Danish statesman informed the Council that his and other Governments wanted "a new and serious effort to arrest the competition in armaments," which if continued would lead to a catastrophe unprecedented in history.[153]

[151] See the debate in *Andra Kammaren* of the Swedish Riksdag, April 30, 1935, in which M. Sandler the Foreign Minister states the principles agreed upon at the Copenhagen Conference. *Riksdagens Protokoll* (1935). *A.K.* 29: 1 *ff.*
[152] *L.N.O.J.*, Vol. XVI (1935), 85C, pp. 555, 561-2.
[153] *ibid.*, p. 562.

CHAPTER XIII

POLITICAL QUESTIONS, MANDATES, MINORITIES, THE SAAR

The Åland Question

SWEDEN had hardly entered the League of Nations in 1920 when she acted in such a way as to strengthen the prestige of the League as an institution for the settlement of disputes. Indeed, the first international conflict of importance submitted to the Council was that between Sweden and Finland concerning the Åland question.[1] The exemplary attitude of Sweden in this controversy was widely recognized when M. Hjalmar Branting loyally accepted on behalf of his Government the decision of the Council recognizing the sovereignty of Finland over the Åland Islands.[2]

The significance of the Swedish action can be appreciated only in light of the keen disappointment which the Swedish nation experienced as a consequence of this decision. Åland had been an integral portion of the Swedish dominions for more than five centuries when she was lost to Russia in 1809. When the dispute with Finland was submitted to the Council "as a result of Swedish action though formally on British initiative,"[3] the homogeneous population of this Baltic archipelago was still united to Sweden by ties of a "common origin, a common history and a common national spirit."[4] Following

---

[1] A useful statement of the facts in the Åland question is to be found in Eric Cyril Bellquist's monograph, *Some Aspects of the Recent Foreign Policy of Sweden,* Chapter III. For further sources see the reference therein cited, especially the *Peace Handbook* of the Historical Section of the British Foreign Office, VIII, No. 148; Correspondence relating to the question of Åland Islands, *L.N.O.J.* (1920), *Special Supplement* No. 1, and *Ålandsfrågan inför Nationernas Förbund,* 3 vols. (Diplomatiska aktstyken utgivna av Kungl. Utrikesdepartmentet), Swedish and French texts, Stockholm 1920, 1921.

[2] *L.N.O.J.,* II (1921), pp. 699-700 (Minutes of the Thirteenth Session of the Council).

[3] Svanström and Palmstierna, *A Short History of Sweden,* p. 377.

[4] See M. Branting's speech in the Council, *L.N.O.J.,* II (1921), p. 699.

the Finnish declaration of independence in 1917, the inhabitants of Åland had declared by a 95 per cent vote their desire for reunion with their mother country. But Finland opposed all pretensions not compatible with her sovereignty over the islands, and the quarrel grew so bitter that the Swedish Minister in Helsingfors was eventually recalled.[5]

After the Council had listened to the arguments of M. Branting and M. Enckell in July 1920,[6] and after a committee of international jurists had upheld the Swedish contention that the matter was not solely within the domestic jurisdiction of Finland, the *rapporteurs* appointed by the Council declared that Finnish sovereignty over Åland was incontestable.[7] In the Council on June 24, 1921, M. Branting, after accepting the recommendations of the *rapporteurs,* declared that Sweden had not been influenced by a desire to increase her territory. She had sought to defend the principles of self-determination, which, although not recognized as a part of international law, had received a wide application in the formation of the new Europe. The Swedish Government had hoped that the Ålanders would not be refused the rights which had been recognized in respect of their Schleswig brothers.[8]

Another delicate aspect of the dispute, important for the security of Sweden, was that of the non-fortification and neutralization of the islands. The Swedish demands on this point were met, and on October 20, 1921, an agreement between ten interested States was signed at Geneva.[9]

An appreciation of the Swedish behaviour in the Åland dispute was expressed in the *New York Times* as follows:[10]

> At any rate the Swedes have done a good deal to rehabilitate
> the principle of settling disputes by discussion instead of war.
> Many nations have invoked arbitration lately, but the willingness
> to let disputes be decided by arbitration always rests on the

[5] Bellquist, *op. cit.*, pp. 289, note 11, pp. 292-7.

[6] *L.N.O.J.*, I (1920), pp. 247-250. (Seventh Session of the Council at St. James's Palace, London.)

[7] *L.N.O.J.*, I (1920), Pt. 11, p. 396.

[8] *supra,* note 4.

[9] C. N. Gregory, "The Neutralization of the Åland Islands," *A.J.I.L.*, XVII (1923), at pp. 72 *ff. League of Nations Treaty Series,* IX, 211.

[10] Quoted in the *American-Scandinavian Review,* IX (1921), p. 625.

major premise that our side is right; and if the arbitration fails to recognize that, so much the worse for the principle of arbitration. The Swedes are not the only people who feel that they have been unjustly treated, but they are seemingly the only people who have realized in recent years that the reign of law must depend on the willingness of the loser to stand by the decision.

The Corfu Affair

The Corfu Affair of 1923 ably demonstrates the vigour of Scandinavian statesmen in their defence of the new principles of international morality embodied in the Covenant of the League of Nations. The bombardment and occupation of a Greek island by Signor Mussolini's forces challenged the fundamental conception of the new order; for a member of the League had resorted to violence against a fellow-member without first submitting the dispute to some form of pacific settlement.[11] No representative on the Council opposed the Italian challenge with so much determination and force as did M. Branting of Sweden, who energetically denied the Italian claim that the affair did not concern the League. M. Branting emphasized the vital interest which the smaller countries had in ensuring that a breach of the Covenant should not be allowed to pass without protest and without the taking of definite action by the League.[12]

Although Lord Robert Cecil supported the Swedish stand, M. Branting was unable to get a definite pronouncement from the Council concerning its competence to deal with the dispute.[13] The outspoken defence of the Swedish representative provoked a burst of applause in the Assembly. Although the conflict was terminated by the mediation of the Conference of Ambassadors before the 1923 Assembly adjourned, the settlement was made, as Professor William Rappard has written, "clearly at the expense of justice."[14] In view of

[11] In reply to M. Salandra, the Italian representative, M. Branting said: "It seems to me that the public opinion of the world will have some difficulty in understanding how these reprisals, which have been called pacific reprisals, can be altogether innocent and can be in conformity with the spirit of the Covenant." (In the Twenty-Sixth Session of the Council, September 18, 1923.) *L.N.O.J.*, IV (1923), p. 1316. See also *ibid.*, V (1924), pp. 525-6.

[12] *L.N.O.J.*, IV (1923), pp. 1280, 1281.

[13] *ibid.*, p. 1306.

[14] Rappard, *International Relations as viewed from Geneva*, p. 198.

these circumstances, especially of the unwillingness of the Great Powers to act as champions of the League, a number of the delegates of the smaller States expressed their disapproval of the Council's behaviour in the closing session of the Assembly. Dr Nansen, "whose courage, energy and manly frankness have won him the affectionate veneration of all justice-loving friends of the League,"[15] spoke as follows:

> ". . . In the sanctity of the Covenant and in the rule of right lies the whole future of the League of Nations. . . . It is only by the loyal application of the solemn Covenant which we have undertaken that we can safeguard the vital interests of each of our nations and of humanity as a whole. . . .[16]

M. Zahle of Denmark joined Dr Nansen in support of the Swedish insistence that it was vitally important that the League should be able to take action for the solution of international conflicts.[17] M. Branting, who explained to the Assembly the position which he had taken, concluded a forceful speech as follows:

> The maintenance of peace is, it is true, the object of the League of Nations, but a peace which is not founded on justice contains within itself the seeds of future conflict.[18]

A natural consequence of M. Branting's resolute defence of the League's authority in the Corfu affair (coupled with his previously gained reputation for impartiality and good sense), was the subsequent enlistment both of him and other Swedish representatives as mediators between parties in dispute. When in 1924 the Mosul question was referred to the Council by the British Government, M. Branting was designated as *rapporteur*.[19] In this dispute, both parties, at the suggestion of the Swedish statesman, acknowledged the jurisdiction of the Council. Following M. Branting's death in February 1925, M. Undén succeeded to the position of *rapporteur*, and sustained the high reputation which his predecessor had won for Sweden since the founding of the League. M. Undén was successful

[15] Rappard, *op. cit.*, p. 200.
[16] *4A.P.*, 140.
[17] *4A.P.*, 141-2.
[18] *4A.P.*, 138.
[19] Compare Bellquist, *op. cit.*, pp. 341-2.

in obtaining the submission of certain questions related to the Mosul affair to the Permanent Court of International Justice for an advisory opinion. Notice should be taken that the Norwegian and Swedish efforts for the development of the bilateral conciliation technique did not apparently diminish their efforts for strengthening the Council as mediator in disputes threatening peace.[20]

The Manchurian Affair

When the Sino-Japanese conflict came, in September 1931, Norway was the Scandinavian State represented on the Council.[21] Although M. Braadland, the Norwegian Foreign Minister, desired to maintain respect for the Covenant, he did not take as forward a position as M. Branting had done during the Corfu Affair. The circumstances of the two cases, however, were not entirely parallel, as Japan did not dispute the competency of the Council to act under Article XI. The Norwegian representative supported the Council's efforts as a friendly and impartial mediator during the autumn of 1931, but in view of the attitude of the Great Powers, he refrained from taking any lead against the aggressor.[22]

Open disapproval of the Japanese action, however, was clearly expressed by the Scandinavian delegates on March 5, 1932, at the Special Assembly called at the request of the Chinese Government.[23] By that time, Manchuria was in Japanese control, and hostilities had spread to the vicinity of Shanghai; China had invoked Articles X, XI and XV of the Covenant. M. Löfgren declared that what was taking place in the Far East was "war in everything but name."[24] Supporting the Swedish thesis advanced during the Corfu affair,[25] he said that the landing of troops and their use in military operations on the territory of another Power were contrary to the provisions of the Covenant and the Kellogg Pact. In the Scandinavian view the way in which Japan was attempting to extend the conception of legitimate

---

[20] *supra,* Chapter XI, pp. 191 *ff.*

[21] Norway was a member of the Council from 1930 to 1933.

[22] See the Minutes of the Sixty-Fifth Session of the Council. *L.N.O.J.,* XII (1931), No. 12.

[23] *Records of the Special Session of the Assembly convened in virtue of Article XV of the Covenant at the Request of the Chinese Government,* Vol. I, pp. 47, 49, 51.

[24] *ibid.,* p. 49.

[25] *supra,* p. 254, note 11.

self-defence threatened the whole international legal order. Dr Munch asked for a clear affirmation by the Assembly that, by virtue of the establishment of the League and the adoption of the Pact of Paris, no new right could be created by force.

The Scandinavian delegates declared that the first duty of the Assembly was to obtain the cessation of hostilities by the submission of clear recommendations to the parties. M. Braadland added that if either party failed to accept or respect the recommendations submitted by virtue of Article XV, paragraph 4, the League ought to take appropriate action in accordance with the provisions of the Covenant. He did not specify what action he envisaged.[26] Dr Munch favoured application of the procedure laid down in the Convention for Strengthening the Means for Preventing War. In other words, "the violation of the measures prescribed to bring about a cessation of hostilities would involve a presumption that the State violating them was the aggressor."[27] He thought that it was only a question of time until that convention, adopted by the Assembly in September 1931 would be ratified.[28]

The general view at the time was that Article XI of the Covenant did not allow such provisional measures without the consent of the parties to the dispute, and the Assembly acting on this assumption, was powerless to compel a cessation of hostilities in the face of Japanese policy. Without declaring Japanese action contrary to the Covenant or the Kellogg Pact, as M. Löfgren had done, the Assembly on March 11, 1932, declared it "incumbent upon members of the League of Nations not to recognize any situation treaty or agreement which may be brought about contrary to the Covenant of the League of Nations or to the Pact of Paris."[29] A Committee of Nineteen was set up to prepare, if necessary, the draft of the report provided for in Article XV, paragraph 4, of the Covenant.

The Committee of Nineteen was in no hurry to proceed along this path, but continued efforts for mediation while awaiting the report of the Commission of Enquiry, which had previously been sent to the Far East to make first-hand enquiry into the conflict. When an exten-

[26] *Records of the Special Session of the Assembly* (1932), Vol. I, p. 47.
[27] *ibid.*, p. 51.
[28] This was, however, a miscalculation.
[29] *ibid.*, p. 87.

sion of time was requested for the Commission on July 1, 1932, M. Sandler, the Swedish delegate in the Special Assembly, placed responsibility on the League for the *impasse* in which it found itself. "From the outset," he declared, "it was obvious that the Sino-Japanese affair called for firm and rapid action." But "the League has put itself in the position of being obliged to wait, and to wait long and patiently, for the report of one of its own organs."[30] Without calling names, the future Swedish Foreign Minister seemed to reproach the Great Powers for their unfaithfulness to the Covenant.

When at last in December 1932, the report of the Lytton commission was submitted to the Special Assembly, the Scandinavian delegates urged the Assembly to base its action on the findings of the commission.[31] The report had upheld the Scandinavian view that the Japanese hostilities could not be justified as acts of self-defence.[32] M. Undén asked the Assembly to associate itself with the declarations of the Commission of Enquiry to the effect that recognition of the new régime in Manchuria was not compatible with existing international obligations.[33] In conjunction with the delegations of Czechoslovakia, the Irish Free State and Spain, the Swedish delegation proposed that the Committee of Nineteen should be authorized to solicit the cooperation of the United States and the Union of Soviet Socialist Republics for the purpose of getting in touch with the parties, with a view to ensuring a settlement of the dispute on the basis of the findings of the Lytton commission.[34]

This proposal was deemed premature; but finally on February 24, 1933, the Assembly adopted a similar proposal, which constituted the report called for in Article XV, paragraph 4, of the Covenant.[35] Although the League in effect morally condemned Japan for her violation of treaty obligations, the sanctions of Article XVI were not

---

[30] *Records of the Special Session of the Assembly* (1932), Vol. II, p. 14.

[31] *ibid.*, Vol. III. See the speech of M. Undén (December 6, 1932) at pp. 38-9; the speech of M. Lange, of the same day, at pp. 39-40; and the speech of M. Borberg (December 7, 1932) at p. 52.

[32] For the report of the Commission of Enquiry dated October 1, 1932, see *L. of N. Doc.*, C. 663, M. 320, 1932, VII.

[33] *Records of the Special Session of the Assembly* (1932), Vol. III, p. 39.

[34] *ibid.*, p. 167 (Appendix X).

[35] *ibid.*, Vol. IV (1933), pp. 56 ff. See especially the recommendations of the Assembly, *ibid.*, p. 75.

put into operation. As Dr Christian L. Lange has written, "it is a well known fact that the leading members of the League held back from applying sanctions against Japan; they contented themselves with a moral protest, because there was too great a risk in employing sanctions against a strongly armed Great Power."[36]

The Italo-Ethiopian Conflict

The Italo-Ethiopian conflict of 1935-1936 was a more revealing test of Scandinavian loyalty to the principle of collective security.[37] The Scandinavian States, whose past record indicated an understandable hesitancy to extend the scope of sanctions, now demonstrated their good faith by urging fulfilment of the obligations of the Covenant. In the face of Signor Mussolini's preparations for war, the Foreign Ministers of the Scandinavian States and Finland met in Oslo on August 28 and 29, 1935, to consider the attitude they should adopt at the coming Assembly.[38] At the conclusion of this conference a *communiqué* was issued stating that the Ministers "assume that this conflict will be handled in accordance with the directions of the Covenant," and that "they will support every effort to guard the peace and maintain the legal principles of the League."[39] The Scandinavian Governments realized that one more defeat for the League would conclusively demonstrate its inability to impose its principles in the political world, except perhaps in case of disputes between small States.[40]

Prior to the Italian rejection of the Council's proposal for settlement of the dispute made under Article XV, paragraph 4, Scandinavian opinion was being prepared for sanctions. At Upsala on August 31, M. Undén, who commanded high respect throughout the country, was stressing the collective responsibility of the League's

[36] See Dr Lange's article "Utbygging av fredspolitikken," in *Mellanfolkligt Samarbete* (1936), Årg. 6, nr. 2, pp. 45-6.
[37] For the development of the Italo-Ethiopian conflict to September 19, 1935, see The Royal Institute of International Affairs, *Abyssinia and Italy* (Information Department Papers, No. 16), third edition, September 1935.
[38] *Morgenbladet*, August 30, 1935 (Oslo).
[39] *ibid.*
[40] See M. Halvdan Koht's speech in the Assembly on September 11, 1935, *16A.P.*, 57.

members, small as well as large, to uphold the Covenant. He indicated that the entry of Sweden into the League in 1920 signified the turning point in her policy of neutrality. "Peace-loving people insisted now not on neutrality in the sense of impartial passivity but the prevention of war or the stopping of hostilities by common effort."[41]

The day after Sir Samuel Hoare made his widely acclaimed defence of the Covenant before the Assembly, M. Sandler, the Swedish Foreign Minister, urged the League and its members to be ready to shoulder their responsibilities in the grave situation at hand. He warned the Assembly against the possibility of a solution "which under the combined pressure of superior material force and of the ardent and general desire to safeguard peace, may sacrifice the legitimate rights of a weak country in the interests of peace but to the detriment of justice."[42] M. Halvdan Koht, Norwegian Foreign Minister, whose political party had proposed the withdrawal of Norway from the League every year from 1921 to 1934, aligned himself with the defenders of the League and branded war as an unsuitable instrument for advancing the cause of civilization.[43] The month before, Dr Munch, the Danish Foreign Minister, had been criticized in the Italian press because he commended the British attitude in the Abyssinian dispute.[44]

In view of the Italian "resort to war in violation of the Covenant," the Assembly in its Resolution of October 10, 1935, set up a Coordination Committee to effect the application of sanctions. The Danish, Norwegian and Swedish Governments speedily accepted the five proposals approved by the committee. These included an embargo on the export of arms, ammunition and implements of war designed for Italy or Italian territory; certain financial measures; a prohibition of the importation of Italian goods; an embargo on certain exports to Italy; and an organization of mutual support between States applying sanctions.[45]

[41] This is a quotation from the *Times* correspondent at Stockholm, in *The Times*, September 3, 1935.
[42] *16A.P.*, 62-4 (September 12, 1935).
[43] *16A.P.*, 57.
[44] *The Times*, August 30, 1935.
[45] See *L.N.O.J.*, *Special Supplement*, No. 147, pp. 12-17. (Report of the Committee of Experts to the Chairman of the Coordination Committee, approved by the Committee of Eighteen on December 13, 1935.)

In Norway and Sweden the imposition of sanctions was taken by the Governments without consultation with the national parliaments. After a meeting of the Swedish Riksdag Committee on Foreign Affairs, M. Hansson, the Social Democrat Prime Minister, stated on October 20, 1935, that all the important political parties were in entire agreement with the Government's determination to employ economic sanctions.[46] Professor Bagge, to whom leadership of the Conservative Party had passed, made a speech, however, in which he said that his party would ask for a reconsideration of Sweden's position towards the League and its obligations, after this conflict was ended.[47]

In Denmark, where the National Assembly normally convenes in October, rather than in January as in Norway and Sweden, the Social Democrat Government introduced a bill in the Rigsdag providing for the application of the specified sanctions.[48] All of the political parties supported the view that Denmark must fulfill its obligations as a member of the League by imposing sanctions; but the Conservative Party objected to the provisions of the bill giving legal authorization to the Government to apply sanctions in future cases.[49]

M. Ole Bjørn Kraft explained that Conservatives wanted the law limited to this individual instance. The Government's bill, however, was adopted by the Folketing with 78 votes against 5.[50] In the Landsting, although no negative votes were cast, only 24 members of a total of 76 actually supported the measure.[51]

Meanwhile the British and French Governments had been authorized by the Committee of Thirteen to seek a conciliation between the contending States. When the ill-fated Hoare-Laval plan was disclosed in December 1935, a howl of indignation arose in Scandinavia. It is significant that the strongest criticism of these proposals came from

[46] *Anglo-Swedish Review,* November 1935, pp. 389-90.
[47] *ibid.* See also *American-Scandinavian Review,* December 1935, p. 362.
[48] *Forslag til Lov angaaende Iværksættelse af Foranstaltninger i Henhold til Folkeforbunds-Pagtens Art. 16 Stk. I. Rigsdagstidenden* (1935-1936), *Tillæg* C, p. 1.
[49] See the Report of the Select Committee of the Folketing, of November 15, 1935 (*Folketinget* 1935-1936, II, *Afdeling,* Blad. nr. 17). Also the Report of the Select Committee of the Landsting of November 16, 1935. (*Landstinget,* 1935-1936, Blad. nr. 5.)
[50] *Rigsdagstidenden* (1935-1936) *Folketinget* I, p. 209 (November 13, 1935).
[51] *ibid., Landstinget,* p. 31 (November 16, 1935).

those quarters which hitherto had supported the British point of view.[52] M. Sandler, the Swedish Foreign Minister, declared in a speech on December 19 that the dismemberment of independent States had not needed the League in the past, nor was it required for that purpose now. Practically all of the Scandinavian press felt that the suggested "handing over of Abyssinia to Signor Mussolini" could not be justified.[53] Even the Conservative *Svenska Dagbladet* said:

> We must wait and see what is going to happen, but when in the twentieth century the first guardian of international order and right calls on Signor Mussolini with peace preliminaries which put a premium on the violation of treaties and pacts, and on aggression, this means bending the knee to robber morality. Lord Beaconsfield once gave England peace with honour; has not Mr Baldwin to fear peace with dishonour?[54]

The subsequent triumph of Mussolini over the forces of Emperor Haile Selassie increased disillusionment in the Scandinavian countries. Public opinion, doubtful of the efficacy of collective security in the face of new political realities, turned towards isolationism. On July 1, 1936, the Foreign Ministers of the six former neutral European States and Finland recognizing altered conditions issued a communiqué declaring that they did not think it right that certain articles of the Covenant, especially the article dealing with the reduction of armaments, should remain a dead letter while others were enforced. They placed it on record that so long as the Covenant is applied only incompletely and inconsistently they are obliged to bear that fact in mind in connection with the application of Article XVI.[55] In a letter from the Swedish Government to the Secretary-General, dated August 29, 1936, fears were expressed that in the future difficulties would arise regarding the effective application of even economic and financial sanctions.[56]

---

[52] See *The Times*, December 16, 1935, also an article by Professor Axel Møller entitled "Fredsforslaget" in *Dagens Nyheder* (Copenhagen), December 12, 1935.
[53] *The Times*, December 19, 1935.
[54] *The Times*, December 16, 1935.
[55] Communication from the Government of Sweden to the Secretary-General (dated August 29, 1936). *L. of N. Doc.*, C. 357, M. 233, 1936, VII (Annex), p. 5.
[56] *ibid.*, p. 4.

If there still remained a doubt of a new Scandinavian attitude towards the obligation upon members to impose economic sanctions, it was dispelled by M. Undén on January 31, 1938, in the special committee set up to study the application of the principles of the Covenant. He bluntly stated that "for the time being, the system of sanctions is in fact suspended," and added that, "in practice, the League no longer possesses the characteristics of a coercive League corresponding to the provisions of Article XVI of the Covenant." A practice has become established whereby members of the League do not consider themselves bound to take coercive action against an aggressor State. M. Undén hoped that the Swedish view would be accepted by the other States as a loyal and legitimate interpretation of the Covenant in view of the recognized impossibility of acting in conformity with the letter of its provisions. His conclusion was that "the League is not weakened by the recognition of the actual fact of its weakness. It is weakened rather by affording the peoples of the world repeated opportunities for remarking the difference between theory and practice."[57]

Mandates under the League

The peoples of Scandinavia greeted with favour the principles expressed in Article XXII of the Covenant that the well-being and development of backward peoples (inhabitants of the former German colonies and certain Turkish territory) "form a sacred trust of civilization," and that the tutelage of such peoples should be exercised by advanced nations as mandatories on behalf of the League. At Geneva the representatives of the Scandinavian States have been extraordinarily active in guarding the sanctity of this principle. The method employed, beginning at the First Assembly, by Dr Nansen and M. Löfgren, was to assert the right of the Assembly to some control over the League's mandates. In an earlier chapter reference was made to Dr Nansen's insistence that the Assembly should discuss the question of mandates despite the Council's objections, because the "Assembly was more or less responsible morally for the terms of

[57] *Report of the Special Committee Set Up To Study the Application of the Principles of the Covenant* (Minutes of the Third Session of the Committee, January 31 to February 2, 1938). *L. of N. Doc.*, A 7, 1938, VII, pp. 9, 10.

the mandates and how they were carried out."[58] In the sub-committee of which Dr Nansen was chairman, M. Löfgren took the position that, as the Council had not taken steps to bring the mandates into effect, the Assembly had rights and obligations in connection with the whole matter, including the terms of the mandates.[59]

The competence conflict between the Council dominated by the principal Allied Powers and the Assembly arose from the ambiguity of paragraph 8 of Article XXII, which the Scandinavian delegates and Mr Doherty of Canada interpreted as meaning that the Assembly should have an opportunity of settling the terms of the mandates before action was taken by the Council.[60] This view was overruled by the Council, which not only refused to submit the draft mandates to the Assembly, but also intimated that the mandate question was vested wholly in the Council. To this latter position Dr Nansen ably replied by quoting a resolution approved by the Council that either body may discuss and examine any matter within the sphere of action of the League. Although the Assembly "reluctantly recognized that under the Covenant control of mandates is given to the Council,"[61] the Assembly's right and obligation to enquire into the League's work in this matter was successfully maintained, largely as a result of the determined stand taken by Dr Nansen. Year after year the Norwegian delegate moved a resolution during the general debate of the Assembly that the report of the Permanent Mandates Commission should be referred to the Sixth Committee for consideration. The success of Dr Nansen's initiative is demonstrated by the attitude taken by the Mandates Commission, which, according to Professor Quincy Wright, "feels obliged to consider all matters relating to the observance of mandates raised by the resolutions of the Assembly as well as of the Council."[62] As an additional means of assuring the influence of the Assembly over mandates, Dr Nansen on one occasion proposed that the Minutes of the Sixth Committee be trans-

[58] Chapter X, p. 156. *1A.6C. (II)*, 306.
[59] *1A.6C. (II)*, 300, 305.
[60] *St. med. nr. 9* (1921). *Om Folkenes Forbunds første delegeretmøte: Genf november-desember 1920*, p. 55.
[61] Quincy Wright, *Mandates Under the League of Nations*, p. 51. See also *ibid.*, pp. 133 ff.
[62] Wright, *op. cit.*, p. 135.

mitted to the Council in order to call its attention to observations made in the Assembly.[63]

The purpose of the Scandinavians in extending the Assembly's supervision over mandates was to ensure the faithful performance of the sacred trust mentioned in Article XXII of the Covenant. Efforts were made to strengthen the influence of the Permanent Mandates Commission over the Council and the Mandatory Powers. M. Branting, as the Council's *rapporteur* on the question of mandates, on December 11, 1923, defined the attitude which the Council should adopt towards the Commission, as follows:

> The Council, which is called upon to take a decision concerning the recommendations of the Permanent Mandates Commission, will doubtless attach great weight to the authoritative opinions of the Committee of Experts on colonial questions which it has itself constituted for this purpose. . . . I believe that it would be wise to carry out its recommendations whenever political considerations—with which, necessarily, our Advisory Committee is not concerned—do not render such a course impossible.[64]

In the Seventh Assembly, Dr Nansen came to the defence of the Permanent Commission after Viscount Cecil had said that its function was to cooperate with and not to criticize the Mandatory Powers. The Norwegian statesman replied that in view of the authorization of the Covenant, it would seem difficult for the Commission to confine itself to cooperation, for if it were not allowed to make remarks on the reports of the Mandatory Powers its work would be worthless.[65] On another occasion Dr Nansen, who was habitually *rapporteur* to the Assembly on mandates, congratulated the Mandates Commission on the courage it had shown when it had sometimes felt obliged to express views disagreeable to certain Mandatory Powers.[66] In other instances the Norwegians and Swedes have assumed the rôle of special guardians of the Commission's welfare. In 1932, for example, efforts were made in the Assembly and Council to prevent the reduction

[63] *7A.6C.*, 25.
[64] *L.N.O.J.*, IV (1923), 28C., p. 385.
[65] *7A.6C.*, 24, 25.
[66] *3A.P.*, 143.

of the number of sessions of the Commission, despite the financial difficulties which all nations were experiencing.[67]

An important condition necessary for the beneficial working of the mandates system (as envisaged in Article XXII of the Covenant) is the willingness of the Mandatory Powers to carry out their obligations and to report sincerely and fully on their administration. In the Scandinavian view, as expressed in the 1920 Assembly by M. Löfgren, the League rather than the principal Allied Powers, should have elected the Mandatory Powers.[68] In order to guarantee the good stewardship of the Mandatory Powers, the Swedish delegate urged that the terms of the mandates should be so stated that there would be a clear possibility of withdrawing a mandate in case of necessity.[69] Although uncertainty remains as to the location of the power, if it exists, to revoke a mandate, it may be noted that Mme Anna Bugge-Wicksell of Sweden, when a member of the Mandates Commission, supported the view that the Permanent Court of International Justice should be the agency of such removal in case of a breach of contract by maladministration.[70]

An important contribution to the successful administration of the League's mandates was rendered by the Swedish representatives on the Council from 1923 to 1926, when they acted as *rapporteur* for the Council on this question.[71] Mention should also be made of the two women who served on the Permanent Mandates Commission. The first of these was Mme Anna Bugge-Wicksell of Sweden, who was particularly interested in questions of education, hygiene and child welfare.[72] Following her death in February 1928, a Norwegian, Mlle Valentine Dannevig, principal of the Vestheim College for Young Ladies at Oslo, succeeded to the Commission. In the Assembly Dr Nansen, whom Mr Philip Noel Baker described in 1930 as "perhaps the only man alive who could venture to say whatever he thought right to any prince, prime minister, or president,"[73] unquestionably

---

[67] See the speech of M. Andvord, *13A.6C.*, 19.

[68] *1A.6C. (II)*, 279.

[69] *1A.6C. (II)*, 371.

[70] This was also the view of Sir Frederick Lugard, Wright, *op. cit.*, p. 440, note 11.

[71] These were M. Branting, M. Sjöberg and Dr Undén.

[72] See Mme Bugge-Wicksell's report on the education of backward peoples which was endorsed by the P.M.C. at its Fourth Session. Wright, *op. cit.*, p. 257.

[73] Vigness, *op. cit.*, p. 129.

occupied the place of first importance when the Assembly discussed mandates questions.

Minorities

Although the Scandinavian representatives in the League have always shown a deep interest in the protection of the rights of racial, religious and linguistic minorities,[74] the best expression of their attitude is found after the beginning of Nazi persecution of the Jews in Germany. In the Council's meeting of May 30, 1933, M. Lange emphasized that the protection of minorities was not only a legal duty imposed upon the League by the minorities treaties, but also a moral duty which the League ought never to forget. In his view no nation could argue that treatment of racial minorities was an exclusively internal question.[75]

The same position was taken by M. Sandler the following September in the Assembly, where he argued that the wording of the Covenant and the practice of the League have shown that "so far as the cause of peace is concerned, no absolute distinction can be made between external and internal questions." He continued with these significant words:[76]

> Each country remains the master of its fate. It is for each country to give its own national social institutions the form which accords with its own particular conditions, requirements and intentions. The League can never set itself up as judge in the conflict of ideas, systems, and parties. But there exist nevertheless unquestioned human values, the conservation of which the League, in the interest of peace and humanity, cannot neglect.
>
> Long before the League was set up, it was realized that the victims of war could not be excluded from the rights of man under international law. It is essential that, at a time of great political and social disturbance, the voice of humanity should be raised no less clearly on behalf of the victims of civil conflict.

[74] See for instance M. Zahle's speech in the Second Assembly, 2A.P., 835; Nansen's speech in the Third Assembly, 3A.P., 60; M. Branting's speeches in the Twenty-Fifth Session of the Council, L.N.O.J., IV (1923), pp. 882, 935; and M. Undén's speech in the Thirty-Fourth Session of the Council, L.N.O.J., VI (1925), p. 876.

[75] L.N.O.J., XIV (1933), 73C., p. 842.

[76] 14A.P., 43-4. (September 29, 1933.)

Referring by name to the Jewish minority problem, the Swedish Foreign Minister asked for a discussion on "the possibility and methods of a more general application of the principles of the special treaties as a means of introducing the conception of equality in this connection also." He introduced these questions in the Assembly because "the conception of the equality of men and nations is at the basis of this institution of the League of Nations." Describing Immanuel Kant as the spiritual founder of the League, M. Sandler said that "any effort, the object or the effect of which is to divide humanity into separate species, necessarily goes counter to the ideas out of which the League of Nations was born. To proclaim the principle of inequality in the world is, in effect, to renounce the League."[77]

Earlier in 1933, M. Lange urged equal treatment of racial minorities on the ground that the diversity of development within a nation was a source of wealth and blessing which ought to be developed.[78] The exemplary attitude of Denmark in regard to the small German minority in South Jutland derives from the view that, by putting minorities at ease, they may become loyal citizens of the countries in which they are living.[79]

The Saar Territory

One final topic will conclude this treatment of the Scandinavian attitude towards the more important political questions dealt with by the League prior to 1938. The policy adopted by the Swedish representatives on the Council from 1923 to 1926 concerning the administration of the Saar territory was characteristic of the general Scandinavian outlook towards political questions. The Treaty of Versailles had conferred the administration of the Saar territory on the League for a period of fifteen years. M. Branting resolved to make certain that the League would properly fulfil this obligation. In the face of recognized difficulties he earnestly endeavoured to provide a truly international character for the Saar administration.[80] At the

[77] *14A.P.,* 43-44.

[78] *L.N.O.J.,* XIV (1933), 73C, p. 872.

[79] See M. Moltesen's speech in the 1932 Assembly, *13A.6C.,* 38. See also *The German Minority in South Jutland* (a summary of Danish Legislation) published by the Danish Foreign Office. April 15, 1924, J. H. Schultz.

[80] For French policy in the Saar see Rappard, *International Relations Viewed From Geneva,* pp. 209-10.

time of the French invasion of the Ruhr the Swedish statesman stressed in the Council that the Governing Commission of the Saar was collectively responsible to the League and independent of the Governments of various member States.[81] He worked to effect the withdrawal of foreign troops of occupation and for the substitution of a local *gendarmerie*; he regretted that it had seemed necessary to establish in a territory administered by the League a régime justifiable only in time of war.[82]

Recognizing the importance of winning the confidence of the people of the Saar, the Scandinavian representatives supported the cause of democratic government for the territory. In this connection Dr Nansen in the 1922 Assembly expressed approval of the suggestion of Lord Robert Cecil that the Council should nominate the Saar member of the Governing Commission in collaboration with the Advisory Council of the Saar.[83] The following April in the Council of the League M. Branting and the British representative abstained from voting for a member of the Advisory Council proposed by M. Hano-toux, because they thought that the nominee did not possess the con-fidence of the loyal population of the Saar.[84] In July 1923, and at later times, the Swedish representative in the Council advised allowing elected representatives of the population of the Saar to present their views directly to Council.[85]

Especially when the Governing Commission issued a decree on March 17, 1923, instituting severe measures in the Saar, did M. Branting criticize the administration for ill-chosen tactics. It was the Commission's function, in his opinion, to endeavour to understand the mentality of the people and to conciliate, rather than to increase tension by imposing measures restricting freedom of speech and the press.[86]

When in January 1935 the plebiscite provided in the Treaty of Versailles was held to determine the future status of the Saar, Sweden, despite her traditional unwillingness to undertake foreign commit-

---

[81] *L.N.O.J.*, IV (1923), 25C., p. 932.
[82] *L.N.O.J.*, V (1924), 28C., p. 507.
[83] *3A.P.*, 61.
[84] *L.N.O.J.*, IV (1923), 24C., p. 598.
[85] *L.N.O.J.*, IV (1923), 25C., p. 871.
[86] *L.N.O.J.*, IV (1923), 24C., p. 595. *ibid.*, V (1924), 27C., p. 352.

ments and responsibilities, assumed a part of the collective police action for maintaining law and order in the Saar. A contingent of two hundred and fifty Swedish troops, voluntarily recruited, was sent to the Saar to cooperate with the British, Italian and Dutch troops on behalf of the League.[87]

[87] *The Times,* December 13, 1934. For the attitude of Swedish opinion to participation, see also *The Times,* January 16, 1935.

Volunteers were recruited because of the provision in the Swedish Constitution, which prohibits the sending of conscript troops abroad without the sanction of the Riksdag. *The Times,* December 13, 1934.

CHAPTER XIV

INTERNATIONAL COOPERATION

I T is beyond the scope of this study to consider the detailed activity of the Scandinavian States in the separate fields of international cooperation, generally referred to as the technical work of the League. Such questions as health, refugees, opium, slavery, unemployment, transport and education, should receive special treatment by experts in the respective fields. This treatise is concerned with these and similar questions only so far as the Scandinavian attitude towards them reveals the Scandinavian conception of their importance to the general theory of the League.

When the Danish, Norwegian and Swedish Governments nominated commissions to investigate the means of safeguarding the interests of the neutral States at the close of the War, the primary concern of these commissions was to draft a proposed convention for an "International Juridical Organization." Little attention was devoted to the problem of positive international cooperation in questions not immediately concerned with procedure for the settlement of disputes and with the development of international law. Yet before the Covenant was drafted, considerable sentiment had been aroused in Scandinavia which opposed a possible limitation of the League's activity to the negative function of preventing conflicts. Such bodies as the Comité Hollando-Scandinave Socialiste and the Norwegian League of Nations Association recognized as early as 1917 and 1919, respectively, that the problem of peace was closely related to the promotion of international cooperation, even in fields apparently quite removed from the question of war.[1]

The Scandinavian Governments, moreover, quickly accepted the view that the maintenance of international peace and justice, the primary function of the League, should be supplemented by the development of technical cooperation on all questions of common

[1] *supra,* Chapter III, pp. 33, 45.

concern. It was not difficult for States such as Denmark and Sweden, who had already taught the world advanced lessons in agricultural and economic cooperation, to subscribe to the principle of international cooperation.

Especially in the economic realm did the Scandinavian States recognize the advantages that might be achieved if nations were prepared to work together. In the Assemblies they pled for nations to understand that it was the interest of every State to cooperate under the auspices of the League and to realize that nations are like individuals in that "the prosperity of one spells the prosperity of all."[2] Possessing a foreign trade greater in relation to population than that of most countries, and recognizing the ill effect which economic war has on good international relations, the Scandinavian States consistently urged, in the period from 1920 to 1933, the lowering of barriers to trade.[3] Unable to obtain the application of the principles adopted by the Economic Conference of 1927,[4] they proceeded, with the cooperation of Belgium, Luxemburg and the Netherlands, to effect in December 1930, through the Oslo Convention, a regional agreement for preventing an increase of tariffs. Tremendously affected by the economic instability of the early 1920's, the Scandinavian delegations urged the settlement of the Reparations and War Debt problem.[5] Indeed, few, if any, countries have been more eager to support the League's efforts for economic cooperation.

In other spheres of technical activity, Scandinavian participation has been characterized by the same willingness to strengthen the bonds of mutual collaboration. The energy and devotion with which

[2] See the speech of M. Moltesen of Denmark on September 7, 1927, in the Eighth Assembly, *8A.P.*, 52.

[3] See Munch, *La Politique du Danemark dans la Société des Nations*, pp. 33-7.

[4] On September 7, 1927, in the Assembly, M. Löfgren said that the commercial policy of Sweden was in all essential points in complete agreement with the principles adopted by the conference; but he pointed to the difficulty which secondary Powers have in applying these principles, unless they are generally adopted by States whose economic influence is greatest. *8A.P.*, 47-8. The Danish and Norwegian delegates also approved the work of the conference. *8A.P.*, 52, 57.

See especially M. Trygger's speech in the Tenth Assembly, *10A.P.*, 90-1.

[5] See the reference made to the efforts of M. Löfgren in the Second Committee, in the report on the work of the finance committee presented by the Second Committee to the Assembly. *3A.P. (II)*, 183. See also Dr Nansen's speech at *4A.P.*, 61-2 and Dr Munch's speech at *4A.2C.*, 34, 35.

individuals from the Northern countries have applied themselves to the League's service command special notice. The work of Dr Theodor Madsen of Denmark, as chairman of the Health Committee of the League, is a fitting tribute to a country whose own public health administration is widely praised. The contributions of Mme Anna Bugge-Wicksell and Mlle Kerstin Hesselgren of Sweden, and of Mlle Henni Forchhammer of Denmark in behalf of women and children, and the services of Professor Kristine Bonnevie of Norway in the Committee of Intellectual Cooperation, are a high credit to the women of Scandinavia.[6] But it is the name of Nansen which leads all others on the League's scroll of service for humanity. Lord Curzon said of him in 1923 that he was "the only living man to whom the doors of every Chancery in Europe were flung wide open."[7] Yet possibly more accurate in determining his contribution was the Assembly's appreciation that "no appeal was ever made in vain to his active love of humanity."[8] When he faced the problem of repatriation of the War prisoners, "everything was lacking, but Nansen's fertile genius improvised all."[9] The "Nansen stamp" and the "Nansen passport" are emblems of an even greater achievement as High Commissioner of the League of Nations for Refugees.

Conclusion

The consistency of Scandinavian policy in the League, though making a summary of principles unnecessary, deserves an added emphasis in conclusion. In the view of these States the primary duty of the League was to endeavour, by reconciling the conflicting interests of the different countries in every field, to create a political atmosphere out of which the idea of international jurisdiction could

[6] See the Records of the Second and Fifth Committees of the Assembly, and the reports issued by the Danish, Norwegian and Swedish Foreign Offices.

[7] See Vigness, op. cit., p. 129.

[8] From the report adopted by the Third Assembly, see League of Nations, Ten Years of World Cooperation, p. 266.

[9] ibid.; there are numerous tributes to the work of Dr Nansen. In addition to Chapter VIII, "Social and Humanitarian Activities," in Ten Years of World Cooperation, see Philip Noel Baker, Nansen (reprint from the issue of May 31 and June 7, 1930, of The Nation and Athenaeum); Jon Sörensen, The Saga of Fridtjof Nansen (translated from the Norwegian by J. B. C. Watkins).

evolve. But the internationalism which they desired was not intended to bring about the absorption of nations into a cosmopolitan mass. Despite the growing faith, down to 1936, in the collective principle, distinctive nationalism was considered still to serve as a source of enrichment for mankind. Scandinavian statesmanship did not find the clash between nationalism and internationalism irreconcilable. Cooperation, as they understood it, offered the reconciliation of opposing ideas.

At Geneva the Scandinavian delegations acted as a group not because of any forced coalition, but mainly because they found themselves side by side in a common task. Indeed it was only when Denmark, Norway and Sweden were brought into contact with the outer world, that they realized the true extent of their common heritage and their common outlook towards international organization. At Geneva they naturally combined to make their influence of greater weight. No secondary Powers, however active, have taken a more prominent part in the League's work.

To fix responsibility for the failures of the League as an instrument of collective security is a task which may be met more scientifically by tomorrow's historian. M. Undén has rightly said that "when judging the attitude adopted by the different States in the matter of sanctions, account must be taken, not only of the declarations made during the discussion (at Geneva), but above all of the acts of those States." His conclusion, which seems representative of the Scandinavian viewpoint, was that "the smaller States—often regarded as timid and hesitating in the matter of the application of sanctions—cannot rightly be held responsible for the failure of the League. On the contrary," he concluded, "it is rather the States which in theory uphold Article XVI most strongly that have raised objections to the application and continuance of economic sanctions during these years" [i.e. 1931-1937].[10]

The Scandinavian contribution, difficult to evaluate finally, has been to serve as an ever-alert conscience to the Great Powers. Keenly

[10] *Minutes of the Third Session of the Committee set up to Study the Application of the Principles of the Covenant* (January 31 to February 2, 1938). *L. of N. Doc.*, A. 7, 1938, VII, p. 9.

aware of their position as small States, they have attempted in the interest of humanity to fill the rôle of spokesman for justice. It is significant that their combination has raised no ill-feeling among other nations. The explanation is clear: the political ambition of this group begins and ends with the aim for peace, a peace founded upon justice.

BIBLIOGRAPHY

BIBLIOGRAPHY

A. SOURCE MATERIAL

I. *Public Documents Officially Printed*

Denmark:

Beretning til Rigsdagen angaaende de paa Folkeforbundets Første Forsamling i Genève, and subsequent annual reports issued by Udenrigsministeriet. 1921-1935. Copenhagen.

Rigsdagstidenden. Forhandlinger paa Folketing og Landsting og Tillæg A, B og C for Samlingen.

Udenrigsministeriet, *Redegørelse for Danmarks folkeretlige Stilling efter Folkeforbundspagten og Kellogg-Pagten: Udtalelser og Aktstykker.* Copenhagen, 1931.

Forslag til Rigsdagsbeslutning angaaende Danmarks Tiltræden af Folkenes Forbund, anmeldt den 11. Februar 1920 (and annexes).

Rigsdagstidenden Ordentlige Samling (1919-1920), Tillæg A. II.

Udenrigsministeriet, *Folkeforbundets Første Tiaar.* 1930. Levin and Munksgaard, Copenhagen.

Danish Foreign Office Journal.

Danish Foreign Office, *The German Minority in South Jutland.* April 15, 1924. J. H. Schultz, Copenhagen.

Great Britain:

British and Foreign State Papers.

Foreign Affairs Historical Section, "The Åland Islands," *Peace Handbook,* VIII, no. 48.

League of Nations:

Armaments Yearbook, 1924-

Monthly Summary, 1921-

Official Journal, 1920-

Records of the Assemblies, Plenary Sessions and Meetings of the Committees, 1920-

Treaty Series, 1920-

Records of the Conference for the Reduction and Limitation of Armaments, 1932-1934.

International Labour Organization:

Records of the Proceedings of the International Labour Conferences, 1919-

Norway:

Kongeriket Norges Stortings Forhandlinger

Forhandlinger i Stortinget, 1919-

Innstilling fra konstitusjonskomiteen angående meddelelse om Folkenes Forbunds første delegeretmøte i Genf november-desember 1920, and subsequent reports on the work of the Assembly.

Innstilling fra Utenriks- og konstitusjonskomiteen.

Stortings Proposition nr. 33 (1920). Om innhentelse av Stortingets Samtykke til at Norge tiltrer den for Folkenes Forbund vedtatte Pakt som inneholdes i Versaillestraktaten av 28. juni 1919.

Utenriksdepartementet, *Stortings meddelelse om Folkenes Forbunds første delegeretmøte i Genf november-desember 1920,* and subsequent annual reports on the work of the Assembly.

Permanent Court of International Justice:

Publications de la Cour Permanente de Justice Internationale, Series A/B no. 53.

Permanent Court of International Justice, Advisory Committee of Jurists, *Documents presented to the Committee Relating to the Existing Plans of a Permanent Court of International Justice.*

Procès-Verbaux of the Proceedings of the Committee, June 16-July 24, 1920.

Sweden:

Aktstycken utgivna av Kungliga Utrikesdepartementet. 1920-Stockholm.

Ålandsfrågan inför Nationernas Förbund, 3 vols., Swedish and French texts. 1920, 1921. Stockholm.

Årsbok för de Nordiska Interparlamentariska Grupper. 1910-
Stockholm.

*Betänkande rörande en internationell rättsordning, avgivet av
därtill av Kungl. Maj:ts utsedda kommitterade, jämte förslag till
konvention, utarbetat av ovannämnde kommitterade i samarbete
med motsvarande av danska och norska regeringarna tillsatta
komitteer.* 1919. Stockholm. (Utrikesdepartementet, January 21,
1919.) P. A. Norstedt & Söner.

Försvarsdepartementet, *Utredning rörande Sveriges försvars-
politiska läge samt behov av försvarskrafter, avg. av sakkunniga
tillkallade av statsrådet och chefen Försvarsdepartementet
den 13 mars 1929.* 1930. Stockholm. (Statens offentliga utredningar 1930: 12.)

*Betänkande rörande det S.K. Genèveprotokollet angående av-
görande på fredlig väg av internationella tvister avgivet av tillkallade sakkunnige.* (Statens offentliga utredningar 1925: 17,
Utrikesdepartementet.) 1925. Stockholm.

Nationernas Förbunds Första Församling i Genève (and following reports, 1920.) 1921- . Stockholm.

Nationernas Förbundsråds Verksamhet under år 1923 (and following reports, 1923-1926). 1924-1927. Stockholm.

*Rapport du Comité d'Experts chargé par le Gouvernement
Suédois de l'Examen du Protocole dit le Genève, relatif au
Règlement Pacifique des Différends Internationaux.* 1925. Stock-
holm. (Documents Publiés par le Ministère des Affaires
Étrangères.)

*Riksdagens Protokoll: Första Kammarens Protokoll, Andra
Kammarens Protokoll, Bihang till Riksdagens Protokoll.*

*Kungl. Maj:ts proposition till riksdagen angående Sveriges
anslutning till nationernas förbund; given Stockholms slott den
14 februari 1920. (Bihang till Riksdagens Protokoll, 1920, 1
Saml. 75 haft, nr. 90.)*

Sveriges Överenskommelser med Främmande Makter.

Löfgren, J. Eliel, *De Nordiska Förliknings- och Skiljedomsavtalen
i deras ställning till det internationella rättsystemet.* 1927. Published by Utrikesdepartementet, Stockholm.

II. *Other Primary Sources*

Aarbog for Rigsdagssamlingen, 1920-21, and following years.

The Norwegian League of Nations Association (Publication no. 1). *Pronouncements concerning the Principles of the League of Nations as passed by the Council of the Association. (January 30, 1919.)* 1919. Oslo.

Organisation Centrale pour une Paix Durable, *Recueil de Rapports sur les différents points du Programme-Minimum.* 4 vols. 1917. La Haye.

Det Nordiske Interparlamentariska Förbundets Åttonde Delegerademöte. August 1916. Stockholm.

Hoffner, Wilhelm, *Stortinget,* 1922-1924, 1925-1927, 1928-1930, 1931-1933, 1934-1936. J. W. Cappelens Fordrag, Oslo.

Scott, James Brown, editor, *The Proceedings of The Hague Peace Conferences. Conference of 1899, Conference of 1907.* 3 vols., 1920. Carnegie Foundation for International Peace, Washington.

B. SECONDARY MATERIAL

I. *Books and Pamphlets*

Arnoldson, K. P. *Pax Mundi.* 1892. London.

Bajer, Frederik. *Fredsförelse* (Nordisk Interparlamentarisk Forbunds Småskrifter). 1913. A/S J. H. Schultz Forlagsboghandel, Copenhagen.

Baker, P. J. Noel. *The Geneva Protocol for the Pacific Settlement of International Disputes.* 1925. P. S. King and Sons, London.

Bassett, John Spencer. *The League of Nations.* 1928. Longmans, Green and Co., New York.

Beales, A. C. F. *The History of Peace.* 1931. G. Bell and Sons, London.

Bellquist, Eric Cyril. *Some Aspects of the Recent Foreign Policy of Sweden.* 1929. University of California Press, Berkeley.

Björkman, Edwin [August]. *Scandinavia and the War.* 1914. (Oxford Pamphlets.) Oxford University Press, London.

Brierly, J. L. *The Law of Nations* (second edition). 1936. Clarendon Press, Oxford.

Castberg, Johan. *Nationernes Forbund og Den Norske Delega-tions Konferancer i Paris.* (Den Norske Forening for Nationernes Liga, Skrift nr. 2.) 4 de juni 1919. Centraltrykkeriet, Christiania.

Consett, M. W. W. P. *The Triumph of Unarmed Forces: 1914-1918* (revised edition). 1928. Williams and Norgate, Ltd., London.

Conwell-Evans, T. P. *The League Council in Action.* 1929. Oxford University Press, London.

Dickinson, Edwin DeWitt. *The Equality of States in International Law.* 1920. Harvard University Press, Cambridge, Mass.

Falnes, Oscar J. *Norway and the Nobel Peace Prize.* 1938. Columbia University Press. New York.

Figgis, John Neville. *From Gerson to Grotius.* 1916. Cambridge.

Fischer, Williams, Sir John. *Some Aspects of the Covenant of the League of Nations.* 1934. Oxford University Press, London.

Gjerset, Knut. *History of the Norwegian People.* 2 vols. 1915. The Macmillan Company, New York.

Hallendorf, Carl, and Schück, Adolf. *History of Sweden.* 1929. Cassell, London.

Habicht, Max. *Post-War Treaties for the Pacific Settlement of International Disputes.* 1931. Harvard University Press, Cambridge, Mass.

Hambro, Carl J. *Folkeforbundet og dets arbeide.* 1931. H. Aschehoug and Co., Oslo.

Heckscher, Eli Filip, and others. *Sweden, Norway, Denmark, and Iceland in the World War.* 1930. Yale University Press, New Haven.

Hershey, Amos. *The Essentials of International Public Law and Organization* (revised edition). 1927. The Macmillan Company, New York.

Hudson, Manley O. *The Permanent Court of International Justice: A Treatise.* 1934. The Macmillan Company, New York.

de Jong van Beek en Donk. *Neutral Europe and the League of Nations.* 1917. Nederlandsche Anti-Oorlog Road, The Hague.

Jørgensen, Theodore. *Norway's Relation to Scandinavian Unionism, 1815-1871.* 1935. St. Olaf College Press, Northfield, Minn.

Kluyver, C. A. *Documents on the League of Nations.* 1920. A. W. Sijthoff's Uitgeversmaatschappij, Leiden.

Lange, Christian L. *Centralorganisationen för Varaktig Fred: dess Arbete och Hittilsvarande Resultat* (Svenska Fredsförbundets Skriftserie XXI-XXII). 1917. Håkan Ohlssons Boktryckeri, Lund.

————. *Exposé des Travaux de l'Organisation.* 1917. La Haye.

————. *L'arbitrage international en 1913.* 1914. Union Interparlementaire, Bruxelles.

————. *Mellemfolkelige Retsmidler* (Interparlamentarisk Forbund). 1916. Det Mallingske Bogtrykkeri, Kristiania.

————. *Rapport présenté par le Président de la Commission Internationale d'Études,* no. IV, "Développement de l'Oeuvre de la Haye." 1917. Organisation Centrale pour une Paix Durable, La Haye.

Lauterpacht, H. *The Development of International Law by the Permanent Court of International Justice.* (No. 11, Publ. Grad. Inst. of Internat. Studies, Geneva.) 1934. Longmans, Green and Co., London.

————. *The Function of Law in the International Community.* 1933. The Clarendon Press, Oxford.

Secretariat of the League of Nations. *Ten Years of World Cooperation.* 1930. Geneva.

Lindström, Rickard. *På Helgeandsholman: Den Svenska Riksdagen och dess Arbete.* 1933. Kurt Lindberg Boktryckeriaktiebolag, Stockholm.

Lundstedt, Anders Vilhelm. *Superstition or Rationality in Action for Peace?* 1925. London.

Madariaga, Salvador de. *Disarmament.* 1929. Oxford University Press, London.

Maury, Lucien. *Le Nationalisme suédois et la Guerre, 1914-1918.* 1918. Librarie Académique Perrin et Cie., Paris.

Miller, David Hunter. *The Drafting of the Covenant.* 2 vols. 1928. G. P. Putnam's Sons, New York.

————. *The Geneva Protocol.* 1925. The Macmillan Company, New York.

Mohn, Paul. *Sverige i Utrikespolitisk Perspektiv, 1937.* Marinlitteraturföreningens Förlag, Stockholm.

Møller, Axel. *International Law in War and Peace.* 2 vols. (translated by H. M. Pratt). 1931, 1935. Levin and Munksgaard, Copenhagen.

Montarroyos, E. *Le Brésil et la Crise de la Société des Nations en 1926.* 1926. Imprimerie Albert Kundig, Geneva.

Morley, Felix. *The Society of Nations.* 1932. Faber and Faber, Ltd., London.

Morris, Ira Nelson. *From an American Legation.* 1923. New York.

Munch, Peter. *Le Projet danois de Désarmement at la Société des Nations.* 1927. A. Pedone, Paris.

—————. *La Politique du Danemark dans la Société des Nations.* 1931. Kundig, Geneva.

—————. *Norden og Folkenes Forbund* (Udgivet af Dansk Freds- of Folkeforbundsforening). 1935. Levin and Munksgaards, Copenhagen.

Munch (editor). (See under Rask-Ørsted.)

Nordlund, K. *The Swedish-Norwegian Union Crisis.* 1905. Almquist & Wiksell, Upsala.

Oppenheim, L. *International Law,* Vol. II (fifth edition, edited by H. Lauterpacht). 1935. Longmans, Green and Co., London.

Palmstierna, Baron E. *An International Police Force* (International Congress for the Study of the Principles of a Durable Peace). 1916. Berne.

Petersen, Niels, and Nielson, Ingvard. *Halvtreds Aars Fredsarbejde.* 1932. Levin and Munksgaard, Copenhagen.

Problems of the International Settlement, with an Introduction by G. Lowes Dickinson. 1918. George Allen and Unwin, Ltd., London.

Problems of Peace. Eighth Series. 1934. Oxford University Press, London.

Rask-Ørstedfondet (Sous la Direction de P. Munch). *Les origines et l'oeuvre de la Société des Nations.* (2 vols., edited by P. Munch.) 1923, 1924. Gyldendalske Boghandel, Copenhagen.

Rappard, William E. *International Relations as Viewed from Geneva.* 1925. The Yale University Press, New Haven.

Ray, Jean. *Commentaire du Pacte de la Société des Nations selon la Politique et la Jurisprudence des Organes de la Société.* 1930. Librairie du Recuil Sirey, Paris.

Royal Institute of International Affairs, *Abyssinia and Italy.* (Information Department Papers, No. 16.) Third edition, September 1935.

Sandler, Rickard. *Ett Utrikespolitisk Program.* 1934. Tidens Förlag, Stockholm.

Scelle, Georges. *Une Crise de la Société des Nations.* 1927. Les Presses Universitaires de France, Paris.

Schück, H., and Sohlman, R. *The Life of Alfred Nobel* (translated by B. and B. Lunn). 1929. William Heinemann, Ltd., London.

Soares, José Carlos de Macedo. *Brazil and the League of Nations.* 1928. A. Pedone, éditeur, Paris.

Sörenson, Jon. *The Saga of Fridtjof Nansen* (translated from the Norwegian by J. B. C. Watkins). 1932. American-Scandinavian Foundation, New York.

Spaight, J. M. *Pseudo-Security.* 1928. Longmans, Green and Co., London.

Svanström, Ragnar, and Palmstierna, Carl F. *A Short History of Sweden* (translated by Joan Bulman). 1934. The Clarendon Press, Oxford.

Svenska Freds- och Skiljedomsföreningen. Jubileumsskrift: 1883-1933. 1933. Falun A.-B. Dala- Tidningens tryckeri, Stockholm.

Svenska Fredsförbundets Skrift Serie. 1911-. Lund.

Thermaenius, Edvard. *Sveriges Politiska Partier.* 1933. Hugo Gebers Förlag, Stockholm.

Trygger, Ernst. *Några Ord om Genèveprotokollet 1924 angående avgörande på fredlig väg av internationella tvister.* 1924. P. A. Norstedt & Söner, Stockholm.

Vigness, Paul G. *Neutrality of Norway in the World War.* 1932. Stanford University Press, Stanford.

Webster, Charles Kingsley. *The League of Nations in Theory and Practice.* 1933. London.

Wehberg, Hans. *The Limitation of Armaments* (Pamphlet Series of the Carnegie Endowment for International Peace: Division of International Law. No. 46). 1921. Washington.

Wilson, Florence. *The Origins of the League Covenant.* 1928. The Hogarth Press, London.

Wright, Quincy. *Mandates Under the League of Nations.* 1930. University of Chicago Press, Chicago.

Zimmern, Sir Alfred. *The League of Nations and the Rule of Law.* 1936. The Macmillan Company, London.

II. *Signed Articles in Periodicals and Newspapers*

Bajer, Fredrik, "Skal Neutraliteten ofres for Folkeforbundet?" *Fredsbladet,* 27 Aarg. nr. 6 (June 14, 1918).

Baker, Philip Noel, "Nansen," *The Nation and Athenaeum,* May 31 and June 7, 1930.

Bellquist, "Possible Effects of Danish Disarmament," *American-Scandinavian Review,* May 1931, p. 299.

Bellquist, Eric Cyril, "Finland's Treaties for the Peaceful Settlement of International Disputes," *American Journal of International Law,* Vol. XXVI (1932), p. 176.

Brandes, Georg, "Scandinavian Sympathies and Destinies." *Foreign Affairs,* I, (June 15, 1923), p. 34.

Branting, Hjalmar, "The League of Nations," *The American-Scandinavian Review,* October 1919, p. 343.

Branting, Hjalmar, "The Peace Movement After the War," *American-Scandinavian Review,* September 1922, p. 533.

Brierly, J. L., "The General Act of Geneva," *The British Year Book of International Law,* 1930.

Brüel, Erik, "Norden og den Internationale Arbeidsorganisation" *Nordisk Tidskrift för Vetenskap, Konst ock Industri,* Vol. V (6), p. 417.

Brusewitz, Axel, "Parliamentary Control of Foreign Affairs in Sweden," *Foreign Affairs* (London), Vol. III (1922), p. 103.

Büscher, Alfred, "Der Skandinavismus," *Nordische Rundschau,* Vol. V, January 1929.

Castberg, Frede, "Le Droit International et la Défense," *Acta Scandinavica Juris Gentium,* Vol. I (1930), No. 2.

Christensen, Severin, "Det Første Udkast til Folkenes Forbund" *Retsstaten,* B.D. III, (nr. 4), (April 30, 1919).

Cohn, Georg, "La Guerre est-elle une Maladie?" *Revue Universitaire Internationale,* No. 13, October 1935, p. 11.

Dillon, E. J., "Sweden and the Belligerents," *The Contemporary Review,* June 1916, p. 704.

Drummond, Sir Eric, "The Secretariat of the League of Nations," *Public Administration,* April 1931, p. 234.

Elviken, Andreas, "The Genesis of Norwegian Nationalism," *Journal of Modern History,* Vol. III, No. 3, September 1931, p. 365.

Essén, Rutger, "Svensk Utrikespolitik," *Svensk Tidskrift,* Vol. XIX (3), 1929, pp. 205-18.

Falnes, Oscar J. "The Scandinavian Peoples in the League of Nations," *American-Scandinavian Review,* Vol. XXII (September 1934), p. 201.

Friedlander, Lilian M., "The Admission of States to the League of Nations," *The British Year Book of International Law* (1928), p. 89.

Gregory, C. M., "The Neutralization of the Åland Islands," *American Journal of International Law,* Vol. XVII (1923), p. 63.

Grønberg, Andre Th., "Fredsmonumentet paa den skandinaviske Grænse," *Fredsbladet,* 23 Aarg., September 15, 1914.

Hambro, Carl J. "Folkeforbundet Idag," *Nordisk Tidsskrift för Vetenskap, Konst, och Industri,* Arg 10, (June 12, 1934).

Hambro, Carl J., "The Rôle of the Smaller Powers in International Affairs Today," *International Affairs,* XV, No. 2 (March-April 1936), p. 167.

Hudson, Manley O., "The Prospects for Future Codification," *American Journal of International Law,* Vol. XXVI (1932), p. 137.

Lange, Chr. L., "Préparation de la Société des Nations," *Les origines et l'oeuvre de la Société des Nations* (Munch, editor), Vol. I, p. 1.

Lange, Chr. L., "Scandinavian Cross Currents," *Atlantic Monthly.* Vol. CXXI, January 1918, p. 128.

Lange, Chr. L., "Utbygging av freds-politikken," *Mellanfolkeligt Samarbete* (1936), Årg. 6, nr. 2, p. 45.

Lie, Mikael H., "L'entrée de la Norvège dans la Société des Nations," *Les origines et l'oeuvre de la Société des Nations,* Vol. I, p. 345.

Long, Robert Crozier, "Anglo-Swedish Oppositions: A Letter from Stockholm," *Fortnightly Review,* Vol. CV, February 1916, p. 235.

Madariaga, Salvador de, "The League Staff," *The Times* (London), September 4 and 5, 1928.

Mogens, Victor, "Norsk Utenrikspolitikk Igjennem 25 år," *Vor Verden,* 1930, nr. 6, p. 245.

Møller, Axel, La Société des Nations et La Réduction des Armements," *Acta Scandinavica Juris Gentium,* Vol. I (1930), No. 2, p. 19.

Munch, Peter, "Les États neutres et le Pacte de la Société des Nations," *Les origines et l'oeuvre de la Société des Nations,* "Will Denmark Disarm?" *Headway,* Vol. II (July 1929), p. 128.

Nansen, Fridtjof, "Aspects of Peace," *North American Review,* Vol. CCXXVIII (November 1929), p. 565.

Nansen, Fridtjof, "The Mission of the Small States" (An Authorized Interview), *American-Scandinavian Review,* Vol. VI (January-February 1918), p. 9.

Pedersen, Oscar, "Foreign Policy Control in Norway," *Foreign Affairs* (London), Vol. II, December, 1921.

Petersen, Niels, "Nordens Indsats i Fredsarbejdet," *Nordisk Tidsskrift for International Ret,* Vol. I (3) (1930), p. 159.

Pyke, Geoffrey, "Denmark and the Great War," *Fortnightly Review* (January 1916), p. 35.

Rappard, William E., "Small States in the League of Nations," *Political Science Quarterly,* Vol. XLIX (December 1934), p. 544.

Rappard, William E., "L'Entrée de la Suisse dans la Société des Nations," *Les origines et l'oeuvre de la Société des Nations,* Vol. I, p. 361.

Sweetser, Arthur, "The First Ten Years of the League of Nations," *International Conciliation Pamphlet,* No. 256.

Stauning, Th. "Danmark og Folkenes Forbund," in *Folkeforbundets Første Tiaar.*

Trygger, Ernst, "L'entrée de la Suéde dans la Société des Nations," *Les origines et l'oeuvre de la Société des Nations,* Vol. I, p. 428.

Vallentin, Hugo, "What Sweden Thinks Today," *New Europe,* March 27, 1919, p. 257.

Wuorinen, John H., "Denmark's Disarmament Program," *Current History,* Vol. XXXI (October 1929), p. 182.

von Würtemberg, E. Marks, "L'oeuvre commune des Pays scandinaves relative à la Société des Nations," *Les origines et l'oeuvre de la Société des Nations,* Vol. II, p. 205.

IV. *Newspapers and Periodicals*

American Journal of International Law (Washington).

American-Scandinavian Review (New York).

American Political Science Review, Menasha, Wis.

Annals of the American Academy of Political and Social Sciences (Philadelphia).

Anglo-Danish Journal (London).

Anglo-Swedish Review (London).

Berlingske Tidende (Copenhagen).

The British Year Book of International Law (London).

Contemporary Review (Oxford University Press).

Current History (New York).

Dagens Nyheder (Copenhagen).

The Forum (New York).

Foreign Affairs (London).

Foreign Affairs (New York).

Fredsbladet (Copenhagen).

Fortnightly Review (London).

Göteborgs Handels-och Sjöfarts Tidning (Gothenburg).

Headway: The Monthly Progress of the League of Nations Union (London).

Herald of Peace (London).

International Affairs (London).

Journal of Modern History (Chicago).

Labour Magazine.

Manchester Guardian (Manchester).

Mellanfolkligt Samarbete (Stockholm).

Morgenbladet (Oslo).

Morning Post (London).

Nordische Rundschau (Berlin).

Nordisk Tidsskrift for International Ret (*Acta Scandinavica Juris Gentium*). (Copenhagen).

North American Review (New York).

The New York Times.

Nordisk Tidskrift för Vetenskap, Konst ock Industri (Stockholm).

The Peace Movement (the fortnightly organ of the International Peace Bureau in Berne), 1912-1914. Berne; (from 1915-1918, published as *Le Mouvement Pacifiste*).

Political Science Quarterly (Lancaster, Pa.)

Public Administration (London).

Retsstaten (Copenhagen).

Revue Universitaire Internationale (organe de la Féderation Universitaire Internationale pour les Principes de la S.D.N.) (Copenhagen).

Svenska Dagbladet (Stockholm).

Svensk Tidskrift, Stockholm.

Le Temps (Paris).

The Times (London).

Vor Verden (Oslo).

INDEX

INDEX

(Some words, including Denmark, Norway, Sweden, League of Nations, Scandinavian States, appear so frequently in the text that it was thought best to omit them from the Index. The names of Political Parties are also omitted.)